Masterpiece Theatre
and
the Politics of Quality

Laurence A. Jarvik

The Scarecrow Press, Inc.
Lanham, Maryland, and London
1999

SCARECROW PRESS, INC.

Published in the United States of America
by Scarecrow Press, Inc.
4720 Boston Way
Lanham, Maryland 20706

4 Pleydell Gardens
Kent CT20 2DN, England

From "Masterpiece Theatre and the Politics of Quality: A Case Study," UCLA dissertation, 1991. University of Michigan, Ann Arbor (microfilm).

British Library Cataloguing-in-Publication Information Available

Library of Congress Cataloging-in-Publication Data

Jarvik, Laurence Ariel, 1956–
    Masterpiece Theatre and the politics of quality / Laurence A. Jarvik.
    p.   cm.
    Includes bibliographical references and index.
    ISBN 0-8108-3204-6 (hardcover : alk. paper)
    1. Masterpiece Theatre (Television program)   I. Title.
PN1992.77.M293J37   1999   98-34464
791.45′72—dc21   CIP

♾ ™ The paper used in this publication meets the minimum requirements of American National Standard for Information Sciences—Permanence of Paper for Printed Library Materials, ANSI Z39.48-1984.
Manufactured in the United States of America.

To Nancy

Contents

Acknowledgments   vi

Preface: Russell Baker and *Masterpiece Theatre*   vii

1. Introduction   1

2. WGBH and the Origin of *Masterpiece Theatre*   27

3. Alistair Cooke and *Masterpiece Theatre*   47

4. PBS and *Masterpiece Theatre*   91

5. British Television and *Masterpiece Theatre*   117

6. *Mobil Masterpiece Theatre*   165

7. *Masterpiece Theatre* and the Nixon Administration   203

Bibliography   219

Index   245

About the Author   261

Acknowledgments

This book is based on research conducted for my doctoral dissertation at UCLA. I would like to thank Paul Von Blum, Albert Boime, Paul Rosenthal, Teshome Gabriel, Howard Suber, and especially my cochairs Ruth Schwartz and Peter Wollen for making it possible. I am grateful to those who cooperated with the research, especially Herb Schmertz, Frank Marshall, and most notably Frank and Arlene Goodman, who as press agents for *Mobil Masterpiece Theatre* provided a wealth of information, access to interview subjects, and a donation of several hundred hours of videotapes to the UCLA Film and Television Archive. I would also like to thank all those who permitted me to interview them on both sides of the Atlantic, and the archivists and librarians in the United States and in England who opened their collections for research.

Preface

Russell Baker and *Masterpiece Theatre*

The original research upon which this book is based was first published in a different version in 1991, before Alistair Cooke retired as *Masterpiece Theatre* host at the end of the 1992 television season and Russell Baker took over as master of ceremonies. Also since 1991, Mobil ceased funding *Mystery!* and in 1997 announced that the Corporation for Public Broadcasting (CPB) had made a multimillion-dollar grant to WGBH-TV for the production of American dramas, to be presented under the banner *Mobil Masterpiece Theatre's American Collection.* In recent years, it has seemed at times that the series might be trading its British accent for an American one.

While all this news appears to have created a dramatic change, however, the reality has been somewhat less seismic. The Traveler's insurance company took up Mobil's *Mystery!* sponsorship and the series continued, and the *American Collection* project was in keeping with 1971 plans by producer Christopher Sarson to schedule American episodes for *Masterpiece Theatre.* At the outset of the series, American productions could not compete with British product because they were too expensive. Rising demand for British product on cable television has since raised the price per hour to the point where American productions appear to be competitive, especially with a CPB subsidy. *Mobil Masterpiece Theatre*'s stated intention to use *Hallmark Hall of Fame* producers to create the American programs shows a desire to schedule high-quality television drama in the tradition of the 1950s "golden age." A sponsor-supplied program like *Masterpiece Theatre* began under the direction of Sir Maurice Evans, the English Shakespearean actor.

WGBH will coproduce new episodes of *Masterpiece Theatre,* as it has coproduced the British series for over a quarter century. The three titles announced by Mobil in 1997 were Langston Hughes's *Cora Unashamed,* Willa Cather's *Song of the Lark,* and Henry James's *The American.* All are period costume dramas and some will be coproduced with British television companies. Nine films will be shown over a three-year period, a relatively small fraction of *Masterpiece Theatre* programming.

Mobil, however, will still have final say over the quality of the program. The company has acted before to ensure the integrity of its series. In 1982, Mobil declined to acquire *Brideshead Revisited* for *Masterpiece Theatre* partially because the frank treatment of homosexuality raised concerns among public broadcasting stations as well as sponsors. So William F. Buckley Jr. assumed Alistair Cooke's role for the presentation of *Brideshead Revisited* at New York's WNET/Channel 13 as part of Exxon's *Great Peformances* series for PBS. With Buckley as host, there was little chance of a firestorm.

"They just called me and asked me if I would do it," Buckley recalled. He had tried to telephone Alistair Cooke prior to accepting, but could not reach him. "Having made the decision, I was glad of it," Buckley later said, "and all the more glad . . . on seeing it whole, inasmuch as it seemed to me to have a most fearfully anti-Catholic impact." Buckley's commentary and interviews at the beginning and end of each episode helped to neutralize content that might have offended some viewers. The program drew a cult following and high ratings, but it was never part of *Masterpiece Theatre.*

The Corporation for Public Broadcasting (CPB), the Public Broadcasting Service (PBS), and WGBH, Boston, have questionable track records in choosing original dramas. Should the oil company further reduce its support and creative involvement in the future, *Masterpiece Theatre* might very well follow such CPB-funded series as *Hollywood Television Theatre, Visions, The Adams Chronicles, The Scarlet Letter,* and *American Playhouse* into oblivion. As this book shows, *Masterpiece Theatre* has tried coproductions and material from countries other than England in the past, airing Australian and German productions, as well as an adaptation of the American-themed novel *The Buccaneers.* Each venture to another land was unsuccessful, however, because the franchise held by the series is for British drama. At this time, the CPB project is not large enough to jeopardize the quality of the series—only three programs a year—and WGBH is still reliant upon Mobil for the bulk of series financing.

The choice of *New York Times* columnist Russell Baker to take over as master of ceremonies from Alistair Cooke in 1992 was perhaps the most significant development of the 1990s. The host, after all, is the human embodiment of the series' personality. While Baker is no Alistair Cooke, he is cut from the same cloth. Herb Schmertz, who handled public relations for Mobil and helped establish the series, felt that using a working journalist to host Mobil's program added to the company's credibility on issues of the day, in other words the "halo effect." After Cooke's departure, a number of English actors were used as temporary hosts prior to Baker's joining the program, none successfully. The choice of Baker must have been approved by Mobil, whatever the public claims by WGBH, in order to enhance Mobil's image. Baker was as close to Cooke as any substitute host could be.

Baker is a well-known *New York Times* columnist. Cooke was a correspondent for the English newspaper the *Manchester Guardian* (and earlier in his career for the *Times* of London) and a regular commentator on BBC with his "Letter from America." Baker, like Cooke, is a pillar of the establishment. He presided over the Pulitzer Prize board, which awards the most prestigious honor in American journalism. Like Cooke for the *Guardian,* Baker had covered the Washington political scene for the *New York Times* in the paper's capital bureau. Both Baker and Cooke are known for a wry wit. And like Cooke, Baker was in his sixties when he began hosting duties and had been a reporter in London.

There are some significant differences, however. Unlike Cooke, who is a naturalized American citizen born in England, Baker is American born and bred. Although he spent some time in Great Britain as a correspondent, Baker's persona simply cannot add the international and cosmopolitan sophistication that Cooke conveyed to the *Masterpiece Theatre* audience. While Cooke could plausibly comment on the Edwardian events that formed the basis for dramatic plots based on his own life experience, Baker must take a different approach. He cannot himself pass, like Cooke, for a character out of *Masterpiece Theatre*. This changes the series chemistry. As host of *Masterpiece Theatre,* Baker appears to have more in common with the American audience viewing the series than with the characters in the dramas.

Alistair Cooke had long experience as a performer on radio and television. He was comfortable in front of the television camera and brought with him a loyal audience from *Omnibus* and the BBC. Cooke had helped found a Cambridge theatrical troupe. Where Cooke could pass for one of the British actors in the series, Baker will have to play the American cousin, a rather different role. While Baker is renowned as a writer, he does not have Cooke's experience on radio and television. He appears more nervous in his role than did Cooke, and perhaps a bit edgy.

Nevertheless, the replacement of British immigrant Alistair Cooke with American native Russell Baker makes one thing perfectly clear—that *Masterpiece Theatre,* despite its British accent, is an American institution, a 1950s-style anthology television drama sponsored by a major corporation. As this book will show, in its stylistic nostalgia for American television of the 1950s, even the choice of outspoken Nixon critic Russell Baker as host reflects the cultural legacy of the Nixon administration—the notion of quality television that finds its repesentation in *Masterpiece Theatre* as a dignified weekly anthology drama with a high moral purpose.

1

Introduction

But first and foremost quality meant weight, history . . . tradition.
>—Jonathan Powell, personal interview

A valuable work, a powerful work at least, is one which challenges codes, overthrows established ways of reading or looking, not simply to establish new ones, but to compel an unending dialogue, not at random, but productively.
>—Peter Wollen, *Signs and Meaning in the Cinema*

This book tells the story of the origins of *Masterpiece Theatre,* which has been on PBS for more than a quarter century. It describes the manner in which the concept of "quality" became the site of an ultimately political struggle between a number of contending interests. The history of this series demonstrates how cultural capital, in Bourdieu's sense, is not without its importance in American political life.[1] In the case of *Masterpiece Theatre,* such cultural capital, defined as quality, was exchanged for social and economic capital by the interest groups involved in its creation, dissemination, and reception. The founding struggles took place in the historical context of the Nixon administration's confrontation with public television.

Among the interest groups competing for control of the series were: 1) the BBC, the British ITV companies, and other program producers, which were seeking to enter the American television marketplace; 2) WGBH-TV, Boston, the American presenting station on PBS, which was aiming to become a national programming

1

source; 3) the Corporation for Public Broadcasting and PBS, which were trying to expand the role of public television; 4) Mobil Corporation, which, as sponsor, was working to counteract bad publicity faced by oil companies as a result of the Santa Barbara oil spill and the OPEC boycott; 5) the *New York Times,* which as newspaper of record was attempting to serve as arbiter of cultural consensus for elite taste in the United States by promoting the series as a worthy alternative to Hollywood products; and 6) the highly educated upper-income audience for the series, defined by PBS and Mobil as consisting of "opinion leaders." These audiences sought Bourdieu's "distinction" through viewing *Masterpiece Theatre* and contributing to local public television stations.

Each of these groups had goals that association with *Masterpiece Theatre* as "quality" programming fulfilled. The main purpose of this book is to investigate the process of negotiation whereby—in relation to the American context—meanings of "quality" are established in *Masterpiece Theatre* over time. Therefore, this is not primarily a critical study of the individual programs broadcast in the series, nor a theoretical analysis of the ideological project represented by *Masterpiece Theatre.* The purpose is to set forth the historical record. The pages that follow are in the form of a largely chronological narrative, based on interviews, documents, and the programs themselves.

Why study a television series in this way?

One reason is that *Masterpiece Theatre* has come to represent, to certain influential critics, the best television has to offer in an American cultural landscape often portrayed as a desert. This is due, in part, to its traditional character, as noted by Jonathan Powell. Such a sense of heritage is a form of the very "cultural capital," described by Pierre Bourdieu in his research on the sociology of taste.[2] It is perhaps the cultural "inherited wealth" that passes from generation to generation.

In his social critique of the judgement of taste, Bourdieu says "cultural products are (relatively) international." He equates the social role of educational television (WGBH in particular) in the United States with France-Musique, a French radio service.[3] As this sort of comparison between television and radio shows, Bourdieu's sociometric analysis of taste and class is of limited use in understanding the American context of *Masterpiece Theatre,* for he restricts his empirical research to his own culture and society.

The Cartesian coordinates of French taste and social rank cannot be unproblematically translated into the American context.

Nonetheless, the history of *Masterpiece Theatre* does demonstrate that even in America, the programs in the series represented a trading commodity valued in the markets of economic, social, and cultural capital, with an exchange value determined by negotiation between Mobil, the British, the middlemen of PBS and the press, and the highly educated and affluent audiences of public television.

Masterpiece Theatre has served as a market stall in the cultural forum of television described by Horace Newcomb and Paul Hirsch.[4] In this forum, its trade was in cultural commodities. Often programs representing an oppositional culture in England, such as teleplays by Marxist screenwriter Trevor Griffiths, were exchanged for such cultural distinction in an American public television subculture of corporate sponsorship and elite audience. Yet, in another sense, the public television subculture can be seen as an oppositional subculture itself, a contrast to the profit-driven world of commercialized network television. In this sense, *Masterpiece Theatre* serves to import cultural capital (as cultural commodities) from Britain (and elsewhere) into an American market.

One can draw a parallel to the import of oil from countries with large reserves to an energy-hungry United States. The crude must then be refined to meet the needs of American consumers, and marketed and distributed to specific target demographics in accordance with government regulations. In this model, Mobil would be playing the same role in television as it does in the oil business where Britain would be Saudi Arabia, providing cheap programs; WGBH would be the refinery preparing the crude for the American market; PBS would be the equivalent of the Department of Energy; and Mobil would control marketing and publicity, just as it does in the oil industry. Indeed Herb Schmertz, who as vice president for public affairs was in charge of Mobil's *Masterpiece Theatre* sponsorship, briefly took charge of Mobil's shipping operations in 1973.

Culture as a commodity, a form of capital, is an important element of the appeal of *Masterpiece Theatre*. In cultural capital, the United States is seen by some to run a deficit. Raymond Williams, for example, writes of the United States, "you do not feel you are in a rich country, materially or culturally. Indeed, you feel you are in a deprived area." That is, America lacks cultural capital, especially in television. Williams blames this state of affairs on the commercial nature of broadcasting, and contrasts the American networks unfavorably with the British. By importing BBC programming on *Masterpiece Theatre,* Williams credits PBS with creating a rich cultural oasis, an antidote to the Hollywood productions which otherwise dominated American television. He recalls his experiences as a visiting scholar at Stanford, emphasizing the following *Masterpiece Theatre* enjoyed among elites: "No, the intellectuals told me (as they do everywhere but in Britain), we don't watch television. Yet they did. . . . The most admired programme, which would even empty parties, is called *Masterpiece Theatre* and turned out to be a selection of BBC-2 classic serials. . . . But then this is the moment to recall what an intelligent Californian said as we were leaving . . . 'Don't let them californicate the world.' "5

In Williams's view, *Masterpiece Theatre* can be seen as a form of alternative noncommercial television, which challenges the hegemony of the advertiser and the marketplace, and the domination of the audience by what Williams describes as the relentless mediocrity of network broadcasting. *Masterpiece Theatre* is valuable precisely because, in its rejection of commercial interruptions and the "machine-turned police serials, the exploitative parlour games,"6 it belongs to what Bourdieu calls "the Aristocracy of culture."7

However, Erik Barnouw argues strongly against Williams's conception of culture on television as a necessary prophylactic against "californication." Barnouw states, "'Culture,' like 'entertainment,' is a term used for strategic purpose rather than to convey a precise meaning. In the case of public television, 'culture' has come to mean the safe area the system is urged to focus on to keep it free of the pitfalls of 'public affairs.' "8 And he goes on to specifically critique the Eurocentrism of Williams's anti-Hollywood position, claiming "it is a throwback to a time when 'culture' meant Europe, and artists went to Europe for training and apprenticeship. Most artists thought that this attitude had vanished, but public television has tended to revive it."9

Here, British cultural studies and the importance of "negotiated readings" in the tradition of Stuart Hall might provide a mode of analysis.10 But in determining the "dominant meanings" and the "oppositional position" one must still have some sense of a particular social space, and the precise coordinates of the discourse under examination. The main purpose of this study is precisely to investigate this negotiation of dominant meanings in the American case through concrete negotiations for creative control of the series and its programming.

French and English scholarly traditions, while valuable, cannot unproblematically provide the specificity needed for analysis of *Masterpiece Theatre.* Therefore, American traditions, rooted in sociology, history, and the study of communications, might provide some theoretical context for the narrative that unfolds in the following chapters.

The work of Herbert Gans, especially his *Popular Culture and High Culture,* is of interest. In this examination of American cultural pluralism, Gans classifies various "taste cultures" in relation to income and social standing. He places what he calls "subcultural programming" on PBS at the "upper-middle" level stating "public television has created a national network for upper-middle cultural fare."[11] Gans goes on to describe the PBS subculture in some detail, noting "people who read *Harper's* or the *New Yorker* are also likely to prefer foreign movies and public television, to listen to classical (but not chamber) music, play tennis, choose contemporary furniture, and eat gourmet foods."[12]

In *The Tastemakers,* an earlier account of American cultural hierarchy from which Gans draws, Russell Lynes points out that, like the stock market, the value of cultural commodities shifts dramatically over the years. Lynes defends the staying power of "middlebrow" art against its critics, tracing the rising and falling fortunes of Whistler, Gerome, Van Gogh, and D. W. Griffith. He concludes by quoting Brander Matthews's maxim, "a highbrow is a person educated beyond his intelligence." He warns against any permanent assignments of any work to any particular brow level.[13]

C. Wright Mills's sociological analysis of *The Power Elite* explains why the programming chosen by Mobil for its PBS series was both British and nostalgic. Mills said that the American elite would need to import what he characterized as "conservative" culture from abroad, for "classic conservatism has required the spell of tradition among such surviving elements of pre-industrial societies as an aristocracy of noble men, a peasantry, a petty-bourgeoisie with guild inheritances; and these are precisely what America has never had. For in America, the bourgeoisie has been predominant from its beginnings—in class, in status, and in power. In America, there has not been and there can be no conservative ideology of the classic type . . . On the right and in the center, public relations fills any need for 'ideology,' and public relations are something you hire."[14]

Masterpiece Theatre was, and remains, funded out of the public affairs budget of the Mobil Corporation. The corporation's vice president for public affairs from 1969 to 1988, Herb Schmertz, was indeed hired to improve Mobil's image. He chose to use what he called "affinity of purpose marketing," i.e., sponsorship of arts and culture, to do so.[15] This study argues that Mobil, and therefore Schmertz, were central to the struggles over the nature of *Masterpiece Theatre*. In 1983, Schmertz was appointed by President Reagan to the President's Advisory Commission on Public Diplomacy. In effect, the success of *Masterpiece Theatre* led to Schmertz's advising on international public relations for the United States of America.[16] Herb Schmertz, through his relationship with *Masterpiece Theatre,* was a professional tastemaker, operating in a political arena.

There are some particular accounts of the power politics of American television which provide additional theoretical context for this history. Especially relevant, in addition to Barnouw's *The Sponsor,* is Herbert Schiller's *Culture, Inc.,*[17] which details the impact of corporate support for the arts, and Kathryn Montgomery's *Target Prime Time,*[18] which explains how issue-oriented advocacy pressure groups mobilize to affect television programming decisions. In a sense, one might consider this history of *Masterpiece Theatre* a case study of how a corporate advocacy campaign—Mobil's—affected entertainment programming on public television. But there is still another context, in addition to the sociological and the political, for this history of *Masterpiece Theatre*. It is the structural microhistory of PBS, for in some sense the series represents in miniature the values of the American institution of public television.

In *Inside Prime Time,* Todd Gitlin called PBS "the last refuge of old-style television." By this he meant a system of sponsor control where "proprietary concern for the image of the product was a major motive."[19] The narrative that follows gives detailed evidence for Gitlin's claim. It argues that *Masterpiece Theatre* is, de facto if not de jure, a sponsor-supplied program. Programs paid for by government grants can be seen as equivalent to the "sustaining" programs in 1950s network television. It is an undeniable fact that Mobil, through its command of finances and registration of the name as a service mark (later turned over to WGBH), controlled the program from the beginning. Indeed, magazine articles called the show "Mobil's *Masterpiece Theatre*" as early as 1971.[20]

Some history of British film and television in America is also a necessary background to understanding the development of *Masterpiece Theatre*. In one sense, the series can be seen to play the same role in American television as Alexander Korda's films played in the motion-picture industry: "quality" British productions of historical stories for American audiences, which were precursors to what is now called "the heritage industry."[21] Korda's productions had made "British" synonymous with "quality" during his lifetime. Lavish costumes, sets, and subject matter entranced American audiences and earned income for Britain while creating public sympathy.[22] Korda had said "We have tended to produce pseudo-American" but that Britain ought to export Englishness instead. He argued, "America wants to see England on the screen."[23]

With the arrival of television in the postwar era, Korda's model provided one channel for British film and television to enter the American cultural marketplace. Indeed, Korda's production of *Richard III* had its American premiere on NBC in 1955 for a then-record price of $500,000. The Korda lineage is still clearly visible in *Masterpiece Theatre*. Korda's *The Six Wives of Henry VIII* and doomed Von Sternberg production of *I, Claudius* were inspirations for the eponymous *Masterpiece Theatre* series. John Hawkesworth, the producer of *Upstairs, Downstairs* and *Flame Trees of Thika*, among other miniseries, began his career as an art director working for Vincent Korda. Korda's company, London Films, was a major supplier for *Masterpiece Theatre* as well, providing *I, Claudius, Poldark,* and *Testament of Youth.*

In addition to Korda's influence, there is also the legacy of English television impresario Lew Grade, whose ATV productions, such as *Disraeli,* have graced *Masterpiece Theatre*'s schedule. Like Korda's London Films, Grade's ATV company had a history of supplying British imports to American commercial network television long before *Masterpiece Theatre*.

Korda and Grade are not the only ancestors of American-British television coproduction and import-export. In the mid-1950s, for example, Hannah Weinstein's Official Films hired blacklisted Hollywood screenwriters to produce adventure series in Britain to be shown on American network television.[24]

In fact, English television had long had an American audience. During the 1950s commercial network television featured *The Adventures of Sir Lancelot, Robin Hood* and *Sir Francis Drake,* NBC's *Adventure Theater,* CBS's *Dick and the Duchess, The Buccaneers, Somerset Maugham TV Theatre,* ABC's *Mark Saber/Saber of London, O.S.S.,* and *Oh, Boy.* The syndicated *Douglas Fairbanks Jr. Presents, The David Niven Show, The George Sanders Mystery Theater,* and *The Third Man* were all produced in England. English actors were visible in anthology drama of the golden age, and the BBC coproduced episodes of *Hallmark Hall of Fame.*[25] The BBC supplied programs to educational television as well, notably *An Age of Kings,* a 1961 Shakespeare package sponsored by Humble Oil and hosted by USC English professor Frank Baxter, which helped set the stage for the *Masterpiece Theatre* package of oil company sponsorship of drama on noncommercial television. Most relevant to the study of *Masterpiece Theatre* was Alistair Cooke's previous job as host of the Ford Foundation cultural series *Omnibus,* which ran from 1952 to 1961 (without Ford's support after 1957). *Omnibus* has been described as "one of the most ambitious efforts to program for a frankly elitist audience."[26]

In the 1960s, swinging London replaced traditional Britain in the public imagination. The Beatles appeared on the *Ed Sullivan Show* and James Bond movies spawned both domestic imitations such as *The Man From U.N.C.L.E.* as well as British television exports called the "ITV thrillers," which shifted British television production from period costume dramas to contemporary spy stories.[27] Among the English series were ABC's *The Avengers* (starring future *Mystery!* hostess Diana Rigg), *Man in a Suitcase,* and *The Baron;* CBS's *Danger Man, Secret Agent,* and *The Prisoner;* and NBC's *The Man from Interpol* and *The Saint.* British series without spies included ABC's *Court Martial* and *The Piccadilly Palace,* CBS's *Showtime,* and NBC's adaptation of *That Was the Week That Was.*

Variety programs, perhaps inspired by the success of David Frost's *That Was the Week That Was,* were a staple of 1970s British fare and included Frost's *The David Frost Revue, This Is Tom Jones, The Engelbert Humperdinck Show, The Muppet Show,* and *The Benny Hill Show*. All of these were on commercial television, but it was the popular success of the MGM-BBC production of *The Forsyte Saga* on PBS in 1969 that led to the niche for British programming under the title *Masterpiece Theatre*.[28] It is significant that WGBH and Mobil created not a slot for a single show, but an anthology format into which different British series could be programmed and sold, initially, on the basis of their very Britishness. *Masterpiece Theatre* was no "mid-Atlantic" ITV thriller. Instead, it was British television with a British accent, a series in which America was seeing Britain on its screens. No such series existed in England.

International politics played an important part in the development of *Masterpiece Theatre*. Britain had an image problem in the 1970s, especially after Prime Minister Harold Wilson's withdrawal of British troops from the strategically vital Middle East. The United Kingdom under a Labour government initially enjoyed a reputation in the Nixon administration as a "perfidious Albion" more closely aligned to the EEC and the Arabs than to American foreign policies in Vietnam, the Middle East, and elsewhere.[29] William Safire, in his memoir of the Nixon administration, recalls that "it was in the U.S. interest to make a point of this 'special relationship' [with England]; it was in Prime Minister Harold Wilson's interest, as he headed then toward a union with Europe that he later opposed, to separate himself just a little from the U.S. embrace. As Wilson put it [in 1969] at the airport, after Nixon had special relationshipped him, 'Our special relationship is by no means exclusive.'"[30] This British attitude towards America posed a sticky public relations problem with the American people.

What better way to regain the appreciation of American elites than by providing quality television stressing a shared heritage? Not altogether surprisingly, the first series on *Masterpiece Theatre* was *The First Churchills*, a reminder of the "special relationship" that characterized the Second World War. It was advertised by Mobil in a full-page *New York Times* spread as the story of "Winston Churchill's Great Great Great Great Grandmother."[31] This was a public relations coup for a newly conservative Britain—Heath was elected as prime minister in 1970—previously associated in the 1960s media with Russian spies (Kim Philby had defected in 1963), The Beatles, and the Campaign for Nuclear

Disarmament. These television programs also can be seen as a form of promotion for British products as well as advertising for tourism and the "heritage industry." No doubt they served to encourage travel to Britain to see the sights depicted on screen.

Hosted by Alistair Cooke, late of *Omnibus, Masterpiece Theatre* was from its inception a weekly visit to a peaceful little corner of England here in the United States; a civilized club for the cultured television viewer in an America torn by conflicting political, economic and cultural forces. It first appeared on January 10, 1971, and drew substantial audiences from commercial television before cable, syndication, and home video transformed the video landscape irrevocably.

Of course, this quiet and cultivated club was not completely immune from the outside atmosphere of political turmoil in the public television system. From the beginning of the Nixon administration, PBS was in trouble. When PBS was incorporated in 1969, Clay T. Whitehead, director of communications for the Nixon White House, immediately attempted to reduce the influence of the Ford Foundation in public broadcasting.[32] PBS was seen as consisting of "liberal and far-left producers, writers and commentators."[33] The solution was to change the structure of public television to eliminate these producers, writers, and commentators from the production process. Whitehead made the suggestion that PBS be deemphasized and the system shifted to the local level. "This provides an opportunity to further our philosophical and political objectives for public broadcasting without appearing to be politically motivated."[34] Whitehead proposed that funding go directly to local public television stations, which would provide programming independent from centralized control by what he saw as hostile and liberal-dominated National Educational Television and New York station WNET. As an alternative to NET, PBS did set up decentralized production centers, one of which—WGBH in Boston—became the presenting station for *Masterpiece Theatre*. Although by the time of Watergate the only regular public affairs program on PBS was hosted by William F. Buckley, the public television system did not go along willingly with the Nixon directives. Accordingly, on June 30, 1972, President Nixon vetoed the Corporation for Public Broadcasting's budget authorization and Frank Pace resigned as its chairman. The next day Whitehead recommended approval of the CPB budget.

The authors of the official history of public broadcasting note "Whitehead and his colleagues provided graphic demonstration of the political vulnerability that can strike at the core of American public broadcasting."[35] Among the programs cancelled in the wake of the conflict was the controversial series *The Great American Dream Machine*. It featured muckracking reporting and barbed contemporary political satire aimed at the establishment. However, *Masterpiece Theatre* was consistent with President Nixon's vision for public television, and it remained on the air throughout the tumult and confusion of the Nixon years, Watergate, and all subsequent administrations.

As Barnouw points out "the quest for the noncontroversial — the safely splendid . . . has tended to create on public television a fascinating past safely removed from the modern American culture of commercial television."[36] Here is a genuine difference between PBS and the commercial networks. Jane Feuer's study of the politics of quality in commercial network television, in the specific case of MTM, concluded that "Quality TV is liberal TV."[37] However, it is certainly not the case that this is how PBS would have chosen to define "quality TV" during the early 1970s.

The notion of "quality" is important to the Public Broadcasting Service, a private nonprofit membership organization founded in 1969, owned and operated by noncommercial television station licensees in the United States. It is their *raison d'être*. PBS's official slogan was once "TV worth watching" (today it is "If PBS doesn't do it, who will?"). The service promotes itself as a leader in quality programming.[38] One purpose of this book, therefore, is to document the history of *Masterpiece Theatre* as an institutional instance of a quality program.

Although considerable literature on quality television exists, it is not the purpose of this book to define the term in isolation. Researchers working for Corporation for Public Broadcasting (U.S.), the Broadcasting Research Unit (U.K.), the Committee on Financing the BBC (U.K.), the NHK Broadcasting Culture Research Institute (Japan), the University of Lund (Sweden), Laval University (Canada), and Michigan State University (U.S.) have all shared Jay Blumler's conclusion, "Of course, qualitative judgments of cultural goods are difficult to make and establish. It was interesting to find in this connection that most authors of the national reports had independently concurred a) that for a mass medium, such as television, elitist and narrowly high-cultural criteria of quality were inappropriate and b) there were several *sorts* of quality by which television might be judged [original emphasis]."[39]

The notion of "quality" was used politically by different actors, both individual and institutional, in the unfolding drama of the creation and maintenance of *Masterpiece Theatre*. The history of these choices provides the working definition of quality that accompanied such decisions—for particular individuals, institutions, and interests—against considerations of politics, economics, and personality. One can examine the contrasts between the official definitions of "integrity," "independence," and "quality" and the financial and political considerations evidenced by documents and testimony on the part of PBS, WGBH, British broadcasters, and Mobil.

PBS describes its National Program Service as a source of quality cultural television. *Masterpiece Theatre* is listed as one such quality television series. "Quality" is formally defined in the PBS *Program Producer's Handbook,* albeit in a tautological and roundabout fashion. PBS policies explicitly define a detailed responsibility for "program quality," residing in the judgment of television professionals. The official handbook states, "In selecting programs for its service, PBS seeks to obtain the highest quality programs available. Selection decisions require professional judgments about many different aspects of program quality, including but not limited to excellence, creativity, artistry, accuracy, balance, fairness, timeliness, innovation, boldness, thoroughness, credibility, and technical virtuosity. Similar judgments must be made about the program's ability to stimulate, enlighten, educate, inform, challenge, entertain, and amuse."[40] In other words, these criteria are to be used by PBS professionals, and not sponsors, to determine whether programs are suitable for broadcast. The sponsor should have no say in PBS programming decisions. However, as this book makes clear, at no time did PBS professionals successfully overrule Mobil's decisions regarding *Masterpiece Theatre*.

In its handbook, PBS states that it is a private nonprofit membership organization, owned and governed by its member stations, and its specific purpose is "to serve their needs" for quality programming. There are four official "fundamental principles" that shape this quality program service provided by PBS: editorial integrity, program quality, program diversity, and local station autonomy. "Editorial integrity" is defined as crucial to "PBS's reputation for quality." This section explicitly declares, "PBS's reputation for quality reflects the public's trust in the editorial integrity of PBS programs and the process by which they are selected. To maintain that trust, PBS and its member stations are responsible for shielding the programming process from political pressures or improper influences from program funders or other sources."[41] By PBS's own definition, quality is dependent on a programming process insulated from both political pressure and sponsor control.

By these official PBS criteria *Masterpiece Theatre* cannot be classified as a quality series. Mobil's Herb Schmertz clearly saw the program as a part of his political campaign to improve his company's image, and he exercised direct control over program acquisition and promotion, saying, "No one is going to spend Mobil's money but me."[42]

PBS requires two additional elements of "diversity" and "local station autonomy" in its definition of quality to assure 1) that no single supplier controls the content of programming on the service, "providing a bulwark against program domination by any single point of view," and 2) that local stations can select and schedule their own broadcasts with the recognition that "there are wide variations in local program needs and tastes. No one is better qualified to determine and respond to those local needs than the public television station licensed to that community."[43] However, Mobil was partially responsible for WGBH's growth into the largest program supplier in the PBS system. Mobil also asked WGBH to schedule national broadcasts at a fixed time, providing benefits such as publicity and fund-raising tie-ins to local stations.

So important are the quality requirements, according to the official PBS handbook, that "by placing its logo on a program, PBS makes itself accountable for the quality and integrity of the program. Program integrity encompasses not only the concerns addressed in these Editorial Standards, but also the concerns about improper funder influence and commercialism addressed in the National Program Funding Standards and Practices. If PBS concludes that a program fails to satisfy PBS's overall standard of quality . . . PBS may reject and withhold its logo from the program."[44] As will be shown, PBS did not withhold its logo from *Masterpiece Theatre,* and never publicly found Mobil's influence to be improper—

although there were private struggles to keep certain shows such as *Upstairs, Downstairs* off the schedule. It may be that PBS's official definition of "quality" is not a very reliable measure of the actual quality of a television program, after all. The criteria used by PBS seem to be bureaucratic rather than aesthetic ones.

PBS does not produce programs itself. Shows are obtained from public television stations, independent producers, television systems, and distributors. These suppliers are solely responsible for the content of programs aired on PBS. PBS is, officially at least a "service," not a network, and PBS is only one institution of several involved in the creation and maintenance of a series such as *Masterpiece Theatre*. The PBS system's role in the politics of quality is only one factor to be examined in this book.

WGBH, Boston, as the presenting station for *Masterpiece Theatre,* is responsible to both Mobil and PBS. The station prides itself on being "broadcasting's best." The WGBH annual report cites *Masterpiece Theatre* as one example of its "program milestones."[45] The notion of "quality" is also important to WGBH, in terms of its internal definition of programming as well as in its relation as a supplier to the larger public television system. The WGBH reputation for excellence is dependent on programs such as *Masterpiece Theatre*. This book will also examine the evolution of WGBH's role in defining the series.

The physical location of WGBH may play a part. Boston elites have a local tradition of respect for British cultural values, and a tradition of intellectual achievement symbolized by the Adams, Lowell, and Eliot families (although Boston is not regarded as an entertainment or theatre capital, perhaps a legacy of its Puritan heritage). In this regard, Digby Baltzell's two studies, *The Protestant Establishment* and *Puritan Boston and Quaker Philadelphia,* suggest that by adding the Boston imprimatur to the series, WGBH added to its reception as a quality program.[46]

Also to be considered in the ascription of quality to *Masterpiece Theatre* is the institutional pedigree of WGBH itself. Harvard is one member of The Lowell Institute, parent of the WGBH Educational Foundation. The other member institutions represented on the Board of WGBH are Boston College, the Boston Symphony Orchestra, Boston University, Brandeis University, the Massachusetts Institute of Technology, Museum of Fine Arts, Museum of Science, New England Conservatory of Music, Northeastern University, Simmons College, Tufts University, University of Massachusetts, and Wellesley College. Certainly the reputations of so many well-respected educational institutions added to the prestige of the station in educational circles.

Headquartered on the grounds of the Harvard Business School, WGBH was in part a creation of Harvard University president James Conant (in public broadcasting lore, the station call letters stand for "God Bless Harvard"). Conant saw radio and television broadcasting as part of his mission to secure Harvard's place as a national institution rather than a regional university. In one of many Crimson ties to England, Conant hired Charles Siepmann from the BBC to teach broadcasting and advocate a British-style public service philosophy for radio and television.[47]

While Harvard might not be able to compete with Broadway and Hollywood or the commercial networks in imagination or in popularity, nor to inform the population in the manner of newspaper and wire services, the university could claim to offer quality television as an alternative. In the same way, Harvard had offered quality education to compete with state universities, which had developed superior football teams and fraternity life (the Ivy League began as a football association). A quality university would seem to be a natural provider of quality broadcasting.

Quality is a central concept for British broadcasters and producers as well. Marmaduke Hussey, chairman of the BBC, declared, "The guiding principle of the BBC must be what it always has been—to provide the widest range of quality programmes right across the full range of license-payers' tastes, interests, and enthusiasm, or, as the [BBC] Charter outlines, to inform, educate, and entertain." And, quoting Lord Reith's remit for the service, "The BBC's role is to bring the best of everything to the greatest number of homes."[48] Commercial ITV franchises literally depended on quality. New franchise bids in past British government auctions for television licenses were solicited based on two criteria alone: "sound financing" and "stringent program quality guarantees." Those companies that passed the quality test were judged solely on the size of a cash bid submitted in a sealed brown envelope. However, the Independent Television Commission or ITC (governing body of the ITV system) had the discretion to award a television license to a lower bidder offering "'exceptionally' greater program quality."[49]

American sales to *Masterpiece Theatre* have directly affected British television companies. A 1984 headline in *Variety* read "Mobil Greases Its BBC Program Link: 17 Hours Annually."[50] By 1988, Mobil was paying up to $200,000 per hour of programming, and foreign sales were calculated in British production budgets. It is clear that some programs were made-to-order in England for sale to *Masterpiece Theatre*. Mobil sponsorship helped convert English program dumping into a profitable export industry. Three types of sales evolved over time: sales of completed shows "on the shelf" became presales of projects already underway, and finally led to coproductions made possible by Mobil's investment, sometimes initiated by corporation vice president Herb Schmertz.

Like PBS, WGBH, Boston, and English television companies, Mobil Corporation defines itself in terms of quality. The *1990 Annual Report* contained a chapter headed "Quality: hallmark of Mobil's operations." In discussing mining, minerals, real estate, and other operations the report notes, "We've taken Mobil's commitment to quality and made it the foundation of the way we do business. Called Total Quality Management (TQM), it's a process for building quality into products, services and relationships with suppliers, customers and other Mobil employees. We're listening to customers' needs in the hopes of exceeding their expectations."[51] Referring to *Masterpiece Theatre,* Mobil says, "Our cultural and community programs are designed to improve relations with the people and governments of the localities and countries where we operate."[52] A quality program like *Masterpiece Theatre* improves the reception of the company in public opinion and on Capitol Hill.

In his memoirs, *Goodbye to the Low Profile: The Art of Creative Confrontation,* Herb Schmertz says that Mobil bought programs from England because PBS could not produce the type of quality programming he wanted to buy for the price he felt he could pay. He notes that *Masterpiece Theatre* was attacked by Ed Asner and the Screen Actors Guild for relying on imported productions and undercutting American talent. Schmertz says he bought English programs based on "two criteria: quality and price. Unfortunately, in our experience, the American television industry isn't competitive in either respect."[53] Mobil wanted "value for money." Schmertz recounted that he was approached in 1970 by Stan Calderwood, president of WGBH, who informed him that Mobil could purchase thirty-nine hours of BBC television drama for $390,000. Even in 1970, notes Schmertz, "that was an absurdly low figure for television, so I was eager to learn more."[54]

As this discussion shows, quality was an important consideration to the national broadcasting service, the local station, the British suppliers, and the corporate sponsor. It was also important to the *New York Times,* which as a cultural arbiter in its reviews sought to evaluate the quality of the television programs, and which saw itself as a quality newspaper.[55] Mobil used the *Times* to express its views on political issues through advocacy advertising. This book seeks to relate the specific uses of quality to the particular agenda of each party to the series, and to the individual shows broadcast as part of *Masterpiece Theatre.*

The method followed in conducting this research into the politics of quality, as it relates to *Masterpiece Theatre,* places historical background at the core of the critical analysis of artistic works.[56] My investigation is based on Glaser and Strauss's conception of "grounded theory."[57] As they suggested, the first step is to ignore the literature of theory and fact on *Masterpiece Theatre* in order to ensure that whatever was discovered in the research would be free from contamination by concepts more suited to different fields of study.

A review of the literature shows there is relatively little scholarly material relating to the history of *Masterpiece Theatre* and only a small body of critical work. In a detailed analysis of the sociology of the series, Timothy Brennan records the overall trend in the development of *Masterpiece Theatre:* the replacement of adaptations from literary classics by original serial melodrama, a move that Brennan calls "downmarket." However, one must be careful before dismissing such series as *Upstairs, Downstairs* merely because they lack literary pedigree, for they maintain a literary sensibility.

Brennan concludes, "In a modest and limited way, *Masterpiece Theatre* is training us to read the 'literary' in a TV culture—to see in America the recurring parable of a rugged American success; to see in England the continued value of good breeding; and to imagine, as it is only possible in the confines of a living room, that a TV literature can raise select groups above the thousands of others who simply aren't tuned to the right channel."[58]

There is also a critique of the role of Edwardian costume drama in American culture by D. L. LeMahieu, which relates *Masterpiece Theatre* to larger cultural trends and argues that the Edwardian television series embody liberal social values typical of the Edwardian age itself.[59]

Books dealing specifically with *Masterpiece Theatre* have mostly been celebratory (and supported by Mobil), including the Museum of Broadcasting's retrospective catalogue.[60] There is a short account of *Masterpiece Theatre* included in former Mobil executive Herb Schmertz's memoir *Goodbye to the Low Profile* (mentioned earlier).[61] There are also books on *Upstairs, Downstairs, The Jewel in the Crown,* and *Piece of Cake,* among others.[62] However, these popular production histories do not relate the individual programs to *Masterpiece Theatre.* An article appeared in *Civilization* magazine about the series, asking "what makes a masterpiece?" But it was a mere five pages long.[63]

Recent literature about PBS does not primarily concern itself with *Masterpiece Theatre.* What histories exist are primarily concerned with public affairs programming or were paid for by public television and written by former public television employees and consultants, including the official PBS history, written by former PBS vice president John Witherspoon.[64] Even the second Carnegie Commission report was written at the initiative of the Corporation for Public Broadcasting.[65] The Carnegie Commission board contained members of the CPB as well as heads of local public television stations, who approved the final draft.[66] The CPB history, *A Report to the People: 20 Years of Your National Commitment to Public Broadcasting 1967–87,* is not, in fact, a history at all. It contains only a timeline, some sample programming descriptions, and the 1986 Annual Report.[67] Such material is self-serving and incomplete. The trade newspaper of the public broadcasting industry, *Current,* is partially owned by WGBH, and its coverage is not complete either.[68] A published dissertation on WGBH ends its history in 1965.[69] More recent books discuss *Masterpiece Theatre* only in passing.[70]

Although there is a massive amount of material on British broadcasting—almost every executive seems to have written a memoir or been the subject of a biography—and the debate over ITV franchises produced a wealth of pamphlets, books, and articles on British television policies and practices, there is very little British material on the *Masterpiece Theatre* coproduction relationship. Much of what literature does exist mistakenly claims that American partners had slight or no influence on the productions they funded. For example, Shaun Sutton—who coordinated BBC coproduction with *Masterpiece Theatre*—wrote that the BBC philosophy was "Just give us the money, and leave us alone. We'll send you a print by and by . . . "[71] Manuel Alvarado and John Stewart's edited volume on Euston Films takes at face value Mike Phillips's statement that Mobil, while informed of casting and other considerations, does not interfere with programs it purchases.[72] On the other hand, Colin McArthur has admitted, "Many of the facts which require to be known about coproduction are [still unknown] . . . the financial terms, the extent of the division of editorial control, the implications for the choice of topics and for the format and content of programmes."[73]

Included in this book are attempts to respond to McArthur's questions, based on the information available at the present time. There is an excellent dissertation by Jonathan Tankel on the history of ITV exports to the United States in the 1960s, and it does refer to the use of ITV programming on *Masterpiece Theatre*. But the PBS series is not the focus of Tankel's study, and therefore McArthur's questions are not answered in detail.[74]

There is a large amount of literature dealing with Mobil's advocacy advertising, including four dissertations dealing specifically with the corporation's *New York Times* op-ed campaigns. However, only passing mention is made of *Masterpiece Theatre*.[75] Herbert Schiller's *Culture, Inc.* discusses the phenomenon of corporate support of the arts, but there is no listing for *Masterpiece Theatre* in the index, and only one reference to Mobil.[76] Erik Barnouw's *The Sponsor* does discuss *Masterpiece Theatre* in relation to Mobil, but his account is derived largely from secondary sources.[77]

Much of the primary research material for this book is based on interviews with public broadcasters, British television producers, actors, officials, and Mobil consultants and executives. Some thirty interviews were conducted in the course of the primary investigation, although not all are quoted. Interviews are of course accepted for what they are, partial and sometimes self-serving accounts. For that reason, and because I was unable to interview certain figures involved in the development of *Masterpiece Theatre* who are now deceased, such as former PBS president Hartford Gunn and WGBH general manager Michael Rice, many of the facts from different interviews were cross-referenced to organize a preliminary account of events.

Then this chronology was compared to available documentation. No document collection permitted unlimited access to all its material. The Nixon, Ford, and Carter presidential libraries restricted access to certain files. For example, correspondence regarding the controversy over the broadcast of *Death of a Princess* by WGBH is sealed for "national security reasons" in the Brzezinski papers at the Carter library. Most sources, including BBC, ITV, Mobil, PBS, and WGBH, did provide substantial access to selected materials, including clippings, newsletters, and program information. Several people, however, requested that I not quote from interviews I conducted with them.

Only the CPB totally prohibited any access to its files and would not release even the minutes of legally mandated open and public board meetings. CPB's stated reason, in a letter from its counsel, was that it "does not permit access to its confidential business records."[78] Certain individuals provided some materials not available from archival collections. In most cases, the available interviews and documents corroborated one another. Where they did not, discrepancies are noted in the text.

This interview and documentary material was compared to published accounts in trade journals and the press, especially the *New York Times, Boston Globe,* and *Variety.* Where there were discrepancies, they are noted in the text. I regarded no single source as infallible, and compared newspaper accounts with documents and interviews.

Finally, I screened a selection of *Masterpiece Theatre* programs from the collection donated by Mobil to the UCLA Film and Television Archive. I have watched at least part of each of the following series: *The Six Wives of Henry VIII, Elizabeth R, Tom Brown's Schooldays, The Unpleasantness at the Bellona Club, Upstairs, Downstairs, Dickens of London, I, Claudius, The Duchess of Duke Street, Lillie, Disraeli, Testament of Youth, Danger UXB, A Town Like Alice, Flame Trees of Thika, Edward and Mrs. Simpson, Flickers, To Serve Them All My Days, On Approval, Private Schulz, The*

Irish R.M., The Jewel in the Crown, Lord Mountbatten: The Last Viceroy, Lost Empires, Silas Marner, The Bretts, Sorrell and Son, A Very British Coup, Piece of Cake, The Charmer, A Tale of Two Cities, After the War, The Dressmaker, Traffik, The Ginger Tree, Jeeves and Wooster, Scoop, House of Cards, The Shiralee, and *Summer's Lease.*

I screened episodes of Alistair Cooke's television series *International Zone* and *Omnibus,* and material from *Mobil Showcase Network* programs, as well, paying special attention to the *Fable for Now* commercials that accompanied them. I then compared them with the surrounding testimony and archival materials. Where no documentation could be found for an interpretation, it is noted in the text as a hypothesis, educated guess, or my own personal point of view.

Notes

1. Pierre Bourdieu, *Distinction: A Social Critique of the Judgement of Taste,* trans. Richard Nice (Cambridge: Harvard University Press, 1984).

2. Bourdieu, *Distinction.* See also *Homo Academicus* (Stanford: Stanford University Press, 1988), and *In Other Words: Essays Towards a Reflexive Sociology,* trans. Matthew Adamson (Stanford: Stanford University Press, 1990).

3. Bourdieu, *Distinction,* xii.

4. Horace Newcomb and Paul M. Hirsch, "Television As a Cultural Forum," in *Television: The Critical View* (New York: Oxford University Press, 1987), 455–70.

5. Raymond Williams, *Raymond Williams on Television: Selected Writings,* ed. Alan O'Connor (London: Routledge, 1989), 26–29.

6. Williams, *Raymond Williams on Television,* 29.

7. Bourdieu, *Distinction,* 11–96.

8. Erik Barnouw, *The Sponsor* (Oxford: Oxford University Press, 1978), 149.

9. Barnouw, *The Sponsor,* 150.

10. Stuart Hall, "Encoding/Decoding," in *Culture, Media, Language,* ed. Stuart Hall et al. (London: Hutchinson, 1980), 123–38.

11. Herbert Gans, *Popular Culture and High Culture: An Analysis of Evaluation and Taste* (New York: Basic Books, 1974). This twenty-year-old study by Gans is far superior to a recent paper reaching similar conclusions filled with Lacanian jargon by Richard J. Schaefer, "Public Television Constituencies: A Study in Media Aesthetics and Intentions,"

Journal of Film and Video 43, no. 1–2 (Spring/Summer 1991): 46–68. Schaefer neglects to cite Gans and omits the official history of public television by Witherspoon and Kovitz.

12. Gans, *Popular Culture and High Culture,* 68.

13. Russell Lynes, *The Tastemakers* (New York: Grosset and Dunlap, 1954), 311–12.

14. C. Wright Mills, *The Power Elite* (New York: Oxford University Press, 1956), 329–30.

15. Herb Schmertz with William Novak, *Goodbye to the Low Profile: The Art of Creative Confrontation* (Boston: Little, Brown, 1986).

16. Official Herb Schmertz biography, The Schmertz Company, New York, 1991. Schmertz resigned from the Presidential Advisory Commission in 1988 when he became public relations advisor to the government of Saudi Arabia.

17. Herbert Schiller, *Culture, Inc.: The Corporate Takeover of Public Expression* (New York: Oxford University Press, 1989).

18. Kathryn C. Montgomery, *Target: Prime Time. Advocacy Groups and the Struggle Over Entertainment Television* (New York: Oxford University Press, 1989).

19. Todd Gitlin, *Inside Prime Time* (New York: Pantheon, 1983), 255.

20. Ed Morris, Director, Public Information, PBS. Memorandum to Promotion Directors. Re: Jude the Obscure. September 23, 1971. The memo comments on an article in *Scholastic Teacher Teleguide,* saying: "We are very unhappy about the way this material is labeled, i. e., Mobil's Masterpiece Theatre, as we were not consulted about this . . . " Photocopy in author's collection.

21. Robert Hewison, *The Heritage Industry* (London: Methuen, 1987).

22. Paul Tabori, *Alexander Korda* (London: Oldbourne, 1959).

23. Alexander Korda, "British Films: Today and Tomorrow" in Alexander Davy, *Footnotes to the Film* (London: Lovett, Dickinson, 1938), 167–68.

24. Howard Suber, "The Anti-Communist Blacklist in the Hollywood Motion Picture Industry," University of California, Los Angeles, dissertation, 1968.

25. Tim Brooks and Earle Marsh, *Complete Guide to Prime-Time Network Shows: 1946–Present* (New York: Ballantine, 1988).

26. Jeff Greenfield, *Television: The First Fifty Years,* (New York: Crescent, 1981), 107.

27. Jonathan Tankel, *The ITV Thriller,* University of Wisconsin dissertation, 1984.

28. Schmertz and Novak, *Goodbye to the Low Profile,* 222.

29. Robert Hathaway, *Great Britain and the United States* (Boston: Twayne, 1990).

30. William Safire, *Before the Fall: An Inside View of the Pre-Watergate White House* (New York: Belmont Tower, 1975), 125–26.

31. Schmertz and Novak, *Goodbye to the Low Profile*, 225.

32. John Witherspoon and Roselle Kovitz, *History of Public Broadcasting* (Washington, DC: Current, 1989).

33. Witherspoon and Kovitz, 43.

34. Witherspoon and Kovitz, 43.

35. Witherspoon and Kovitz, 46.

36. Barnouw, 146–51.

37. Jane Feuer, Paul Kerr, and Tise Vahimagi, *MTM: Quality Television* (London: BFI, 1984), 56.

38. Public Broadcasting Service, *Facts about PBS* (Alexandria: PBS, February 1991), 2–3.

39. Home Office, *Research on the Range and Quality of Broadcasting Services: A Report for the Committee on Financing the BBC* (West Yorkshire Media in Politics Group, Centre for Television Research, The University of Leeds, London: HMSO, January, 1976), 170. Other works on this topic include Sakae Ishikawa, "Quality Assessment of Broadcast Programming," *Studies of Broadcasting (special issue)* (Tokyo: Broadcasting Culture Research Institute, 1991); Bradley S. Greenberg, *Production, Technological, Economic and Audience Factors in Assessing Quality in Public Service Television* (Michigan State University: Department of Telecommunications, February, 1991); CPB, *Proceedings of the 1980 Technical Conference on Qualitative Television Ratings, Final Report* (Washington, DC: Office of Communication Research,1980); Broadcasting Research Unit, *Quality in Television—Programmes, Programme-makers, Systems* (London: John Libbey, 1989).

40. Public Broadcasting Service, *Program Producers Handbook* (Alexandria: PBS, August, 1990), 2.

41. PBS, *Program Producers Handbook*, 2.

42. Herb Schmertz, personal interview, 15 March 1991. After conflicts with Mobil and WGBH, PBS withdrew entirely from creative participation in *Masterpiece Theatre*, leaving decisions to WGBH. Herb Schmertz said, "I think PBS would have liked to have had a larger role in all these activities, but basically we were dealing with the station of entry and PBS didn't give us anything of any use. They couldn't deliver the network for the other stations on specific dates and times 'cause the other stations wouldn't agree to that, so they really didn't deliver anything. There was nothing. I would have been happy to deal with them if they had anything to offer, but they really, basically, didn't really have anything to offer."

43. *Program Producers Handbook*, 2.

44. *Program Producers Handbook*, 2–5.

45. "National Television Productions," *WGBH/Boston Annual Report* (Boston: WGBH, 1989), 4.

46. Digby Baltzell, *Puritan Boston and Quaker Philadelphia* (New York: Free Press, 1979), and *The Protestant Establishment* (New Haven: Yale University Press, 1987).

47. Richard Norton Smith, *The Harvard Century: The Making of a University to a Nation* (New York: Simon and Schuster, 1986).

48. Marmaduke Hussey, "Chairman's Foreword," *BBC Annual Report and Accounts 1989/90* (London: BBC, 1990), 2–3.

49. Adam Dawtrey, "40 ITV License Bids Expected Today," *Hollywood Reporter,* 15 May 1991, 4.

50. *Daily Variety,* 10 January 1984.

51. Mobil Corporation, *1990 Annual Report* (Fairfax, 1990), 23.

52. Mobil, *1990 Annual Report.*

53. Schmertz and Novak, *Goodbye to the Low Profile,* 225.

54. Schmertz and Novak, *Goodbye to the Low Profile,* 222.

55. The paper's motto is: "All the news that's fit to print."

56. H. Aram Veeser, *The New Historicism* (New York: Routledge, 1989).

57. Barney G. Glaser and Anselm L. Strauss, *The Discovery of Grounded Theory* (Chicago: Aldine Publishing Company, 1967).

58. Timothy Brennan, "Masterpiece Theatre and the Uses of Tradition," *American Media and Mass Culture: Left Perspectives,* ed. Donald Lazere (Berkeley: University of California Press, 1987), 373.

59. D. L. LeMahieu, "Imagined Contemporaries: Edwardian Costume Drama," *Historical Journal of Film, Radio, and Television,* 10, no. 3 (1990), 243–56.

60. Alistair Cooke, *Masterpieces: A Decade of Masterpiece Theatre* (New York: Knopf, 1981); Museum of Broadcasting, *The Museum of Broadcasting Celebrates Mobil & Masterpiece Theatre: 15 Years of Excellence* (New York: Museum of Broadcasting, 1986); Greg Vitello, ed., *Twenty Seasons of Mobil Masterpiece Theatre: 1971–1991* (Fairfax: Mobil Corporation, 1991).

61. Schmertz and Novak, *Goodbye to the Low Profile,* 221–33.

62. For example, Patty Lou Floyd, *Backstairs with Upstairs, Downstairs* (New York: St. Martin's Press, 1988); Mollie Hardwick, *The World of Upstairs, Downstairs* (New York: Holt, 1976); Bamber Gascoigne, *The Making of The Jewel in the Crown* (New York: St. Martin's Press, 1983).

63. Rachel Shteir, "What Makes a Masterpiece?" *Civilization,* August/September 1997, 46–51.

64. John P. Witherspoon and Roselle Kovitz, *A Tribal Memory of Public Broadcasting: Missions, Mandates, Assumptions, Structure* (Washington, DC: CPB, July 1986).

65. Carnegie Corporation of New York, *A Public Trust: The Report of the Carnegie Commission on the Future of Public Broadcasting* (New York: Bantam, 1979).

66. Carnegie Corporation, *A Public Trust,* i–ii. Among the public television officials on the commission were Henry Cauthen, SECA; Virginia Duncan, CPB; and Bill Moyers, WNET.

67. Corporation for Public Broadcasting, *A Report to the People: 20 Years of Your National Commitment to Public Broadcasting 1967–87* (Washington, DC: 1987).

68. The members of the *Current* Publishing Committee are: Educational Broadcasting Corporation, New York; Maryland Center for Public Broadcasting; WGBH Educational Foundation, Boston; Public Broadcasting Council of Central New York; WNED, Buffalo; WTTW, Chicago; KQED, San Francisco; KCET, Los Angeles; WETA, Washington, DC; and WOSU, Columbus. *Current,* 29 April 1991, 29.

69. Edwin Leonard Glick, "WGBH-TV: The First Ten Years (1955–65)," University of Michigan dissertation, 1970.

70. For example, James Ledbetter's *Made Possible By . . . The Death of Public Broadcasting in the United States* (New York: Verso, 1997) devotes only four pages to the series (143–46). An exception is my own chapter-length study "Mobil's Masterpiece" in *PBS: Behind the Screen* (Rocklin, CA: Prima, 1997).

71. Shaun Sutton, *The Largest Theatre in the World: 30 Years of Television Drama* (London: BBC, 1982), 144.

72. Manuel Alvarado and John Stewart, *Made for Television: Euston Films Limited* (London: BFI, 1985).

73. Colin McArthur, *Television and History,* Television Monograph No. 8 (London: BFI, 1980), 57–58.

74. Tankel, *The ITV Thriller.*

75. Patricia Ann Davis, *A Description and Analysis of Mobil Oil Corporation Advertising on the Basis of Content and Context before, during, and after the Oil Crisis,* New York University dissertation, 1979; Larry Allen Williamson, *Transcendence, Ethics, and Mobil Oil: A Rhetorical Investigation,* Purdue University dissertation, 1982; Janice Walker Anderson, *A Quantitative and Qualitative Analysis of Mobil's Advocacy Advertising in The New York Times,* Penn State University dissertation, 1984; Gary Kurzbard, *Ethos and Industry: A Critical Study of Oil Industry Advertising from 1974–1984,* Purdue University dissertation, 1984.

76. Herbert Schiller, *Culture, Inc.: The Corporate Takeover of Public Expression* (New York: Oxford University Press, 1989).

77. Barnouw, *The Sponsor.*

78. Paul E. Symczak, Corporation for Public Broadcasting, letter to author, 19 April 1991.

2

WGBH and the Origin of
Masterpiece Theatre

Our working arrangement for *Masterpiece Theatre* has always been with WGBH-TV in Boston, which, in the language
of television, serves as the "station of entry." While WGBH
has the final say on program selection, we provide the leadership on advertising, promotion, and publicity.
        —Herb Schmertz, *Goodbye to the Low Profile*

If *Masterpiece Theatre* was "an agreeable form of moonlighting"
to host Alistair Cooke[1] and "simply a tile in that mosaic"[2] of Mobil's public relations effort for Herb Schmertz, it is something far
more important to the Public Broadcasting Service and to WGBH,
Boston. The twenty-seven-year-old series is the longest running
program on the PBS prime-time schedule. It was the first regularly
scheduled drama series to be supported by a major corporation. It
had won twenty-nine Emmys by 1998 and the 1991 Governor's
Award from the Academy of Television Arts and Sciences. It is the
only PBS prime-time drama series to have successfully created a
"spin-off"—*Mystery!* In fact, to this day *Mystery!* and *Masterpiece Theatre* are the only year-round weekly dramatic series during
prime-time on PBS. Perhaps even more importantly, Mobil is the
largest single underwriter of programming on WGBH, accounting
for between 10 and 15 percent of the station's 100 million dollar
budget in 1991 and helping to make WGBH the largest single
source of programming for PBS. Finally, surveys of donors show
that *Masterpiece Theatre* "is at the top of their list of favorites."[3]

It is safe to conclude that, however minor a project the host and underwriter claim the series is to them, *Masterpiece Theatre* is truly "the jewel in the crown" of the American public television system.

John W. Macy Jr., first president of the Corporation for Public Broadcasting, was among the fans of the series. His widow recalls "*Masterpiece Theatre* was our favorite program and we never missed it."[4] John J. O'Connor, television critic of the *New York Times,* said the show was one of the "unmistakable landmarks in the history of American television," showing that "first-class quality television can be done."[5]

Peter Spina, who succeeded Herb Schmertz at Mobil, observed, "if you do a good comprehensive survey, focus group, 'PBS, what does PBS mean to you?' Invariably, it'll be *Masterpiece Theatre.* Not going to be *Nova.* It's not going to be *Sesame Street.* You know. They'll all rate high, but it'll be *Masterpiece Theatre . . . Masterpiece Theatre* is what people first think of when they think of PBS."[6]

Today *Masterpiece Theatre* and *Mystery!* occupy their own suite of offices in WGBH's headquarters building (for which the station pays one dollar a year symbolic rent) on the grounds of the Harvard Business School in Allston, Massachusetts (a reminder of the public broadcasting legend that WGBH call letters stand for "God Bless Harvard"). The executive producer has her own budget of between $10 and $15 million a year, all of which came from Mobil until 1998, when the Corporation for Public Broadcasting made its first grant to pay for programs in the *American Collection.* WGBH spends about $2 million of that budget to cover station overhead. The *Masterpiece Theatre* production unit reports directly to WGBH president Henry Becton. It is independent of national program head Peter McGhee and the other divisions of the station. Promotion and publicity have been handled outside of WGBH by Mobil and its press agents, for many years Frank and Arlene Goodman Associates, who were replaced around the time Russell Baker replaced Alistair Cooke by Owen Comora Associates. Although WGBH has the contractual right to decide which shows are chosen for broadcast, they must consult Mobil on all program decisions. WGBH produces the framing and filler sequences for the programs, and arranges for all the technical requirements of the PBS system. PBS has no direct involvement in the production of the series.[7]

This structure for the production and distribution of *Masterpiece Theatre* is in large measure due to the initiative of Stanford Calderwood, who during the six months he was head of WGBH before resigning under pressure in 1970, put together the enduring elements of *Masterpiece Theatre*. Mobil's Schmertz is the first to give him credit. "You know none of this would have happened without Stan," he says. "It might have happened another way but it probably wouldn't have happened with me if it hadn't been for Stan Calderwood."[8]

In May 1970, Calderwood retired as executive vice president of the Polaroid Corporation, where he had responsibility for advertising and marketing. He says, "I had been at Polaroid for 17 years . . . when I decided to resign to go into 'public service.' My stock options had been good to me, I was bored, and a change was sought by a guy about to become 50 years old."[9] He went to work as president of WGBH, at the urging of friend and neighbor Julia Child (star of *The French Chef*), on June 30th of that year. Impressed by the success of *The Forsyte Saga*, Calderwood felt such miniseries could create a unique franchise for public television. Calderwood wanted to build up presentations of British series as something special public television had to offer viewers.

He brought with him a solid background in corporate support for quality commercial television and other cultural projects. While at Polaroid, Calderwood had "learned to stretch dollars to build the company's image," working primarily with CBS and NBC to sponsor public affairs programs such as *Berlin Blockade* and Leonard Bernstein's New York Philharmonic *Young People's Concerts*. These were financed from what Calderwood called a "slush fund," allocated directly by Edwin Land (Polaroid's founder) to purchase shows that at the last minute still had not found other sponsors and were therefore available at "distress prices." Calderwood's instruction to the CBS advertising sales department was that Polaroid would never pay full price, but after the network had tried and failed to sell a show elsewhere, Polaroid would be interested in buying it.

He not only bought television time, but also paid for art shows at major museums that displayed Polaroid photography. The first was for Marie Cosindas. Calderwood put together a collection of her prints, had the catalog inserted in the *Saturday Review of Literature,* and "convinced" the Museum of Modern Art in New York, the Art Institute of Chicago, and the Boston Museum of Fine

Arts to give Cosindas a show. Polaroid paid for the opening receptions, catalogs, and other related expenses.

Polaroid had been the first national underwriter for Julia Child's *The French Chef* on public television (although the Boston Gas Company sponsored construction of her kitchen and Safeway Stores was production underwriter).[10] In exchange, Polaroid received credit on the show's title sequence. Thus, by the time Calderwood took over at WGBH he had "a long record of squeezing a great deal out of quality programming or exposure." Calderwood's advantage was that he "understood most corporations didn't want to pay for it [quality television], even at reduced prices."[11] Calderwood was convinced that a strategy similar to the one he had used at Polaroid for network television would work to bring quality programs to WGBH.

Before the Nixon administration's confrontation with National Educational Television (NET) and the Ford Foundation, the New York station WNET had been the public television system's major national program supplier. Among its offerings were such highly regarded drama series as *New York Television Playhouse* and *NET Playhouse*. In 1969, NET had successfully presented the BBC's production of *The Forsyte Saga,* for example, with commentary by public television executive James Day. By building on the success of the program, Calderwood took advantage of the slowness of the Ford Foundation to follow up, as well as WNET's relative weakness in relation to WGBH, since the New York station had been singled out for criticism by the Nixon administration, which was seeking to reduce the amount of what it saw as liberal bias on public television.

The new president of PBS, Hartford Gunn, had been Calderwood's immediate predecessor as president of WGBH. Due in part to Gunn's achievement in organizing—as a competitor to NET—the Eastern Educational Network (EEN) of noncommercial stations centered at WGBH, Gunn was chosen to become the first head of the newly formed Public Broadcasting Service in 1970. With a sympathetic Gunn as head of the national system, Calderwood saw the chance to make WGBH into an alternative national supplier for PBS, thereby building up both the finances and public image of the local broadcaster.

The Boston public television station had a long tradition of local program sponsorship throughout the 1960s. Prior to Calderwood's arrival, local companies behind programs included the First National Bank of Boston, the John Hancock Life Insurance Company, and Dick Russell's Pontiac Village (a Boston car dealer).[12] Writing in 1970, Edwin Glick concluded that "regardless of the justification given, any viewer of WGBH's programs or any reader of the station's *Annual Reports* will realize that 'underwriting' or 'sponsorship'—call it what one will—is a major fact of life at WGBH and one of the reasons so many of its major productions have shown the quality which has become a hallmark of so much of the station's output."[13] This local support from sponsors had been one of the accomplishments of Hartford Gunn, a graduate of Harvard's business school.

Under Gunn, corporations had been encouraged to pay for program advertising in newspapers and magazines. Such cooperative advertising promoted the station and the sponsor in tandem. In 1962, WGBH was already receiving $15,000 worth of such advertising support. For example, Beacon Wax paid to promote *Open End*, publishers were paying to publicize a book series called *I've Been Reading,* and a large Boston-based construction company, the Perini Corporation, paid "to plug a film on the construction of the second East Boston Tunnel."[14] The pattern of corporate sponsorship and corporate advertising for public television series found in *Masterpiece Theatre* had already been worked out on the local level at WGBH during his tenure.

In June 1970, before taking over Gunn's job at WGBH and going on the station payroll, Calderwood flew to London, where—while his wife was completing her Harvard dissertation research on Islamic art—he made a "cold call" to the BBC from his hotel room at Claridges. Calderwood told the BBC that he was inquiring about buying programming "off the shelf." He was working unofficially, with no budget and no authority. Calderwood recalls meeting with Robin Scott, then head of BBC-2, to whom he conveyed his enthusiasm for *The Forsyte Saga.*[15] He followed up with a request to see any of the other "good drama" the BBC had "on the shelf." Calderwood told Scott that he was convinced he "could raise the money to put on a 39-week series if they would give us a good price. The *quid pro quo* was that it would be driving a wedge into the American TV market for the BBC." Calderwood characterizes the nature of his appeal as "pragmatic." He recalls telling Scott that discount sales to WGBH would benefit the BBC: "Look,

I said, that good stuff sitting in the can is like a hotel room un-
sold—it's worthless. Why not give us some cut prices and use it as
a loss leader?"[16]

Time-Life Films owned the distribution rights to current BBC
drama productions, but Scott told Calderwood that he would ask
Time-Life to give WGBH the best possible price, "taking less than
they would normally expect from commercial TV." Calderwood
then screened the available programs at the BBC. While he originally had been searching only for drama, Scott insisted that
Calderwood also consider nature series along with drama productions. Calderwood went along, promising Scott "if I got the drama
going, nature would be next." Calderwood returned from London
carrying some 16 mm kinescopes.[17]

When he was officially installed as president of WGBH, Calderwood did not mention to anyone that he had the BBC kinescopes,
and kept silent about "my thoughts about seeking sponsorship for the
BBC material." Calderwood attributes this to what he says was an
atmosphere of hostility to large corporations that confronted him at
the station. Apparently, sponsorship by local companies was one
thing, but seeking the support of big business might provoke a strong
reaction from the politically committed staff at WGBH. Calderwood
characterizes the political situation at WGBH in 1970 as "a sandbox
for overgrown kids. We were coming out of the sixties, and a great
many people with a radical bent found public TV the ideal place
to exercise their private antiestablishment agendas. It seemed to
me they informally dominated the place."[18] Therefore, the former
corporate executive and new station president trod carefully.

Calderwood says he found the station staff to be selfish and un-
interested in "what was best for public television as a whole; instead, it was generally a sense of the 'me' generation. 'What can
you do for my particular bailiwick?' was the response I got most
often as I got to know the staff." Calderwood wanted to use BBC
shows to attract financial support that could benefit producers at
the station, in effect having the British productions serve to subsidize local output. When he presented the idea of using inexpensive
BBC material to build audiences and raise corporate financing and
individual contributions to the station staff, Calderwood met
strong opposition. "There were damn few on the staff—at any
level—that thought much of the idea . . . If I was going to raise corporate money, skip the audience-building, and get the money for

this pet project or that pet project," he recalls. Apparently, the personnel at WGBH wanted Calderwood to raise money directly for their own local productions instead of English drama.

Calderwood says the only two supporters he had at the station were David O. Ives, a former *Wall Street Journal* reporter who was then general manager and later succeeded him as president, and Michael Rice, who was at the time program director and was later promoted to general manager by Ives. They were skeptical at first, he says, but were sympathetic because they too had been impressed by the success of *The Forsyte Saga*. Because of the hostility of the "sandbox," Calderwood says he left the "endless problems at the station" to Ives and Rice and "as frequently as I could I was on the plane getting all the pieces into place [for *Masterpiece Theatre*]."[19]

David M. Davis (who went on to head *American Playhouse* and the documentary series *P.O.V.*) was in 1970 Ford Foundation officer for public television and himself a former manager at WGBH. Davis recalls talking to Calderwood frequently during this period. Calderwood first met with National Educational Television in New York, to ask them if they planned to follow up on the success of *The Forsyte Saga,* which they had purchased with a no-strings Ford Foundation grant approved by Davis. "Stan went right down to New York, talked to the people then running NET, saying 'You got this great hit, what are you going to follow it up with?' And their answer was 'Well, we don't have any money, we can't make any commitments, so we don't have anything to follow it with.' First big hit. Well, this guy was on practically the next airplane to London."

Calderwood's style was different from that of most other educational broadcasters in 1970. Where they saw themselves as educators, Calderwood saw himself as a businessman. Davis recalls just how strange this approach appeared at the time. "He knew the commercial world and marketing and all that . . . In the next six weeks he saw more chief executive officers, chairmen of the boards of major U.S. corporations than anybody in noncommercial broadcasting ever had in the past twenty years. He came out of the commercial world. He had the ad agency contacts. He had access. He could talk to them in their language. What does your corporation need, what do we have to offer? And he made the sale to Mobil directly to the chairman, of this concept, of *Masterpiece Theatre*."[20]

Calderwood's first step, however, was to get a reasonable price from Time-Life. Time-Life Films was a new division of Time Inc. that was formed in 1969 when it acquired Peter M. Robeck and Company, a small distributor of filmed television programming such as *The Roy Rogers Show* and *Death Valley Days.* Time Inc. wanted Robeck's connection to the BBC pipeline for itself as it moved into new television ventures. Robeck had been a BBC distributor since 1959, when Don Taffner—representing London's Thames Television in New York—had introduced the BBC account to him. For ten years, Robeck had been trying to package English programming with a sponsor while distributing primarily to educational television. In his earliest success, he had sold the *An Age of Kings* package to Humble Oil in 1961 for broadcast on NET. This experience gave Robeck the impression that there was a viable market for commercial sponsorship of BBC shows. "I had an ever growing conviction that there was a place in this country for BBC product," he says. "It had been mishandled very badly in terms of public broadcasting . . . but the BBC had this very strong desire to be exposed in the United States." Robeck says that initially the BBC executives were not profit-driven. "They didn't give a damn because they weren't getting any of the money anyway, but the exposure was good for them for credits and all that, because everybody there wanted to come here to work." In one of his first moves to raise revenues, Robeck stopped all sales for almost a year, until NET was willing to negotiate higher prices with him.[21]

Robeck sold Kenneth Clark's *Civilization* to Xerox for PBS broadcast immediately prior to the acquisition of his company by Time Inc. in 1969. At the time Robeck sold *Civilization,* his price of one million dollars was the highest amount ever paid for a BBC show. He had made the deal through a New York public relations company called Marshall and Bloom, owned by Frank Marshall and Phil Bloom. Marshall was a Xerox executive speech writer who had set up his own shop and made television sponsorship one of his specialties as a corporate consultant. Marshall would come to play an important role in the development of *Masterpiece Theatre* as an advisor to Mobil's Herb Schmertz.

Robeck's own background, like Calderwood's and Marshall's, had been in the commercial arena. Since graduating from UCLA, he had worked for CBS, the *Los Angeles Times,* and RKO General before setting up his own business. He sold his company to Time

Inc. for stock valued at $675,000 and the presidency of Time-Life Films.

Time Inc. owned five television stations when Robeck arrived. The company had also invested in MGM, buying five percent of the company's stock in 1967. *Life* magazine had been producing sponsored documentaries for Alcoa and the Hughes Television Network. Time-Life Books was collaborating with MGM and NBC on a series sponsored by General Electric, through Time-Life Broadcast. This division had produced a twelve-part nature series called *The World We Live In,* based on the *Life Nature Library* and the *Life Science Library,* with a second season of fourteen episodes underway. *Sports Illustrated* was also making short television films sponsored by Shell Oil Company, which featured offbeat facts about sports and sports figures, and Time Inc. was negotiating directly with the BBC to coproduce a historical documentary series entitled *The British Empire* with companion volumes from Time-Life Books. However, the company's various television projects were not being managed efficiently, and what was worse from Time Inc.'s point of view, they were losing money. After a management study, they bought Robeck's firm because of its good track record in television sales. Time-Life was looking forward to syndication of BBC material through independent stations and toward securing product for its future in cable television and educational markets. Time Inc.'s management study indicated that of the 5,000 hours of programs produced by the BBC each year, at least 100 hours could be sold in the U.S.[22] In fact, shortly after Robeck's arrival, Time Inc. sold its television stations to develop cable and other markets.[23]

Robeck and Time-Life Films agreed with Calderwood's view that showing BBC series on PBS through WGBH made sense. Calderwood had convinced Robeck that "if he let us have the programs cheap, it would be like getting paid to run what in effect would be commercials for his library of BBC programming."[24] Robeck had not yet been able to sell the shows to anyone else and accepted a price of ten thousand dollars per hour. Robeck says, "I thought it was a very important deal because this was going to get an exposure, and it was going to be in a good time period and all that. And I think it did. I think *Masterpiece Theatre* loosened up the American marketplace very considerably."[25]

With Time Inc. on board, the supply of product was now assured, but Calderwood had other worries. With his experience in advertising and marketing behind him, the WGBH president realized that corporate sponsors required "PBS network guarantees, not the individual indications from a bunch of individual stations to run the programs at their whim."[26] Calderwood claims that the commitment was easily secured because PBS had more hours than they did decent programming." PBS agreed in principle to provide a regularly scheduled time for the program. It may have helped that PBS President Hartford Gunn was former president of WGBH. In any case, Calderwood had put a "package" together consisting of "the programs at a decent price and wide exposure available if we got the right programs." His next step was to find a sponsor, or in the professional language of the public television system, an "underwriter."

Calderwood began his search for a sponsor by working up "some cost-per-thousand figures that even the most skeptical advertising director would find hard to resist." Based on his own personal experience "of successfully reaching small but important audiences with quality programming, I felt sure I had a winner. Some underwriter was going to come off looking very prestigious with only a relatively small cash outlay." Calderwood felt the presence of such prestige programming would also build up audiences for public television "who could write bigger checks when the appeals went out." Thus, the arrangement would be mutually beneficial for WGBH, the PBS system, and the corporate sponsor.[27]

Calderwood contacted advertising agencies to try and sell them on the idea of sponsoring BBC drama on PBS, since they were the best placed source of potential underwriting money. However, Calderwood found opposition from the agencies he approached, who "would only see noncommissionable dollars being spent by their client." That is, support of public television would not come out of an advertising budget because of its statutory noncommercial nature. "Such dollars would cut into their profits, and they would put the whammy on the idea." He managed to get a few screenings, one with AT&T, which expressed interest and gave Calderwood two meetings. However, "the idea got choked someplace 'upstairs.' "

After this rebuff, Calderwood called in a personal favor from Joe Daly, chairman of the Doyle, Dane, Bernbach advertising agency. Daly's friendship with Calderwood resulted from years of handling Polaroid's business—the Land camera was one the agency's first major accounts. Calderwood met with Daly, told him of the resistance he was encountering from other advertising agencies, and asked him "to put me in contact with the right guy at Mobil, one of DDB's accounts." Calderwood asked Daly to promise not to kill the deal because no commissions were involved, if he managed to convince Mobil. "I only asked Joe to make certain Herb [Schmertz] took my call." Schmertz did take Calderwood's call, and Doyle, Dane, Bernbach did not insist on a commission.

Schmertz had for some time been relying on Frank Marshall for advice on finding a niche Mobil might occupy in public television. Marshall, who began his career writing copy for the American Petroleum Institute while still in his teens and had gone on to become the chief speech writer for the top executives of Xerox, was chosen by Schmertz because he had brokered the Xerox sponsorship of the BBC's *Civilization*. Marshall had Schmertz's respect as a businessman, because at one million dollars, Xerox's funding for *Civilization* was (at the time) the largest such corporate underwriting deal ever made for a public television broadcast. The program was well received, and Xerox was enjoying a very good press. *Civilization* literally had been "a million dollars worth of good publicity." Marshall ran all of Xerox's image-building public relations campaigns, as well as the corporation's sponsorship of "socially conscious" programs on commercial television. Marshall was known as an imaginative thinker, a quality Schmertz liked. He had arranged to broadcast one episode of *Civilization* on NBC in an unprecedented cross-promotion deal with public television. He had also chosen the award-winning television film *The Autobiography of Miss Jane Pittman* for Xerox in 1974. For Mobil, he consulted on programming destined for the Mobil Showcase Network and other venues as well as PBS, and continued to have other corporate clients for his consulting practice. In 1976, Marshall became vice chairman of Reeves Communications. He retired in 1982.[28]

Before Calderwood's offer was presented to Schmertz, Mobil had already decided to do "something" in public television, but Marshall had not yet found the specific programming niche that would make Mobil distinct. Calderwood's sales visit fit in nicely with Mobil's desire to carve out its own distinctive corporate identity through support of PBS. The chance to be identified with quality British drama would differentiate Mobil from other corporations. In Marshall's words, it would allow Mobil to create a "franchise."[29]

From Calderwood's point of view, the Mobil deal would be only the first of many. "I was most anxious to have the best possible deal to set the precedent for others I had planned (a movie series, a science show, and so on)," Calderwood says. "My unabashed plot was to get the best possible deal for Mobil to pave the way for more support."[30]

After taking the call from Calderwood, Schmertz called Marshall and asked him to come along to a screening of the BBC material, presented by Robeck. According to Marshall, Calderwood showed *Portrait of a Lady,* starring Richard Chamberlain, who was at that time living in England. Marshall thought it was a terrible show, but told Schmertz it was a good idea for Mobil to sponsor a series of BBC dramas, especially because Calderwood had indicated there were many hours of inexpensive material sitting "on the shelf" in England. "If they've got a hundred hours, there's got to be, you know it's the old optimist's story: 'With all this shit around there's got to be a pony somewhere,'" says Marshall. "So we felt it was at least worth exploring."[31]

After the showing, Calderwood recalls that "Herb was interested." Marshall commented that his view was that "you couldn't do demographics on who the audience would be on public television, because public television was—in the network sense—brand new . . . Well, we knew if we drew an audience it would be an upper-income well-educated audience. But how big it would be, or where it would be, was almost impossible to figure out, because if you went back to shows like *The Forsyte Saga* or *Civilization,* the Nielsens said that the audiences were below measurable limits. You had no way of measuring." For that reason, Mobil would take a "public service" approach to the series.

According to Marshall, that meant "anything designed not to have a measurable profit return. From advertising, from commercial advertising you've got a direct profit motive. You're trying to sell product. There's a certain measurability between how much advertising you do and how much sales you have. That does not exist in public television . . . So if I can make a distinction, it's probably an economic distinction."[32] There was a difference between product advertising and image advertising, and sponsorship of *Masterpiece Theatre* would be in the latter category.

Making that distinction was important, because in 1970 Mobil's public relations budget was a fraction of their advertising budget. It was only in 1973—because of the oil crisis—that Mobil canceled all product advertising and turned over its entire promotion budget to Schmertz. However, in 1970 Calderwood still had a very convincing argument as to why Mobil should back the WGBH series of BBC dramas instead of other projects. According to Schmertz, the reason he agreed to supply the financing was simple: Mobil said yes to the show because "it was cheap. . . you could run your shows without having to buy time. So you could put all your money into the content."[33] Mobil would have a national audience on PBS for far less than a commercial network might charge.

Calderwood says that Schmertz invited him back "a day or two later . . . [to] help him make the pitch to the chairman, Rawleigh Warner, and the other top brass. My memory is that the president of Mobil International and Mobil Domestic were in the room. Before I left, Warner had given the nod and we began all the details needed to get going."[34] Calderwood says "had Calderwood not met a soulmate in Herb Schmertz, there would have been no *Masterpiece Theatre*. What he was doing at Mobil was very akin to what I had been doing earlier at Polaroid. We both recognized the importance of attaching corporate names to quality. He understood what I was offering at the very outset, listened to each idea that would cost more (support advertising and so on), and was very encouraging on the one hand, not demanding on the other."

With Mobil in place, the deal was set, although the details of the series still needed to be worked out. Marshall, who worked closely with Schmertz, recalls: "We got the concept, and then said to WGBH, 'Now, who's going to do it? This is what we'd like to do. What would you like to do?' They said,'We like your thinking here.' And we said, 'Now who's going to do it?'"[35] Calderwood asked Michael Rice to assign a WGBH staffer to the project to serve as executive producer. Rice picked Christopher Sarson, a British subject and former Granada Television *World in Action* director, and assured Calderwood that Sarson "was not one of the 'sandbox kids.'" Among Sarson's television credits for WGBH would be *Zoom,* an award-winning children's program that premiered the year after *Masterpiece Theatre.*[36]

As recounted by Marshall, "We have a man on the staff named Chris Sarson, and we said, 'We'd like to meet him.' And we liked him very much, nice guy. So he was given the task of evolving the on-air concept, and we held for ourselves the prerogatives of promotion and advertising."[37]

Calderwood credits Sarson with knowing "the limits to what public television could accept." Since many of the BBC programs contained nudity, language, and other material not normally found on American television, this was a concern in 1970. No doubt Sarson's personal experience with the English television industry was a factor in his selection.

Calderwood and Sarson traveled to London together to look through BBC shows and begin making their selections, and Schmertz and Marshall joined them there. Calderwood recalls the process as follows: The first day he and Sarson watched the first episodes of several different series to get an across the board sampling. The second day, they watched second episodes of the shows that had interested them the first day and first episodes of new programs. After the screenings Sarson and Calderwood would go to the theatre. But they made no decisions until Schmertz had arrived in London. Once the Mobil executive was present, "we selected most of the first year's series at that time."[38]

Sarson recalls that Samuel Holt, vice president for programming at PBS, was present for the London screenings.[39] "We all went over to England in the fall of 1970," recalls Sarson, "and in those days they didn't have cassettes and that kind of thing, so we all had to sit down and they'd all very ceremoniously play these tapes of stuff that they thought was going to be appropriate . . . We concentrated, and I knew this from when I'd been in England, we were able to concentrate on the serialized drama slot which had been a prominent feature of BBC-2 . . . and it really started shooting in color in about 1965 . . . So we had a backlog of three or four years, maybe even five years of programs. Which was terrific, because we had a very good choice."[40]

Marshall recalls that on the first trips to London, he and Schmertz were not yet looking for any particular type of British drama. At that point, they were just seeing if there were sufficient quality material to construct a series. "If we could put enough together and get a pipeline going, there was something valuable . . .We were just exploring," he says. "We had our Geiger counter out to find, to see if we could sift any gold."[41]

Schmertz and Marshall discussed the screenings between themselves while in London. "Herb and I sat down and said, 'What do you think?' and I said, 'I think I like it a lot.' And he said, 'I do too.' And then we started thinking of how to try to package it, and I eventually came up with the name *Masterpiece Theatre*."[42] Marshall says he registered the name as a service mark with the U.S. Patent and Trademark Office, later assigning it to Mobil.[43] According to Calderwood, it was Schmertz who named the show. This is consistent with Marshall's claim, since at the time Marshall was working for Schmertz. It was not until 1974 that Schmertz registered the title in Mobil's name. He says he did so because he thought "the day may come when we may want to use *Masterpiece Theatre* on commercial television . . . it was done in a moment of whimsy and reality, I suppose."[44] Although Patent Office records do not show Marshall's claimed registration and assignation to Mobil, they list the date for first use of *Masterpiece Theatre* as 1971. The records also show that the *Masterpiece Theatre* service mark was not assigned to WGBH until 1980.[45] Pete Spina, who replaced Schmertz as Mobil's vice president for public affairs, says the rights were eventually transferred as a result of complex negotiations with WGBH that prevented the station from having another sponsor use the name, and that Schmertz was mistaken to surrender ownership. "I would have kept the trademark," he says. "Absolutely. What flexibility. That, and I don't think it would have been a problem with the PBS system at all."[46]

Whether first protected by Marshall in 1971 or Schmertz in 1974, with the name registered as a service mark in the Patent Office, the "franchise" for *Masterpiece Theatre* was clearly established as belonging, initially, to the sponsor—since both men worked for Mobil, not WGBH. Their views, therefore, would be paramount.

Marshall and Schmertz agreed that the focus of the series would be on the theme of "quasi-literary masterpieces, the concept of doing Dickens and Thackeray and Henry James and that sort of thing. Nobody had ever done it. Not even the BBC realized that there was a theme to what they were doing. They never identified it. They just thought of it as books to drama. So putting that package together resulted in a combination of known factors, mixed in a different way, that made it unique."[47] This was the "franchise" Mobil had been looking for, which would enable the corporation to be associated with quality. Next came the task of putting the finishing touches on the package.

According to Marshall, Mobil needed a series with the following elements: "Theme. Host. National network. Heavy promotion and advertising."[48] And to organize these elements, Mobil would have to work very closely with WGBH. "You must understand that as our relationship with 'GBH developed, we earned each other's trust," says Marshall. "Like any new relationship there were always glitches and arguments and wondering about the other's motives and that kind of thing, but by and large the relationship evolved into a comfortable, communal relationship, where we really did have the same objective, that is, to get as much audience as we could, and to build a long-term series . . . a long-term franchise."[49]

The theme of the series would be found in the type of programs chosen for broadcast. The first year's selections were consistent with the *Masterpiece* theme and consisted of *The First Churchills*, followed by *The Spoils of Poynton, The Possessed, Pere Goriot, Jude the Obscure, The Gambler, Resurrection,* and *Cold Comfort Farm.* Sarson says that the series began with the Churchill story for several reasons. Sarson had hoped to play off the success Susan Hampshire had as Fleur in *The Forsyte Saga.* He thought "the reasons for running *Churchills* were just so compelling . . . with Susan Hampshire, with Churchill as a name, the fact that it was in color, the fact that it was this costume drama, the fact that it was something that it was very much expected by an American public that was going to watch something called *Masterpiece Theatre.*"[50] Frank Marshall adds another reason, that in his view *The First Churchills* was the weakest of the season's offerings, "so rather than go with your strongest show first, we felt it would be wiser to go with a weaker show and build, than to go with a strong show and disappoint."[51] Sarson does not claim any personal favorites in the first set of selections, saying "these decisions were decisions that everyone can take credit or blame for."[52] Schmertz describes the working relationship in similar terms. "It was very collegial. There was no them and us . . . I rarely had any differences of opinion."[53]

However, Marshall remembers personally pushing for the inclusion of *The Spoils of Poynton* and *Cold Comfort Farm* in the first season. "Martin Lisemore [who made *The Spoils of Poynton* and later *I, Claudius*] . . . seemed to have a great talent for interpreting James," says Marshall, who picked *Cold Comfort Farm* "because I thought it was the funniest thing I ever saw. Nobody else in the world, except one film editor and my wife, thought it was funny. No. I don't even think my wife thought it was funny. It failed abysmally. The accents were inscrutable, and everybody hated it. Period. Critics hated it. Audience hated it. I thought it was wonderful."[54] In a sense, the inclusion of the program (which had been well received in England), over the objections of the others involved in selecting *Masterpiece Theatre* episodes, served as Marshall's personal signature on the series.

Sarson recalls that once the programs were selected, he took care of the nuts and bolts, including the payments to Time-Life Films. "I did it, actually," he says. "Mobil wrote the check to WGBH and then GBH paid the BBC . . . I guess we paid Peter [Robeck]. Sure. We'd pay the agent and then the agent would pay them." The price was ten thousand dollars an hour for thirty-nine hours, on a one-year contract. Sarson was under the impression that the purchase of BBC programs was a temporary measure, "that we should start importing British drama for a couple of years, and then gradually introduce American-made productions. That was a very important part. The idea was not just to stay on this importing line, it was to encourage American production."[55] That may have been Sarson's understanding, but no one else mentioned such a deal.[56]

In any case, the selection of programs put the "theme" of *Masterpiece Theatre* in place as the package was being assembled during November 1970. However, the second element, the host, still remained to be decided. As Calderwood recalls, "To give you some sense of how rushed, and how personal the whole thing was in the early stages, we had to come up with filler to round out the hour. We didn't have Alistair Cooke at this moment. Because my wife was a collector of Persian pottery, I bummed off the BBC some short filler that featured an art historian talking about pottery as an art form."[57] Fillers were needed because BBC drama was not timed to the regular one-hour slots of American television.

Fillers were *not* part of the packaging concept Mobil had in mind. Indeed, they were to be a source of recurring disagreement between Mobil and WGBH because Schmertz and Marshall did not like paying for what they saw as unrelated material. On the other hand, Marshall said that he and Schmertz certainly agreed with WGBH that the shows in the series "needed explanation." The program would have to have a host. This was to be a change from *The Forsyte Saga,* which was presented without an introduction (but with fillers starring public television executive James Day). Schmertz and Marshall felt that for their package to be acceptable to a wide viewing public, which might not know British history as well as English audiences, "it would be nice to put the novels in a social context, a social-historical context."[58] Schmertz wanted a journalist, not an actor, to host the program. His position was that "actors don't really have as much credibility as journalists when they're talking about these kinds of shows." According to Marshall, Sarson may have first proposed Alistair Cooke.[59]

Sarson takes credit for picking Cooke as well, saying "I wouldn't be at all surprised if Mobil didn't say 'and we've got to have a personality to introduce the show.'" However, Sarson still needed Schmertz's approval for his choice. Calderwood points out that Schmertz "either initiated or went along gladly with all the subsidiary aspects to the show: the Cooke contract, advertising on TV pages in key markets, I think posters for schools, and so on. In short, once I had the handshake deal from Herb, he was the key element. Obviously, without his convictions and money there would have been no program . . . I suspect it was an unprecedented deal that did set the stage for what we now have on public television."[60]

All involved agreed that Alistair Cooke would host the series. Marshall says "the concept came to be that we would do something called *Masterpiece Theatre* with Alistair Cooke as the host, as he hosted *Omnibus*."[61] Schmertz and Marshall may have been delighted with Cooke, but Schmertz characterized their relationship as "arm's length." He says of Cooke: "I think that he did not feel comfortable being associated with Mobil. And he went to great lengths to avoid being associated beyond what was necessary for the show. From his vantage point, and what he wanted out of the world, he didn't want to be, appear to be flacking for an oil company."[62]

To this day Cooke maintains his relationship with Schmertz and Mobil was "very cordial and very slight."[63] The reason, according to Cooke, is simple: "I do not do TV or radio commercials, or institutionals, or any sort of appearance which suggests a commercial promotion (I surely don't have to go into that; any journalist known for his opinions who does a commercial for anything loses all credibility at once)."[64]

The next chapter examines the significance of Alistair Cooke's credibility as a journalist and literary celebrity to the enduring success of *Masterpiece Theatre*.

Notes

1. Alistair Cooke, personal interview, 19 June 1990.
2. Herb Schmertz, personal interview, 15 March 1991.
3. Jeanie Angier, WGBH, memo to author, 11 March 1991.
4. Mrs. John W. Macy Jr., letter to author, 4 August 1990.
5. John J. O'Connor, *"Masterpiece Theatre* Salute," Museum of Broadcasting, *The Museum of Broadcasting Celebrates Mobil and Masterpiece Theatre: 15 Years of Excellence* (New York: Museum of Broadcasting, 1986), 10–17.
6. Pete Spina, personal interview, 17 April 1991.
7. Schmertz, personal interview.
8. Schmertz, personal interview.
9. Stanford Calderwood, memo to author, 27 January 1991.
10. Edwin L. Glick, *WGBH-TV: The First Ten Years (1955–1965)*, University of Michigan dissertation, 1970, 113.
11. Calderwood, memo to author.
12. Glick, *WGBH-TV,* 116.
13. Glick, *WGBH-TV,* 117.
14. Glick, *WGBH-TV,* 125.
15. *The Forsyte Saga* was sold into commercial syndication on independent stations by MGM Television after its run on PBS. Les Brown, *Encyclopedia of Television* (New York: Zoetrope, 1982), 161.
16. Calderwood, memo to author.
17. Calderwood, memo to author.
18. Calderwood, memo to author.
19. Calderwood, memo to author.
20. David M. Davis, personal interview, 12 January 1991.
21. Peter Robeck, personal interview, 15 March 1991.
22. Curtis Prendergast, *The World of Time, Inc.* (New York: Athenaeum, 1986), 383–85.
23. Robeck, personal interview.
24. Robeck, personal interview.
25. Robeck, personal interview.
26. Calderwood, memo to author.
27. Calderwood, memo to author.
28. Frank Marshall, personal interview, 4 January 1991, and "Personal Resume," photocopy in author's collection.
29. Marshall, personal interview.
30. Calderwood, memo to author.
31. Marshall, personal interview.
32. Marshall, personal interview.
33. Schmertz, personal interview.

34. Calderwood, memo to author.
35. Marshall, personal interview.
36. Calderwood, memo to author.
37. Marshall, memo to author.
38. Calderwood, memo to author.
39. Christopher Sarson, personal interview, 19 June 1990.
40. Sarson, personal interview.
41. Marshall, personal interview.
42. Marshall, personal interview.
43. Marshall, personal interview. Marshall said he would not bluff about a trademark matter and that he gave the paperwork to Mobil when he transferred ownership. In his interview, Schmertz denied Marshall ever owned the name.
44. Schmertz, personal interview.
45. Marshall, personal interview, and Schmertz, personal interview. Service Mark registration documents, Int. Cl.: 41, U.S. Cl.:107, Reg. No. 1,012,457, Reg. 3 June, 1975 [Mobil]. Reg. No. 1,132,403, Reg. 1 April, 1980 [WGBH], U.S. Patent and Trademark Office, Crystal City, Virginia.
46. Spina, personal interview.
47. Marshall, personal interview.
48. Marshall, personal interview.
49. Marshall, personal interview.
50. Sarson, personal interview.
51. Marshall, personal interview.
52. Sarson, personal interview.
53. Schmertz, personal interview.
54. Marshall, personal interview.
55. Sarson, personal interview.
56. After his interview, Sarson said he would provide documents to support his statement that American productions were planned. However, even after several phone calls to request them, no documents were forthcoming.
57. Calderwood, memo to author.
58. Marshall, personal interview.
59. Marshall, personal interview.
60. Calderwood, memo to author.
61. Marshall, personal interview.
62. Schmertz, personal interview.
63. Alistair Cooke, personal interview, 19 June 1990.
64. Alistair Cooke, letter to author, 5 April 1991.

Alistair Cooke and *Masterpiece Theatre*

The *Masterpiece Theatre* Sunday evening debauch of Englishness is one of the standbys and continual referents for students of Anglophilia and its American mystique. When Alistair Cooke assumes the leather armchair, the free association
begins and Englishness takes on its varied guises and incarnations: the civilized country house; the strained but decent
colonial civil servant; the regimental mess; the back-to-the-
wall wartime coolness under fire; the stratified but consider-
ate social system; the eccentric but above all literate milieu of
London in assorted moods and epochs.
    —Christopher Hitchens, *Blood, Class and Nostalgia*

Although he was the last element of the package to be confirmed
(and was eventually replaced), Alistair Cooke is linked indelibly
with *Masterpiece Theatre*. Cooke is the enduring host who has given
continuity and personality to the weekly presentations of British
drama. His life history overlaps the events of many *Masterpiece
Theatre* programs, giving added dimension to his commentaries. As
a television celebrity Cooke spawned parody on *Sesame Street* with
"Alistair Cookie," on Disney's *Mouseterpiece Theater,* and on *Saturday Night Live* as burlesqued by Dan Ackroyd, who appeared as
"Leonard Pinth-Garnell . . . a tuxedoed master of ceremonies who
made Alistair Cooke seem positively plebeian."[1] Kay Gardella of
the *New York Daily News* has said Cooke is partly responsible for
the series' "snob appeal,"[2] while John J. O'Connor of the *New York
Times* gave the "urbane and unflappable" Cooke credit for making
the series "a national institution."[3]

Mobil's Herb Schmertz says he had four reasons to choose Alistair Cooke as host: 1) Cooke's personal history as host of *Omnibus,* 2) his credibility as an Englishman, 3) his personal authority as a journalist and critic, and 4) a natural talent for making audiences comfortable with watching difficult material and explaining what might be missing. Cooke was indispensable to the show for these reasons. "He can't make bad material look good, but he can make good material look better," says Schmertz.[4] In the opinion of this observer, Russell Baker does not quite fill his shoes and it is doubtful that anyone else ever could do so.

Since *Omnibus* played so large a role in the choice of Cooke, an examination of that weekly cultural television program is in order. *Omnibus* was the Ford Foundation's demonstration project for the possibilities of noncommercial public service television, a microcosm for public broadcasting. Like PBS, *Omnibus* had corporate sponsors, called "subscribers," presumably buying time on the program for educational and noncommercial reasons. As of 1955, the Ford Foundation reported a mix of subject matter on *Omnibus* very similar to the program types PBS airs today.[5]

In the series, Cooke played the same role he does on *Masterpiece Theatre,* introducing the material and providing wry commentary. However, the performances originated in New York and focused on the cultural life of the eastern seaboard instead of that found in London. The shows were also done live, rather than on tape. Although not solely limited to drama, *Omnibus* was, for example, the venue for a five-part miniseries about the life of Abraham Lincoln, written by James Agee. In other ways, too, the program was similar to *Masterpiece Theatre.* It was "upper-middle-class." *Time* quoted Alistair Cooke saying the program was consciously aimed "at middlebrow audiences."[6] Like *Masterpiece Theatre, Omnibus* aired on Sunday evenings. And as with *Masterpiece Theatre,* Cooke was the master of ceremonies who came to symbolize the program to audiences and critics alike. Producer Robert Saudek had similar reasons for choosing Cooke to those given by Sarson, Herb Schmertz, and Frank Marshall. He said that Cooke was picked for *Omnibus* because, "we wanted someone who would be distinguished and distinctive and highly intelligent. We did not want just a handsome actor or actress who simply mouthed the words. We wanted someone who could write or speak his own material." According to writer Christina Adam,

Cooke was the "backbone of the program."[7] *Time* said that Cooke gave *Omnibus* an identity, noting that he "strolls from experience to experience, doing his urbane best to lace a heterogeneous program together."[8] Cooke would do the same for *Masterpiece Theatre,* seated.

Alistair Cooke likes to point out that *Omnibus* ran from 1952 through 1961, "[It] started . . . the Sunday after Eisenhower was elected and it finished after Kennedy was inaugurated. No connection whatever, an entire accident." The series time slot moved from CBS (1952–56), to ABC (1956–57), and to NBC (1957–59, 1960–61) on Sunday afternoons and evenings—after 1957, without any Ford Foundation funds. Cooke recalls the series as "a vaudeville show of the arts and sciences and entertainment and literature and everything . . . that's why it was called *Omnibus,* something for everyone."[9]

Dwight MacDonald devotes a considerable portion of his book-length study of the Ford Foundation to an analysis of *Omnibus,* which he characterizes as "an hour-and-a-half miscellany."[10] Although MacDonald credits the series with having attracted a large audience—seventeen million viewers, far larger than the average *Masterpiece Theatre* rating—he feels "its success in raising program standards and the level of public taste is debatable." As mentioned earlier, similar complaints have been voiced by critics about the programs on *Masterpiece Theatre.* MacDonald attributes the lack of true cultural distinction to program producer Robert Saudek's stated mission of realizing a show aimed at the middle-brow American public, the average person, "neither highbrow nor lowbrow."[11] And the perfect middlebrow host, according to Mac-Donald, was Alistair Cooke, whom he describes as "an inspired choice. Mr. Cooke is a kind of cultural headwaiter who simultaneously intimidates and flatters the customers, being impeccably dressed (but in a casual way), fluently articulate (but easy to follow), British as to accent (but American in the easy bonhomie of his manner: 'My name—by the way—is Alistair Cooke'). The brochure [about the program published by the Ford Foundation] presented Mr. Cooke as a mental heavyweight ('perhaps the century's foremost interpreter of America') with a style guaranteed to extend the lightest-weight brain in his audience ('He will be the good companion always welcome in your home for his fresh and witty slant . . . the kind of fellow you will be glad to have drop in every Sunday afternoon, because he always leaves you with a new story to tell, a new subject to talk about, a new sense of expanded horizons')."[12] Later Cooke would incorporate MacDonald's "headwaiter" remark into his own description of his role on *Masterpiece Theatre*.[13]

MacDonald's assessment of *Omnibus* shows, which included Orson Welles in *King Lear* and Leonard Bernstein's *The World of Jazz,* was that "the great majority of the passengers on '*Omnibus*' have been run-of-the-mill . . . The show has a disturbing habit of falling flat on its face when it tries to soar."[14] Among the worst programs, in MacDonald's view, was a travelogue cohosted by Charlton Heston and Cooke, described by MacDonald as operating "in his suavest this-won't-hurt-a-bit manner." Also very bad was a condensed version of *The Iliad,* which MacDonald called "painlessly (or painfully, depending on the point of view) emceed by Mr. Cooke ('The story is about a buccaneer named Paris who went cruising in the Aegean Sea')."[15] The tone was vintage Cooke, familiar to any *Masterpiece Theatre* viewer.

MacDonald argues that, with Cooke as host, *Omnibus* avoided becoming highbrow, "but there is some disagreement as to what else it has accomplished."[16] Like Barnouw's uncharitable description of the role of Mobil in *Masterpiece Theatre,* MacDonald criticizes the relationship between the commercial sponsors of the *Omnibus* and the middlebrow content of the show. MacDonald attributes this to the sponsor's mission: to make advertisements that would blend into the show itself. This, he argues, "is still a further blurring of the increasingly tenuous boundary between commercials and entertainment in TV, a 'fuzzing-it-up' process that goes beyond anything the ordinary, or nonphilanthropic, programs have yet ventured."[17] As with complaints over Mobil's role in the 1970s, MacDonald objects that *Omnibus* put its loyalties to its "subscribers" (that is, sponsors) above any and all other considerations.

According to MacDonald, the resulting problems were "an over fondness for 'names,' a lack of originality (not long ago, the program's 17,000,000 viewers were taken Behind the Scenes at Grand Central Terminal to see How a Great Railroad Is Run, a theme that might have interested the editors of *St. Nicholas Magazine* back in the nineties), and an exaggerated fear of boring an audience whose capacity it may well underestimate. Mr. Saudek [the producer] seems honestly convinced he is bringing culture—or a reasonable facsimile thereof—to the masses, and thinks criticism of *Omnibus* must proceed from intellectual snobbishness . . . In an effort to avoid snobbery, one may fall into condescension."[18] The charges of snob appeal and downmarket sensibility, combined with dullness, are similar to complaints that have been levied by critics such as Barnouw against *Masterpiece Theatre.*

Yet despite MacDonald's strictures, *Omnibus* received generally good reviews from the *New York Times* during its original run (as does *Masterpiece Theatre*). Jack Gould, the influential *Times* critic of the 1950s,[19] called the *Omnibus* debut featuring Rex Harrison and Lilli Palmer in *The Trials of Anne Boleyn* (one of the six wives of Henry VIII, and protagonist of a *Masterpiece Theatre* episode) "one of television's most exciting and important events since the introduction of commercial video . . . the debut of a fresh state of mind toward TV." Gould called Alistair Cooke an "engaging and knowing host."[20] He praised the series for such efforts as a dramatization of the life of Samuel Johnson starring Peter Ustinov.[21] In a more contemporary mode, *Omnibus* broadcast *American Trial by Jury* with Joseph N. Welch, nemesis of Joseph McCarthy (recalling Cooke's own book on the Alger Hiss case, *Generation on Trial*), as well as costume drama such as *Dear Brutus,* a Roman drama starring Helen Hayes and Susan Strasberg (Rome would feature in *Masterpiece Theatre*'s production of *I, Claudius*). There was classical music, too. Leonard Bernstein presented *The Jazz World, The History of Musical Comedy,* and *On Opera.* Ballet found its representative in Agnes de Mille's program on the *Evolution of the Dance;* and Gene Kelly in *Dancing.*

Omnibus even presented a unique, bowdlerized version of *A Streetcar Named Desire* with Hume Cronyn and Jessica Tandy as Mitch and Blanche. Curiously, Stanley Kowalski was entirely cut from the *Omnibus* adaptation, and Cooke, smoking a cigarette and standing suavely in a spotlight, interjected himself as a stand-in to explain what transpired in the interim. The replacement of the crude Stanley with the erudite Cooke, and the emphasis on the more middle-class Mitch at the expense of the lower-class Kowalski is symptomatic of the very "middlebrow" prejudice detailed by MacDonald.[22]

In a similar way, *Masterpiece Theatre* would refrain from airing "kitchen sink" dramas presenting contemporary English working-class life. Cooke's personality helped set the tone for both *Omnibus* and *Masterpiece Theatre.*[23]

Another example of Cooke's open critique of the lowbrow, this time made apparently in jest, is found in the appearance of Jack Benny in the antiwar drama *The Horn Blows at Midnight*.[24] This show, broadcast on *Omnibus* from Hollywood in 1953, featured patter between Cooke and Benny remarkable for Cooke's declarations of middle-class condescension. After an initial wisecrack that "after a substantial shipment of gold from Fort Knox . . . [Benny] agreed to come on *Omnibus* purely for the sake of art," the dialogue went as follows:

> Cooke: It is time to take a rest from highbrow plays, ballets, and high priced talent and bring in a really solid, down to earth, in the gutter, low comedian.
> Benny: I had the opportunity of doing *The Horn Blows at Midnight* or *Hamlet*.
> Cooke: *Hamlet*? Oh, you were going to play the grave digger, right?
> Benny: No, no, no. King Lear.
> Cooke: Wait a minute. King Lear in *Hamlet*?
> Benny: Yes. We're very flexible out here, you know.
> Cooke: This makes me all the more grateful you made the choice you did.
> . . .
> Cooke: If you've got a half hour or ninety minutes next Sunday afternoon, will you take a look at us?
> Benny: Well, I will if you look at my show.
> Cooke: You're on television?
> Benny: You know, I'm on next Sunday too.
> . . .
> Benny: Oh, Mr. Cooke, I do want to thank you for coming all the way out here to Los Angeles, just so you could have me on your show.
> Cooke: No, no, no, Jack. We were coming out here anyway.
> Benny: Oh . . . [25]

There is clearly an ironic self-referential element of mockery in Cooke's lines, based on the public images of the two television personalities (there is also an oblique reference to Orson Welles's performance as King Lear, in an earlier episode of *Omnibus* directed by Peter Brook).[26] By condescending to his guest and pretending he does not recognize the status of Jack Benny, Cooke is mocking, while acknowledging his own reputation as a snob. As it turns out, many years earlier Cooke had actually treated Charlie Chaplin with the same whiff of disapproval he displays for comic effect towards Jack Benny (this episode will be discussed later in this chapter). By playing a dunce, Benny is drawing on his vaudeville past. Yet the reality was that Benny was doing Cooke the favor. Jack Benny was one of the major stars of American television as well as radio, film, and stage. Cooke was less well known. That Cooke, even as a joke, feigned ignorance of this reveals the essentially snobbish screen persona of the host of *Masterpiece Theatre*—once described by Mobil's Herb Schmertz as a television program "for people who don't ordinarily watch television."[27]

In another program, cementing its ties to the same journalistic institution on which Mobil spent a great portion of its multimillion dollar op-ed advertising budget, *Omnibus* devoted itself to the theme of How a Great Newspaper Is Put Together—emanating directly from the offices of the *New York Times*. Yet such extraordinary consideration on the part of producer Saudek did not always guarantee freedom from criticism on the part the paper. Complaints about condescension in the series were raised in 1956, when the *Times* asked Cooke about "an objection raised by some viewers who believe that *Omnibus* has been too 'highbrow' in its program concepts." Cooke dismissed the charge. "'That's ridiculous,' he said, 'the great thing *Omnibus* did was to prime the pump for a great many people whose interests were not being met by television. There can be nothing more patronizing than to say that it's 'highbrow.' I know this from traveling to many parts of the United States.'"[28]

By 1960, Cooke was described by *Times* critic Jack Gould as "a national figure by reason of his role as host on *Omnibus*."[29] It was this celebrity to a national audience as well as his genius for moderation and snob appeal that Cooke would bring to his role on *Masterpiece Theatre*.

Omnibus coincidentally paralleled *Masterpiece Theatre* in another respect. It was classified as an "export-import" product, produced in the United States, exported to Canada for an initial showing broadcast because of sponsorship by Aluminium of Canada, Ltd., and reimported to the United States for airing on American networks. Like *Masterpiece Theatre,* it was part of the international television trade.[30]

Meanwhile, the North American representative of the BBC was

following *Omnibus* jealously, delighting in negative reviews of his competition. Basil Thornton, later an executive at WNET, passed along to London a critical attack from Jack Gould, crowing, "this terrific crack at *Omnibus* follows Hamburger's. We think poor Bob Saudek is in bad shape, but I must say *Omnibus* thoroughly deserves everything that Gould has said about it."[31]

Cooke had his own contacts with the BBC, higher up than Thornton, the apparently hostile North American representative. In 1955, while visiting the Dorchester Hotel in London, Cooke was approached by Michael Gill, then producer for the North American Service of the BBC, and asked to appear on a radio program entitled *Dateline London*. The show was supplied by the BBC to over thirty American radio stations "to forward Anglo-American relations." It was produced in cooperation with the English Speaking Union. On the broadcast, Cooke was interviewed about American elections.[32]

But British public relations efforts were not the only official propaganda work with which Cooke was involved. In 1957 Cooke wrote an essay for the United States Information Service—the official foreign propaganda arm of the United States government during what was already being called the Cold War—"for use by newspapers, magazines, or radio stations, with or without credit to USIS," entitled "The American Film: A Visitor Looks at Hollywood." In it he championed the moguls, arguing that "these men have more talent in their little fingers than all the sensitive journalists and foreign writers who come through in a year, stay three weeks, and go back to write a powerful series of pieces on the vulgarity, the absurdity, the tragedy, the artistic bankruptcy of Hollywood."[33] Cooke was soon to become involved in other official propaganda efforts.

In 1959, *Omnibus* broadcast a film produced and supplied by the United Nations called *Power among Men*. It told four different stories "of man's will to endure—and to grow—despite wars and the threat of atomic bombs." The countries covered were Italy, Haiti, Canada, and Norway, as well as the Soviet Union.[34] Then, in late 1960, Cooke was singled out by the *New York Times* for his BBC coverage of the United Nations. Jack Gould called Cooke's reporting a "gem," and felt that his analysis of "the importance of recognizing the virtues of tedium" at the UN should be commended because "tediousness . . . is preferable to a final war."[35] That Cooke preferred stability to strife is in perfect congruence with his public image and private life as a pillar of the establishment.

The next month an article headlined "Alistair Cooke to Host Series Designed to 'Personalize' the UN" appeared in the *Times*. The series, produced and paid for by the United States Broadcasters Committee for the United Nations, was *International Zone*. Cooke announced the goal: "We hope to get people genuinely interested in the United Nations and what it does . . . What I would like to do is make vivid what people look upon as a bureaucratic organization." Cooke was unapologetically partisan in his interview, noting that the show would concentrate on the human-interest stories of people who work for the UN as soldiers, delegates, interpreters, and the like. *International Zone* was produced under the auspices of the United Nations, in UN television studios. It was provided free to local stations and aired Sunday afternoons in New York on WNBC.[36]

Two years later, the *Times* placed the program in the context of James Bond and the Kennedy era. "*International Zone,* a title that bespeaks trench-coated correspondents, fleeing furtive spies, perhaps in hot pursuit of intriguing, svelte ladies, is really a series by the United Nations about the United Nations." Correspondent Richard F. Shepard commented that "the United Nations has more in the way of drama—quiet and noisy—than the usual run-of-the-mill TV adventure strip." The article goes on to quote Cooke as saying the program was "an essential thing to do."[37]

One episode in the series, called *UN Dateline,* detailed the activities of foreign correspondents assigned to cover the activities of the international organization, that is, people like Cooke. Much of the narration took place from Cooke's own *Manchester Guardian* desk in the UN newsroom. Filmed in a cinéma vérité style in grainy black and white, using hand-held cameras, zooms, and much panning and tracking of delegates and press officers giving press conferences both formal and informal, the film bears stylistic testimony to the 1960s. Cooke's breathless narration begins, "In the next half hour you are to be gently immersed in the broth of news-gathering at the UN" and complements the fly-on-the-wall approach in which Cooke is both protagonist and observer.[38]

Perhaps due to the success of *Omnibus* and *International Zone,* Cooke had been suggested to the Board of Governors of the BBC in 1961 as a possible English television personality. By contrast to his experience with American television, he was rejected as unsuitable. According to the official minutes, "It was generally agreed that whilst he had an excellent sound personality, he was not quite as effective on television. There were also difficulties in that all material had to be prefilmed as there was no direct television link with the United States. C.P. Tel. considered that Alistair Cooke would be too busy to undertake any further engagements."[39] Cooke and his supporters tried again in 1962. This time Cooke's price of five hundred pounds plus expenses was considered too high.[40]

Rejected by BBC television, Cooke remained at the UN with *International Zone* until 1967. The next year he celebrated his one thousandth *Letter from America* on BBC radio. He flew to London to be the guest of David Bruce, the American ambassador, at a celebratory Charterhouse dinner.[41] The *Times* ran an editorial paying Cooke homage, declaring "the country he describes can be grateful for his objective interpretation of our real, and occasionally unreal, alarums and excursions."[42] In the same year, Cooke published a collection of his radio broadcasts under the title *Talks about America*.[43] The *Times Literary Supplement* praised the author as "not a mere reporter or even a mere book writer—he is a British National Institution."[44]

After this blessing from the *TLS,* the BBC approved Cooke as narrator for a series of thirteen television documentaries about the United States in 1969. The producer was the same Michael Gill responsible for *Dateline London.* Entitled simply *America,* the production was filming in Boston when Christopher Sarson, the English producer at WGBH assigned to *Masterpiece Theatre,* approached Cooke for the first time.

Sarson says Cooke was the first and only choice to host *Masterpiece Theatre,* and getting him to accept the position was "Super-important. Super-important . . . Because if you're doing a series of short programs, a series of short series, the continuity should be other than just an identification symbol, it should be somebody the viewer can turn to. If you believe in Alistair Cooke, you'll tune in to the first episode of the next series, not because the next series has been heavily promoted or that kind of thing, but basically because you trust Alistair Cooke. If you have a host who you have that kind of connection with, then you're okay."

Sarson believes that the choice of Cooke was more important

than the selection of dramas. He feels that audiences watch the host and only secondarily the programs, explaining, "it's the key figure—in *20/20* it's Hugh Downs and Barbara Walters—they tune in for basically. Then if the subject's interesting they watch it."[45]

As mentioned earlier, Cooke had a reputation in Britain as host of the long-running BBC radio series *Letter from America*. He had a simultaneous career as American correspondent for the *Guardian*, from which he retired in 1972. On April 11, 1973, Queen Elizabeth II made Alfred Alistair Cooke an Honorary Knight Commander of the Order of the British Empire (KBE) for his "outstanding contribution over many years to Anglo-American understanding."[46] It was Cooke's third year on *Masterpiece Theatre*, during a season that had featured the premiere of *Upstairs, Downstairs* and the tremendous popular and critical acclaim it enjoyed.

In 1973, however, Cooke was still perhaps best known in the United States as a network television personality. That November 14 had seen the 10 P.M. NBC premiere of his Xerox-sponsored BBC/Time-Life four-million-dollar coproduction, the thirteen-part series *America: A Personal View,* which Cooke wrote and narrated, and Knopf's publication of the best-selling companion volume *Alistair Cooke's America.*[47] The production crew was the same Kenneth Clark had employed for *Civilization,* also sponsored by Xerox. Xerox vice president David Curtin (a client of Frank Marshall's public relations firm, Marshall and Bloom) explained that Cooke's series was intended to encourage patriotism, "Seldom does a series appear that is at once as appropriate and as relevant to the times in which we live as is *America*. At a time when it seems to some people that this country may be losing its way, we believe that *America* may well help to revive faith and pride in our nation among all citizens."[48]

It was a remarkable coup to get a British-produced view of two hundred years of American history onto prime-time network television. The subtitle was designed to forestall another possible Boston tea party on the part of critics: it was *A Personal View*. Cooke went still further, telling the *Times* that the show would be "a very personal view."[49] *Times* critic John J. O'Connor pointed out that, despite his British accent and his work for the BBC, Cooke had been living in the United States for 35 years, had become a citizen in 1941, and "while he has been reporting on American affairs for the

BBC and various British publications, the extent of his involvement in American life has been considerable." O'Connor reminded readers that Cooke had a long American television career extending from *Omnibus* to *Masterpiece Theatre*. Therefore, the critic concluded, Xerox, Time-Life, and NBC need not apologize for letting the English-born Cooke host a pre-Bicentennial American history lesson, although it was "not dazzling. Low-keyed and occasionally pedantic, it is intelligent, provocative, and civilized."[50]

"Civilized" is an adjective often employed to describe Cooke. He brings with his onscreen personality a lifetime of personal experience passing through the elite institutions of English and American culture. Indeed, one might argue that his real profession—one not incompatible with his own claim to be a "journalist and broadcaster"—is that of a "civilized man," at least to the extent such distinction can be conferred by the official recognition of establishment institutions. He is well clubbed and an avid golfer, a member of the Athenaeum, Savile, Royal and Ancient (St. Andrew's), and the National Press Club in Washington, DC. In addition to his honorary KBE, Cooke was made Honorary Fellow of Jesus College, Cambridge, in 1988, and received honorary LL.Ds from Edinburgh in 1969, St. Andrews in 1975, and Cambridge in 1988. He received the Peabody Award in 1952 and again in 1983, the Benjamin Franklin Medal of the RSA in 1973, and the Howland Medal of Yale University in 1977. He has won the Dimbleby Award from the British Academy of Film and Television Arts in 1973, and four Emmy awards from the National Academy of Television Arts and Sciences.[51] On September 25, 1974, he addressed "the first official celebration of the Bicentennial" in a special session of Congress. There Cooke congratulated the Judiciary Committee for its vote of impeachment against President Richard Nixon.[52] He likened them to the first Continental Congress, remarking that both were "watchdogs eager to corner a tyrannical executive." In his conclusion, Cooke shared his personal philosophy: "I have seen the past—and it works!"[53]

Cooke's past certainly has worked for him, and his life story reads like a biography of a character in a *Masterpiece Theatre* series. His lifetime of contacts and clubs, as an establishment pillar, are part of the tremendous respectability of the PBS show. Cooke also personally embodies the Horatio Alger myth Brennan found in his analysis of the *Masterpiece Theatre* series. For Cooke's rise was a spectacular climb from a provincial English lower middle-class existence to the heights of New York society, with a home on Fifth Avenue overlooking New York's Central Park, and a summer house in a fashionable Long Island retreat. Cooke is featured prominently in *New Yorker* writer Brendan Gill's autobiography and memoir of club living, *A New York Life*.[54] He was a frequent visitor to the fashionable New York salon run by publicist Ben Sonnenberg, where a typical dinner-party guest list included Cooke, Brooke Astor, Truman Capote, Bob Dylan, Jacob Javits, Jasper Johns, Jackie Kennedy, Bobby and Ethel Kennedy, and Tom Wolfe.[55]

He is very much a self-made man, who has assiduously carved out his public identity and striven to preserve a star persona of high cultivation, moderation, and reasonableness.[56]

Alfred Alistair Cooke was born on November 20, 1908, in Manchester, England. The son of a Wesleyan lay preacher and metalworker, Samuel Cooke, and his Irish wife, Mary Elizabeth Byrne, as a boy Cooke won a history scholarship to Jesus College, Cambridge, from Blackpool Grammar School. At the time, the Jesus College was under the mastership of Arthur Gray.[57] As "one of the best-known of all broadcasters, particularly successful in presenting the American scene to the British," Cooke is cited glowingly in the official college history to refute traditional accusations that "the College excelled in nothing but rowing."[58]

Cooke founded the Cambridge University Mummers in 1928—the first coed drama club in the history of the University. Cooke was at the time hoping to become an actor, and switched his studies from History to English. His mentor was Basil Willey, author of *The Seventeenth, Eighteenth,* and *Nineteenth Century Background,* a follower of "Q" (Sir Arthur Quiller-Couch) in his approach to literature as well as successor to him in the Edward VII Chair. In his early experience with Willey, there is perhaps the seed of Cooke's own approach to purveying English and American cultures to one another by the judicious sketchings-in of such "backgrounds."

Willey describes Quiller-Couch's approach as one that held that "the grappling with masterpieces, with the intent to discover their total meaning and value, is one of the most difficult tasks the human mind can accomplish . . . it is to the attainment of this discriminating

judgement, this instinctive sense of value, that all education in hu-
mane letters . . . should lead."[59] Willey adds: "My point is that the
subject-matter of literature is Life, and that it was against the divorce
of literature from life that 'Q' contended most vehemently. It was
the reduction of literature to an abstract 'subject,' or science, a dead
carcass for pedants to peck at, that he most detested . . . I think that
to 'Q' this chiefly meant the personal approach to books . . . We are
accustomed now to connect literature with life, not so much by linking books to their authors, as by viewing them in their historical setting, and in relation to their social or intellectual (may I use the hor-
rid words?) 'background' . . . we thus find ourselves compelled to
study history as well, especially social and economic history, and the
history of religious, moral, and political ideas."[60] And it is precisely
this linking of life to literature through personality that Cooke provides in his introductory talks on *Masterpiece Theatre.*

As a student of "Q" and Willey, Cooke naturally fell in with a
crowd holding that it was the duty of the English to proselytize.
Willey wrote "'English must be kept up,' as Keats once said, and
in striving to keep it up you will be helping to preserve that precious
heritage which many of you have risked your lives to defend."[61]
The purpose of education, therefore, is to learn how to spread the
gospel widely, to see English as a faith that must be spread far and
wide. In a sense, it is a low church calling as opposed to a high
church one. Perhaps Cooke's affinity for this style of literary study
reflects the early formative influence of his preacher father. Since
Cooke was on the side of an evangelical approach to English, he
was therefore not a partisan of F. R. Leavis's defense of "minority
culture" and "discrimination" against "mass civilization."[62] Cooke
describes Leavis as "the high priest guarding the oracles . . . in its
most imperious form . . . I myself came very briefly under the wing,
never the spell, of Dr. Leavis."[63] Cooke's split may also have had
a personal element. He says he once went to Leavis "to take a couple of his pupils. And I had a very, very poor time with Leavis, so
he decided not to give his pupils to me." Instead, Cooke got a job
"sort of coaching, supervising in my last year, with my own super-
visor," Basil Willey.[64] So, at Cambridge, the die was cast. Cooke
had sided with the "Q" tradition of criticism, an orientation he was
to maintain throughout his career. In presenting the backgrounds to
English television drama on *Masterpiece Theatre,* Cooke would do
what his master, Basil Willey, had done for English literature.

In 1929, Cooke received a First in the first part of his English tripos. He received a Second on the second part in 1930, and stayed an additional year, becoming editor of the *Granta* in 1931. But Cooke was not satisfied with literary journalism alone and pursued a career as a public performer. He eagerly aimed at a career in broadcasting early on, but his first steps were not without their setbacks.

While looking for a job, Cooke sent a clipping of actor-manager Cyril Maude's remarks about his acting—as printed in a paid advertisement for his summer holiday's theatre troupe—to the BBC. In the summer of 1931, he had appeared on stage in Dartmouth with the Cambridge Mummers, prompting an endorsement from Maude, formerly manager of the Haymarket Theatre, who said he "laughed heartily and enjoyed practically every moment." Cooke was singled out for effusive praise in a reprinted letter to the *Paignton Observer,* in which Maude called attention to "a particularly talented young man of much charm called Mr. Alistair Cooke, who wrote the 'book' as well as the music, it appears!"[65] Along with this cutting Cooke sent a letter asking the Director of Programmes of the BBC Talks Department (J. R. Ackerley) for a chance to work as an on-the-air critic. Cooke also sent in suggestions for dramatic sketches and revues. The reply from the BBC was not encouraging. It noted that the BBC already had theatre and literary critics, a "glut" of supplementary talks by the likes of T. S. Eliot and Harold Nicolson, concluding "we already have about as much as we are able to do on the subject."[66] Ten months later, Cooke tried again, sending a copy of the *Granta* (which he had edited). Again, disappointment. Ackerley threw letter and journal away without reading Cooke's review of *Heartbreak House.* Ackerley replied that he thought the journal ought to have included a review of his own recently published book, and failing to find such a notice, he consigned the unsolicited magazine to the wastepaper basket. Once more, there was no job for Cooke.[67]

However, despite his rejection by the BBC, Cooke did receive a Commonwealth Fund fellowship to the United States in the summer of 1932. The scholarship was provided from funds donated by oil millionaire Edward S. Harkness, son of John D. Rockefeller's partner, and was the start of Cooke's receipt of oil money for transatlantic educational ventures. Cooke was one of twenty-five graduates of British, Empire, and Commonwealth universities to receive the grant for studies in America. He credits his selection to

the chairman, Lord Halifax, being a fellow "North Countryman"
who felt that "on the whole, we are the most reliable types."[68]

At the ceremony in St. James's Palace—much like a scene in
Upstairs, Downstairs—Cooke was personally presented to the
Prince of Wales, Edward VIII. The Prince, a fellow devotee of
jazz, was a model for Cooke. He writes, "To us—to those of us in
particular from Oxford and Cambridge who affected the sophisticated fatigue fashionable in the early thirties—the Prince's little
social rebellions were a heartening sign that he was 'one of the
lads' who would take the starch out of royal protocol and move the
monarch, when his time came, into the twentieth century."[69] In
hosting *Masterpiece Theatre,* Cooke would once again return to
this attitude of sophisticated fatigue. This affected aristocratic de-
meanor was a delightful breath of "stuffy air" to the upper middle-
class seeking some respite from the turbulence of American
society in the 1960s and 70s.

Cooke, who had bought a new double-breasted houndstooth suit
for the occasion from the tailor of "the son of a distinguished West
End actor," recalls feeling "like a country cousin being presented
with his first wine list" while waiting for the prince. When he arrived after a long wait, Cooke "was amazed and comforted to see
that he was wearing a suit of the identical material and cut. This
happy coincidence, on the snobbish Oxbridge scorecard of the day,
put me one up with one hole to play."[70] Already Cooke was acutely
aware of the importance of appearances.

Cooke vividly recalls his conversation with the prince. For Edward exclaimed "My God, my brother!" Cooke says he had long
thought of himself as a look-alike for Prince George, later Duke of
Kent. He characterized their conversation as "one of odd intimacy." He notes that Edward, like himself, moved in Anglo-
American circles, and when he told of his plan to study American
theatre, the prince asked if he would direct musicals. Cooke maintains he was shocked and disappointed by this remark, thinking of
himself as a serious person following Piscator and Meyerhold. He
recalls that Edward "drooped visibly, and rightly, at my earnest ex-
position of the superior discipline of the German and American directors."[71] According to Ronald Wells, Cooke had spent part of
1931 studying theater at the German *Volksbuhne* in Silesia.[72]

The Commonwealth Fund fellowship would prove invaluable to
Cooke's effort to enter the BBC. In the United States, he worked

on his American establishment credentials, attending Yale to conduct "private research in dramatic criticism" and then Harvard, to take Professor Miles Hanley's course on American English and do research for *The American Linguistic Atlas*. While at Harvard, Cooke staged plays by Lennox Robinson and W. H. Auden, a Japanese Noh drama, *Cymbeline*, and a Hasty Pudding Club musical. During the summer, he toured the United States by car.[73]

Upon his arrival in America, Cooke says he wrote to J. L. Garvin, editor of the *Observer*, and suggested a series of Hollywood profiles. The list featured Ernst Lubitsch, Lee Garmes, George Cukor, C. Aubrey Smith, and Charlie Chaplin. Cooke notes, "the choice of Smith as the English star may sound odd, but I was writing for an English paper, and at that time he was symbolizing the British Empire to a gaping world a good deal more heroically than Stanley Baldwin."[74] This admiration of C. Aubrey Smith also perhaps shows the direction in which Cooke's own career would head, as a professional Englishman abroad. Indeed, to many Cooke is a kind of C. Aubrey Smith for our times, the sign and symbol of the British Empire.

However, at this stage Cooke sought identification with quite a different kind of comic character. Still an aspiring theatrical director, he made his way to the Chaplin Studios for an appointment with Charlie Chaplin, at the time the most famous Englishman in America.[75] This was an interview that was to change Cooke's fortunes forever, establishing a relationship that would allow him, at last, a place at the BBC. For Chaplin was also a working-class English lad (although from a lower level than Cooke) who had made good in America, but one who was pursuing a different public image. Where Cooke celebrated middle-class snobbery, respectability, and decorum, Chaplin was a symbol of "the little man." This conflict of visions and personalities, the respectable against the rebellious, would result in a rift between them that sent Cooke back to England.

The relationship between Cooke and Chaplin is worth attention in detail because his experience in Hollywood provides a key not only to Cooke's private trajectory, but to his essence as a public man and television star personality. While Chaplin was self-educated, opinionated, childish, and seemingly unprofessional (with no sense of time), Cooke was a graduate of Cambridge and saw himself as balanced, professional, and punctual. His later reputation for timing his radio talks and television commentaries to the second contrasts with Chaplin's legendary time-wasting while waiting for "inspiration" as a film director.

Chaplin's bohemianism was apparently seen by Cooke as a threat to his own carefully acquired respectability. Already in possession of the hauteur that would become his trademark as host of *Masterpiece Theatre,* Cooke notes that manager Alfred Reeves and Charlie Chaplin made him feel as if he was "suddenly with two optimistic midgets in the office of a failing vaudeville agent. Neither Reeves nor Chaplin could have been much over five feet." Cooke writes that he also found himself shocked by the initial impression of squalor given off by Chaplin's office, which "reflected Chaplin's deep distrust of elegant surroundings whenever there was serious work on hand."[76] The shabby world of vaudeville and low-rent show business—a reminder of the working-class entertainments of the Blackpool of Cooke's youth, a milieu from which he had so assiduously escaped—would be a recurring milieu for series such as *Lost Empires,* episodes of *Upstairs, Downstairs,* and music-hall fillers produced by Joan Wilson on *Masterpiece Theatre.* So would the accompanying conflict between working-class life, aristocracy, and middle-class pretension. Although Cooke behaved agreeably to Chaplin, it is apparent from his written account that he patronized and despised him. One can see in the *Omnibus* sketch between Cooke and Jack Benny mentioned earlier the same tone of highbrow condescension to a low comedian.

Not only was Chaplin's office small and shabby in Cooke's recollection, but so, apparently, was the man himself. Chaplin's diminutive size is noted repeatedly by Cooke: "He certainly is a tiny man."[77] The little tramp was, nonetheless, very friendly. Cooke's explanation is that Chaplin was a friend of his employers, the Astors, who owned the *Observer,* and that he also liked another Alistair, Alistair MacDonald, son of Ramsay MacDonald. "It was as simple as that."[78] Although Chaplin doesn't mention Cooke in his autobiography,[79] Cooke claims to have soon become a fixture *chez* Chaplin. He says he spent every day at the Chaplin home, dined with Paulette Goddard and Chaplin, and weekended on Chaplin's yacht *Panacea.* At the time Cooke refrained from explaining to Chaplin that, in his words, "I was a young man of mixed but lively aspirations to be either a theatrical director of the stature of Reinhardt, Piscator, or Meyerhold *or* a playwright of

deafening fame (I was undecided then whether to be the acknowledged successor to Noel Coward or Eugene O'Neill)." Instead,
Cooke recalls in an essay the feeling of "sitting there for the first
time on anybody's yacht . . . I was a fortunate nobody immersed
in a glow of vanity, wondering, as the reader must be, how I had
got here."[80] Mixed in with Cooke's snobbery towards Chaplin's
vulgarity was genuine admiration of his success.

Cooke maintains that he was not overly impressed, despite
Chaplin's immediate intimacy and confidence in him, "sponta-
neous, generous, gabby, confidential, as if taking up again where
he had left off with a favorite, long lost brother." Cooke says that
this was due to Chaplin's "helpless reflex of egocentricity." He
writes that Chaplin "needed to dazzle a new friend with the whole
panoply of his charm, humor, talent, knowingness, and—which
was a little less impressive to anyone used to thinking—his intel-
lect."[81] Chaplin apparently also ate too quickly, although with
great "deftness."

Cooke says he felt he had done a favor for the millionaire comedian by sharing his presence. "'I am the renowned Charlie
Chaplin,' he seemed to say, 'and you are a new friend who might
well turn into my Boswell.'" He then tried to indoctrinate Cooke
with radical politics, but Cooke says he would not submit to Chaplin's propaganda. In fact, Cooke pleaded complete ignorance of
politics, a state of affairs difficult to believe, in view of his later
work as a political journalist and author of a book on the Alger
Hiss case. "I was at the time about as apolitical as it is possible to
be, and I have been amazed, in going back through the political
history of Britain during the years I was at Cambridge, to see how
casually unaware I was of budget deficits, the American debt problem, the departure from the gold standard and other weighty matters which Chaplin went hotly on about as he sat squeezing the
sand between his toes in the hills above Avalon."[82]

Cooke writes of his growing disappointment in Chaplin's politics. He recalls, "This was not quite what I had expected of the
world's ranking clown, and he must have guessed that my ahs and
ums and other grunting responses proceeded from no very deep
conviction or even from a passing acquaintance with the facts and
dogmas he trotted out." Cooke excuses Chaplin's radicalism, noting that "his much abused 'radical philosophy' was no more than
an automatic theme song in favor of peace, humanity, 'the little

man' and other desirable abstractions—as humdrum politicians come out for mother love and lower taxes," yet mocks, for example, Chaplin's belief that FDR's New Deal is "a promising halfway house on the road to 'true Socialism'. . . . something on which Joseph Stalin had the only legitimate patent."[83]

Cooke says he found it difficult to write about Chaplin's politics in detail. "Certainly, the world's funniest man would have turned into the world's most hectoring bore if he had gone on as long as these recollections."[84] Yet Cooke does remind the reader of "Chaplin the Slacker" press headlines during World War I and the song "Oh, the Moon Shines Bright on Charlie Chaplin," which criticized Chaplin's sitting out the dangers of the war in the comfort of the United States. (Cooke chose to remain in the United States throughout World War II and became a naturalized American citizen in 1941.)

Chaplin asked Cooke back to help him write a screenplay about the life of Napoleon and, during his next summer vacation, Cooke came out to Hollywood for his second encounter with Charlie Chaplin. He stayed at the Mark Twain Hotel, reporting to Chaplin daily on his research. Cooke would have lunch at Musso and Frank's, a famous Hollywood watering hole on Hollywood Boulevard. Later, Cooke claims to have introduced Chaplin to Shakespeare's *Cymbeline* by reading the script to him aloud. So enthusiastic was Chaplin that he stood up Sam Goldwyn. "I read on into the twilight," Cooke writes, "by which time I knew he was supposed to be on his way to a party that Sam Goldwyn was throwing in his honor. I looked at the clock and reminded him. He erupted into a fury and stalked around the room, like the outraged Little Corporal himself . . . 'What is a cocktail party compared to this? . . . keep going!' . . . It was a trait I noticed later in other very poor boys who had grown very rich: a willful desire to flout the idea that there is any such thing as a duty or a social obligation."[85] Cooke's interest in propriety (and perhaps in meeting Goldwyn) is clear. Cooke's civilized respectability is in sharp contrast to Chaplin's lack of social graces.

In a sense, like Hudson in *Upstairs, Downstairs,* Cooke was acting as the disapproving servant of an irresponsible master. Cooke was, in his work for Chaplin, still true to the cinematic tradition of C. Aubrey Smith. Cooke was a loyal retainer, from his own account. Despite his personal disapproval of Chaplin's cavalier approach to social obligations, Cooke recalls continuing reading till midnight and then patronizing a geisha house in Little Tokyo with his boss.

However, Chaplin soon tired of the Napoleon project. When Cooke asked him to be best man at his Pasadena wedding in August 1934, Chaplin said yes—and then stood Cooke up. According to biographer David Robinson, the reason was Cooke's failure to invite Chaplin's live-in companion Paulette Goddard,[86] but Cooke's own written account gives no clue. Chaplin did invite the newlyweds out for an evening wedding party—with Paulette Goddard—and then over to his house. To Cooke, Chaplin once again showed his detestable flouting of convention by failing to provide champagne at home. "Our wedding party ended on a scene that would have warmed the heart of a Southern Baptist," Cooke complained.[87] It was Cooke's most telling critique. The son of a low-church preacher was saying, in a sense, that he did not want to go back down the social ladder. Which meant returning to London.

Cooke had again written to the BBC on Chaplin Studios's letterhead in the spring of 1934 and lined up a job interview. He was leaving Hollywood and Chaplin behind him, despite what Cooke claimed was an offer both to be assistant director on *Modern Times* and Chaplin's promise to make him a movie star. "'If you stay with me,' he said, 'I'll make you the best light comedian since Seymour Hicks.'" Apparently this was an insult to Cooke, because treading the boards as a comedian was not a suitable occupation for a gentleman. Cooke, who had once wanted to be an actor, gave no other explanation for turning down such a generous offer. After Cooke returned to England in the spring of 1934, he did not speak to Chaplin for many years, "not at all during the bad years of the late forties and early fifties" when Chaplin was denied permission to return to the United States in an atmosphere of McCarthyism.[88]

Without mentioning the split with Chaplin, Cooke told his own Boswell, Ronald Wells, that in the spring of 1934 he saw a "front-page" headline in a Boston newspaper saying "BBC fires P.M.'s son." Oliver Baldwin had been film critic for the network, and Cooke says he phoned the director of the Commonwealth Fellowship and asked to be sent back to interview for the post of movie reviewer. He cabled the BBC, was invited to apply by Desmond MacCarthy, and sailed home on the *Aquitania*. On arrival at

Broadcasting House, Cooke auditioned with a review of the last film he had seen and was immediately given the job.[89]

On his return to England, Cooke apparently found the BBC atmosphere much changed from his previous frosty reception. He had a documented interview with the new Director of Talks on April 23, 1934. The next day he received a letter beginning, "I am pleased to be able to tell you that we shall be very glad to have you undertake a series of broadcast talks for us on 'The Cinema.'" Thanks perhaps to his improved resume that included Harvard, Yale, and Charlie Chaplin, Cooke was now attached the BBC, with a remit to report on America as well as films. The Director of Talks expressed the hope that the people of America would assist Cooke "to enable you to interpret America to English listeners. We share your view as to the real importance and social implications of the creation of an intelligent and critical cinema audience in this country."[90] On December 10, 1935, the BBC's Moray McLaren asked Cooke to report on the American theatre as well, in a series entitled "The Drama of Today: Number One: America—Mr. Alistair Cooke." Cooke gave his first BBC talk on Sunday, January 26, 1936. He produced his talks in London, based on his experiences abroad, simulating the American scene with the help of recordings and actors.[91] While preparing one of his shows, he visited Wallis Simpson to procure an Ethel Merman recording of *Anything Goes* not then available in England. While there he enjoyed "the brief courtesy of a drink."[92] His personal involvement with the story of Edward VIII and Mrs. Simpson was just beginning.

Shortly after producing his first BBC broadcast, Cooke started moonlighting, joining the American NBC radio network with a featured weekly talk about Britain aimed at American listeners. The show was called *London Letter* and was produced by Frederick Bate, whom Cooke described as a member of the Anglo-American social crowd found in Paris and on the Riviera, and also as "an intimate of the Prince of Wales, and after January, 1936 therefore the King." Because of this social connection, Cooke soon scored a journalistic coup, reporting the abdication of Edward VIII live over a transatlantic circuit leased from the BBC, beating out CBS. Cooke appeared up to six or seven times a day during the abdication crisis, and poured out an estimated 250,000 (Cooke estimates 400,000) words across the Atlantic.

In his account of the crisis, Cooke says that he was called out of a meeting of the newly formed Research and Discussion Committee of the English Speaking Union on December 1, 1936—a session "adjusting the British stereotypes of America" with MPs, journalists, soldiers, and lawyers in attendance—chaired by Sir Fredric Whyte, later head of the American division of the Ministry of Information during World War II. Cooke's participation in propaganda efforts is here officially recorded as beginning in the mid-thirties. His involvement in propaganda would continue with additional work for the United Nations and the United States Information Agency, before he began to host *Masterpiece Theatre.*

Cooke speaks fondly of the "sinister prestige" of receiving the long-distance call from Fred Bate, then in New York, urging him to rush to the leased studio in the BBC and begin broadcasting news of the abdication crisis to America before CBS went on the air at midnight. With a copy of the *News Chronicle* editorial in hand, Cooke got on the air first and "ad-libbed as best I could."[93]

CBS countered Cooke with talks by H. G. Wells and Harold Nicolson, but Cooke was the sole voice of NBC "putting New York to bed at four in the morning London time, doing the same for California three hours later." Bate arranged for a line to be put into Cooke's bedroom, and Cooke continued to deliver his story over the next ten days. One biographer attributes the CBS decision to send Edward R. Murrow to England as a direct response to the threat from Alistair Cooke, who was perceived to represent competing "youth and swiftness."[94] Assisting Cooke as a researcher was Walt Rostow, then a Rhodes scholar at Oxford and later national security advisor to President Lyndon Johnson.[95]

In 1937, by now an established celebrity as a result of his marathon broadcasts on the abdication crisis, Cooke published his first book, pursuing his identity as an all-rounder. The book was an edited volume of film criticism entitled *Garbo and the Night Watchmen,* put out under the imprint of Jonathan Cape.[96] Cooke's intellectual stance against the "minority culture" is set forth clearly on the first page of the preface. He sees the role of the critic as "a professional star-gazer, a night watchman who must rush away at midnight to state a heartache or a preference against the dawn's deadline."[97] In the 1971 reissue, he added his credo (similar to Q's and Willey's): "what I admired, and admire, most in a critic is a personal point of view and the ability to express it crisply, or passionately, or drolly, or entertainingly, but above all intelligibly."[98]

In addition to printing his own reviews of *Top Hat, Anna Karenina, La Bandera, Things to Come, A Tale of Two Cities, Fury, Mr. Deeds Goes to Town, Born to Dance, Ramona, Fifteen Maiden Lane, Ernte, Manhattan Madness,* and *Love from a Stranger,* Cooke chose additional pieces by writers from both Britain and America. They were Robert Herring of the *Manchester Guardian,* Don Herold of *Life* and *Scribner's,* John Marks of the *New Statesman,* Meyer Levin of *Esquire,* Robert Forsythe of *New Masses,* Graham Greene of the *Spectator* and *Night and Day,* Otis Ferguson of the *New Republic,* and Cecilia Ager of *Vogue* and *Harper's Bazaar.* It can be noted that most of the English critics were on the left of the political spectrum, as were the American contributors. Whatever Cooke's earlier protestations of political ignorance, he was choosing his friends carefully from the socialist side for this volume.

Cooke concludes the volume with a special section where each critic discusses Chaplin's *Modern Times.* Although the others like and admire the film, Cooke gives Chaplin a drubbing. Without revealing any personal relationship with the Little Tramp, he dismisses *Modern Times* with the faint praise that "it should be said with firmness and regret that *Modern Times* is never once on the plane of social satire."[99]

Following on the heels of his anthology, in 1938, Cooke published an essay in *Footnotes to the Film* called "The Critic in Film History."[100] Cooke was in very good company, as the anthology also had essays on direction by Alfred Hitchcock, an exhibition by Sidney Bernstein (later owner of Granada Television, producers of *The Jewel in the Crown*), and acting by Robert Donat. Cooke's article gave his philosophy of criticism: "If a critic is going to write relevantly, he will have to know a great deal about ordinary men and women, even if he knows little about anthropology. It may not be his ambition to spot winners, but if they become winners, and he had never thought it, it's likely he overlooked their essential qualities . . . The film critic seems at his worst when he is aware of literary or theatre comparisons of style, when he is making his own (superior) cultural position clear, when he is apostrophizing the illiteracy that went to the making of a film. To date he seems to be at his best when he is telling himself what he likes about a movie."[101]

In this essay, Cooke disparages the influence of critics—a suitably respectable middlebrow position—mocking "the very personal reactions of Mr. Fink who writes for *New World* and *New Era.*" Although Cooke had chosen the film critic from *New Masses* for this anthology, and though he would go on to work for the liberal *Guardian* and the labor *Daily Herald,* he is at this point attempting to distinguish himself somewhat from the left.

Instead of left politics, Cooke chose free expression as his main criterion of artistic judgment. He likened movies to jazz and celebrated "freedom from inhibition" over cleverness. He concluded with a swipe at all of English criticism, timed beautifully with his move to America: "For time and again in English criticism one reads a clever remark and feels what a good remark it would be if only it were true."[102]

Cooke had already moved away—both figuratively and literally—from his concentration on film criticism and clever English critics with his emigration in 1937 to the United States, made possible "by the fat check" from NBC for his work in London.[103] He would become a news reporter instead of a film critic. After what he describes as a "precarious stretch" as a freelancer, Cooke became special correspondent on American affairs for the *Times* of London from 1938–1940 and served as BBC American correspondent.[104]

One of Cooke's early reports from America was a talk entitled "The Theatre: New York and London."[105] It was a cross-cultural comparison of the sort that Cooke still makes his specialty. It is curious to note that Cooke was the last choice of the BBC at that time. In an internal memo, the North American representative first apologizes, hoping that London does not feel browbeaten into taking Cooke. "I do!" is the penciled notation. He then tells London that "the position here is not one which you could not easily grasp in England."[106] Robert Nathan, the first choice, was too expensive. Robert Benchley would not have bothered about the particular topic of the talk. And Elmer Rice would not have known what to say (this comment is annotated with question marks).

The memo then goes on to refer to a crisis in Anglo-American theatrical relations, citing J. B. Priestley's literary attack on Broadway, "which only added fuel to the already well-burning controversy" (Priestley's writings would form the basis for the *Masterpiece Theatre* series *Lost Empires*). The memo suggests Cooke is the right man to put out the fire because he "has removed himself from passing judgments," and a talk by someone else "might easily have caused us plenty of bother."[107] Already Cooke's public

persona, as a man who refrains from speaking his mind, is in full
flower: Cooke is a reliable intermediary, a safe pair of hands, an
excellent broadcaster who can calm any agitation between feuding
English and American parties, while not causing any bother. In
this case, Cooke's task was to reconcile Broadway to the West
End. On *Masterpiece Theatre* his role would be similar—to bring
the BBC (and other English television) to PBS.

In this early BBC talk, Cooke begins by declaring that there is
no one alive who is qualified to talk about Anglo-American theatrical intercourse, since "nobody lives in New York and London
at the same time, and there has not yet appeared on this planet an
Englishman or American who knows equally well the way the
other feels about life and the values he gives to it."[108] This typical
profession of modesty is similar to Cooke's initial rejection of the
offer to host *Masterpiece Theatre*. At the time he turned the position down, Cooke suggested Alexander Woollcott, John Mason
Brown, or Max Beerbohm as better choices for producer Chris
Sarson. Of course, they were dead, and Cooke took the job. Perhaps the jesting protest was a reminder that Cooke had not forgotten the BBC's reluctance to choose him many years before.[109]

In his first BBC broadcast Cooke immediately puts forth his
own personal qualifications, saying he is uniquely suited to the impossible enterprise of Anglo-American understanding. Cooke
starts his analysis by claiming he covered the West End for several
years in the late twenties and early thirties, and had spent three
years covering Broadway (he does not explain just how he came
by these dates, overlapping his student years at Cambridge, Harvard, and Yale). He goes on to claim to be better qualified than
J. B. Priestley for the job of comparing Broadway to the West End.
His reason is that he is not a playwright (despite having been one
in his student days).[110] In Cooke's opinion, dramatists are "the last
people who should be consulted on the tastes of their foreign audience, though . . . like most people with a grudge they talk loud-
est." Then Cooke puts forth his major critical premise, namely that
he will not come to any conclusions because "there is nothing so
good for foreign travellers as to resist the desire to come to conclusions."[111] Cooke's ability to suspend judgment will be a feature of his introductions to *Masterpiece Theatre* (it is usually very
difficult to tell from his opening remarks which programs he likes
and which he does not).

In the BBC talk, Cooke then summarizes the contemporary cross-cultural situation in 1938—which bears a striking parallel to that of the 1970s—as follows: the Americans know Shaw, Lonsdale, O'Casey, Coward, Maugham, Priestley, etc., but the English know only O'Neill and George S. Kaufman, occasionally Elmer Rice and Robert Sherwood, and very little about Odets, Steinbeck, Irwin Shaw, Mark Connolly, S. N. Behrman, Sidney Howard, and John Howard Lawson. So there is an imbalance. When the British do see American drama, they don't get a real performance of the genuine article—rather "third-rate American actors who had evidently been directed to act as a British director or producer thought Americans acted."[112] In contrast, Americans do a better job with their casting, and "an Englishman has good reason to be proud of the Broadway productions of English plays."[113] Cooke notes that Cedric Hardwicke, Gertrude Lawrence, Maurice Evans, Leslie Howard, Jack Buchanan, and Emlyn Williams are veterans who frequently tread the boards of Shubert Alley. He points out that not only are the stars British, but so are entire casts and crews.

Cooke perceives major problems, "snags that anybody would hit who started to choose the other country's entertainment." The snags are caused by money, and the erroneous belief that success can be discovered only on the basis of financial profit. Cooke says this is "the worst possible criterion," based on a false premise that the biggest hits at home will be the biggest hits abroad, "founded on the presumption, even more naive, that two nations *should* like the same things."[114] As a case in point, he chooses George F. Kaufman, the biggest name on Broadway, whose *You Can't Take It with You* has been running for two years, who is a complete success with the French, who liken Kaufman to Feydeau. However, it was not so popular in London, where "the theatre was warmed by hardly a single smile." To Cooke, the show is not suitable for export because it is based on "local whimsicalities."[115]

Similarly, local English sensibilities are not understood by Americans, who find too much "intense glandular activity of the young people," "sentimentality, of a recognizable brand"—not the American "pretty nauseous way of being sentimental, over friendship, over giving a helping hand, over many a thing you have seen in the movies and blushed at"—but instead the "very special brand of English sentimentality . . . about what we would call 'sensitive young men.'"[116]

Despite his initial promise not to draw a conclusion, Cooke does present one in the guise of a simile about the two different culinary traditions. He says the Americans like ice cream with chocolate sauce and the English like roast beef with horseradish sauce. The problem is that the producers serve the English ice cream with horseradish sauce and the Americans take English roast beef with chocolate sauce. The result is that "you are left with two very sick men. No wonder, therefore, that when their digestion has got to work they are inclined to be petulant until they have got back to their native meals. Good night."[117]

This role, of the headwaiter who keeps the chocolate sauce with the ice cream and the horseradish with the roast beef—the role of a devoted but imperious servant—was to be Cooke's on *Masterpiece Theatre* as well. It is a view of criticism as etiquette, and of good taste as the equivalent of good table manners, which made Cooke the once and future master of ceremonies for television series obsessed, in a sense, with the history of everyday life—the veritable Braudel-style *Annales* school approach—of programs like *Upstairs, Downstairs* and *I, Claudius.*

Cooke's interest in manners also comes across in another typical early BBC broadcast. It was entitled "Living in New York and London" and featured Cooke and his first wife, Ruth, doing a comparison between keeping house in America and England.[118] Here we see Cooke again positioning himself as interlocutor, keeping the chocolate sauce with the ice cream and the horseradish with the roast beef.

As part of his continuing concern with Anglo-American conventions, Cooke befriended H. L. Mencken. He had first contacted Mencken while an exchange student at Harvard. Cooke writes about being struck on first encounter by Mencken's diminutive physical stature in the same way he was by Chaplin's: "a small man so short in the thighs that when he stood up he seemed smaller than when he was sitting down." Cooke had kept up a correspondence with the author of *The American Language* (he would come to edit *The Vintage Mencken*)[119] and, upon returning to America in 1937, he would frequently visit Mencken's Baltimore home. After Mencken's death, Cooke wrote a letter to the *New York Times* asking that the house be granted landmark status.[120] To Cooke, Mencken was "the reigning expert on such things as Anglo-American equivalents." At the time of his relationship with Cooke, however, Mencken was in critical disfavor due to his opposition to Roosevelt and the New Deal. Cooke found himself in an awkward position with his other friends, who forgave him "as you might forgive an apprentice cabinetmaker for having a Ku Kluxer as an instructor." Cooke notes that as an Englishman, a broadcaster, and a lapsed Methodist, he "embodied in one person a good many human types he disliked." It was as a reporter that he related to Mencken, who read his material and "taught me . . . that there is no such thing as ideological truth."[121] It was only with the start of World War II that Cooke saw less of Mencken "because his stubborn refusal to see it as anything but a collision of powers equally fraudulent and hypocritical was something I—as a British correspondent in the United States—would have found too uncomfortable to contend with."[122] This falling off from Mencken in certain respects paralleled Cooke's distance from Chaplin.

England was already at war with Germany, while the United States remained neutral. It was British government policy to attempt to steer American public opinion into aiding her cause.[123] In this context, Cooke made a series of suggestions to his superiors at the BBC for broadcasts designed to improve Anglo-American relations. He suggested talks on New Deal social services, trade unions, and American journalists like James Thurber and Heywood Broun. The response was not enthusiastic. "Whilst I think there is a need for the USA to understand the British, and indeed the European, situation, I do not feel at this stage there is an equivalent need for us to understand the American point of view," wrote one BBC staffer.[124] He added that Cooke's suggestions were "recherche," and that a piece entitled "Homage to a Great Democrat" was not appropriate for an English audience feeling abandoned and alone, victim of American isolationism. "I feel that homage to anything just at present is a bit previous to say the least of it." The BBC executive also dismissed Cooke's ideas for talks about democratic festivals in America as "not likely to appeal here." He concluded that Cooke was losing touch with his obligations, no longer taking "the standpoint of an Englishman" in his reporting. Yet, he acknowledged that Cooke "is indeed a good broadcaster and there are not many of them. We might make counter proposals to Cooke." The memo was passed along to Robert MacDermot for comment. He agreed that Cooke "has adopted the rather irritating American attitude whereby the U.S. is regarded as being the sole guardian of democracy, an attitude which is apt to puzzle the average Englishman who has been nurtured on American-manufactured films and stories of gangster and proto-nazi police methods." MacDermot agreed that Cooke was "an excellent broadcaster" and encouraged counter proposals.[125]

Although Cooke's specific suggestions were not taken up, he continued to report from America, although he noted "it was hard to enchant British newspaper readers with reports of the strength of the American isolationist sentiment."[126] Clearly the British subjects seeking shelter from German bombers during the Blitz had little sympathy for an English correspondent in the safety of the neutral United States.

Meanwhile, Cooke continued his activity as a film critic, writing a favorable study of Douglas Fairbanks for Alfred Barr at the Museum of Modern Art in 1940.[127] The museum was a cultural institution supported by Rockefeller oil money. Cooke's study of how Fairbanks managed his own image can be seen as instructional model for the young Cooke in creating his on-screen personality: Fairbanks was as dapper and sophisticated as Chaplin was rough and raw. Fairbanks was a screen gentleman where Chaplin was a tramp. Douglas Fairbanks was, in Cooke's words, "the ideal twentieth-century American."[128] Unlike Chaplin or Mencken, Fairbanks was a motion-picture icon of respectability.

The study is a biographical account that makes the case that "screen acting is not so much the functioning of an individual talent as a presentation of raw human material."[129] Cooke argues for a direct connection, in Fairbanks's case at least, between the life of the man and his screen persona. This is true to Willey and the "Q" tradition of linking experience with art. And in the way Cooke lived his own life, one might argue that he put his theory of the creation of screen character into practice, living the role which was appropriate for the host of *Masterpiece Theatre*. Indeed, in a way, it was a form of method acting carried to its full and logical conclusion.

In the study, Cooke chastises those who will not admire Fairbanks as being unable to enjoy direct emotional responses because of "the old reflex of 'maintaining one's standards.'" This is a reflex with which Cooke no doubt identifies.[130] His introduction, "Creating a Screen Personality," analyzes the genesis of Fairbanks's star image in direct relation to Hollywood studio politics. In this example of critical writing, Cooke gives the historical background of Hollywood cinema, as Basil Willey did for English literature.

Douglas Fairbanks was Chaplin's partner in United Artists, and Cooke prints a photo of Pickford, Fairbanks, and Chaplin together in his text.[131] Cooke is explicit in building up Fairbanks as an alternative cultural icon to Chaplin, and in wanting his study to serve as a rebuke to film critics who have overlooked Fairbanks in favor of the little tramp. And Fairbanks had this advantage for the critic: "He does not have to be rescued, as Chaplin had, from any cult admiration." That is, Chaplin does not need Cooke, but perhaps Fairbanks does need a critic as his champion.

To Cooke's seeming relief, and unlike Chaplin (who lived in sin with Paulette Goddard), Fairbanks was married to "America's sweetheart," Mary Pickford. Unlike the radical comedian, there was nothing unsavory about Fairbanks. "'Doug stood for the film industry's total respectability. He was not merely inoffensive, which is what the parents were looking for: he was a positive ideal worthy of any small fry's positive emulation."[132] To Cooke, Fairbanks's great achievement was "mating audience and actor."[133] From reading the text, one also gets the sense that Cooke's study of Fairbanks's screen image provided him with a model he would use in crafting his own television personality after the war as one of "total respectability."[134]

On December 1, 1941, Cooke became an American citizen.[135] At that time, the British were stepping up their efforts to bring America into the war. One of the English efforts was a volume entitled *Union Now with Britain,* published with an endorsement from *Time* publisher Henry R. Luce declaring, "No thoughtful American has done his duty by the United States of America until he has read and pondered" the book.[136] Earlier that same year, Cooke had joined the staff of the British *Daily Herald,* a left-wing newspaper allied with the Labour Party. He held the post until 1943. With the entry of the United States into the war after Pearl Harbor, the BBC felt Cooke's work was now of utmost importance, despite the fact that "there was prejudice against Alistair Cooke" within the organization. Past hard feelings—perhaps a result of Cooke's failure to return home when war broke out—should be put aside, said a memorandum. It was "essential now to have a known BBC reporter in America—whom he would term the BBC's Reporter or some such title—a man who would be responsible for doing the kind of things that Murrow and Co. did here, not dealing in the political field at all but handling all the live interest stuff, going out and getting recordings, etc. The only suitable person . . . was Alistair Cooke."[137] As a result, Cooke spent 1942 "reporting from the American grandstand to an audience of embattled Britons."[138] His assignment was to detail the effects of the war on American industry and society.

There were still complaints from England about Cooke's Americanized coverage, and Cooke fired back in kind. Writing to John Pringle in January of 1943, he said, "On principle, I would say that I simply cannot bring myself to satisfy British preconceptions about America . . . But for the same reasons, I think Britain loses valuable respect here by having people go on describing it in terms of fox-hunting, Wedgwood, and the village pub. *Mrs. Miniver,* from this point of view, did Britain here incalculable harm by describing with perfect fidelity a tiny minority of the English and implying (for Americans at least) that this was Britain today, that these were the people of Sheffield and Liverpool, paralysed and cowed by a decorative but inflexible country aristocracy."[139]

These comments parallel Christopher Hitchens's later criticisms of the view of Britain conveyed by the programs shown on *Masterpiece Theatre,* quoted in the epigraph at the opening of this chapter. Over time, Cooke's own television image came to resemble those clichés found in movies put out by Hollywood during World War II, productions Cooke had earlier chastised for deceptive presentations of English life.

In 1943 Cooke was ordered to register with the U. S. government under the Alien Registration Act, an act that Cooke felt would label him "officially lumped as a purveyor of British propaganda along with the employees of the British Information Services [the official public relations arm of the British government in the United States]." As a naturalized American citizen, Cooke felt he must protest. Mencken rallied to his side and Cooke appealed, arguing "that to declare myself a British propagandist would be an affront to both my trade as a reporter and my status as an American citizen." According to Cooke, the matter was dropped. This was not Cooke's last run-in with American authorities, however, for in 1944, Cooke filed a protest against American government censorship of his dispatches on "the industrial home front." (Cooke had been working as a contributor to the London *Times*.) According to Cooke, this action was also supported and encouraged by Mencken.

In 1944, Cooke helped start the BBC program *Transatlantic Quiz,* a game show designed to improve cross-cultural under-standing.[140] Then, in 1945, he began writing for the *Manchester Guardian,* covering the opening session of the United Nations, or-ganized in part by Alger Hiss, about whose trial he would write his first book. Cooke became the paper's American correspondent and remained on the job until his retirement in 1972. In 1947, Cooke began his *Letter from America* on the BBC, the world's longest-running radio show.[141] Already Cooke was being called America's "ambassador without portfolio to Great Britain."[142]

Cooke soon had a chance to renew his contact with Basil Wil-ley, as the Cambridge don notes in his memoirs. Willey saw Cooke when he attended the inauguration of Dwight D. Eisenhower as president of Columbia University in 1948, as the representative of Cambridge University. Seeing Willey's name in the paper, Cooke invited him to dinner. Willey notes that he had not seen Cooke since his student days at Cambridge "though like everyone else I had followed his meteoric rise to Anglo-American fame. I found him now living in a luxurious apartment just off Fifth Avenue, and the dinner he provided (complete with colored maid-service) was as stylish as himself. It was interesting to find in him the same qualities, though now in full blow and exerted in far wider fields, as he had shown before: great cleverness, wit, imagination, and the up-to-the-minute alertness of the born journalist. I admired, too, his refined American accent (he was born in Lancashire), adopted with characteristic finesse so as to offend neither American nor British ears."[143] Willey's writings provide further evidence for Cooke's remarkable ability to adapt to his role as a transatlantic personality, a professional middleman.

In 1950 Cooke, who pleaded political naïveté with regard to Chaplin, wrote about a crucial political drama of the postwar con-frontation with communism—the trial of Alger Hiss. *A Genera-tion on Trial: USA v. Alger Hiss* was published by the prestigious publishing house—and Mencken's publisher—Alfred A. Knopf. The study was based on reporting he had done for the *Guardian.* It was hailed by the American press, which saw in it a critique of witch-hunting.[144] Although Cooke may have been sympathetic to the plight of the eggheads—after all, Hiss had been an architect of the United Nations—in his account of the "generation on trial" Cooke's approach is rather detached. He spends a great deal of time quoting and paraphrasing transcripts, but rarely shows his own hand, and does not take a stand as to whether Hiss is guilty or innocent of perjury.

In the conclusion, Cooke quotes William Empson on "irony" and "ambiguity." And in his introduction, Cooke suggests that "a useful dialectic job could be done by substituting the word 'Nazi' wherever the word 'Communist' appears in this affair; it would probably teach us a good deal about what was interchangeable and what was not, in the attitudes of the Left to Fascism in the late 1930s, and the attitudes of the Right to Communism in the late 1940s. I suspect they are much closer than we know, for anybody's comfort; one's willingness to credit somebody else's brutality has a lot to do with who you think is being mistreated."[145] Again, Cooke is the man in the middle. He is reasonable, respectable, safe, and secure. He is sympathetic to Hiss's plight, but will not go out on a limb—not for him or against him. Cooke has occupied a place safely above the fray, removed from the din of the crowd below.

The British perceived that Cooke was engaging in a form of social history, not political polemic. The *Times Literary Supplement* noticed that "the theme is not Hiss's guilt at all. It is the way in which American institutions can treat an American-born American official, of the white race and the 'right' social background, at a time when fear of Communism has let loose those violent strains of hysteria which, in earlier and successive stages of American history, marked the 'Native Americans,' the 'Know-Nothings,' the Ku Klux Klan and many other xenophobic associations. That is why his book is called *A Generation on Trial* . It is as much about the methodology of American trials as about Hiss's (and Mr. Cooke's) generation in America."[146] By sidestepping the issue of Hiss's guilt, Cooke achieved a diplomatic victory from which he apparently would benefit when Hiss's chief accuser, then Senator Richard Nixon, became president.

Nixon, in his own account of the House Committee on Un-American Activities hearings, describes Hiss as looking somewhat like Alistair Cooke does when hosting *Masterpiece Theatre:* "tall, elegant, handsome, perfectly poised."[147] But also as "too suave, too smooth, and too self-confident to be an entirely trustworthy witness."[148] No wonder, then, that Cooke takes the view that his study is about the tragedy of "the trials of a man who was judged in one decade for what he was said to have done in another."[149] Cooke begins his volume with a background study of FDR's America of the New Deal and World War II, and denounces what he sees as the American trap, where "a public man . . . may be confronted at any time with inconsistencies from his past that are not the permissible inconsistencies of the time."[150] Cooke had been careful to try and steer clear of such impermissible inconsistencies. At the 1948 Progressive Party convention that nominated Henry Wallace, Mencken had jokingly introduced Cooke to a Minnesota Youth for Wallace battalion as covering the event for "the London *Daily Worker*."[151] The wisecrack wounded Cooke sufficiently for him to remark that "an Englishman naturalized in America must in his own lifetime resign himself to be thought a renegade in his native country, a British spy in his adopted one."[152]

There is another level to Cooke's book, one not mentioned by either the English or American reviewers. It is Cooke's kindly treatment of Richard Nixon, "a dark, intense man, younger than Hiss, whose tenacity in pursuing this whole affair brought it in the end into the courts."[153] Indeed, Cooke is scrupulously fair to Nixon as well as to Hiss. He writes, "Mr. Nixon just wanted to know if Hiss thought the Government should make every effort to look into the alleged subversive acts of Communists in the United States."[154] He blames the media, not Nixon, for any excesses of patriotic zeal. "The worst indignities were done by the headline writers . . . It was the feature writers who did a serious disservice to the motives and even to the legitimate procedures of the Committee, and such irreparable damage to Hiss."[155] Later, Cooke describes the broadcast of HUAC sessions as a problem in itself, with "television's peculiar and terrifying gift for casting an intensely private eye on scenes of the utmost publicity; elbowing along the Committee table and taking long, revealing glances at the darkly handsome Mr. Nixon . . ."[156] Again, Cooke does not criticize Nixon for pursuing Hiss, but instead calls for laws to "limit public hearings, ban all forms of news photography . . . A revision of the libel and slander laws has long been overdue."[157] Despite the rather un-American tone of Cooke's censorship plea, that Cooke could write an account of the Hiss case without condemning either

Hiss or Nixon shows his mastery of the role of reasonable, detached, even-handed, civilized observer.

Knowing how carefully Nixon kept track of the doings of his antagonists, and of Nixon's personal involvement in driving news
correspondent Sander Vanocur off the air at PBS during the 1970s
because of his sympathies to the Kennedy clan, one cannot help
but hypothesize that Cooke's scrupulous fairness to Nixon did not
go unheeded. Cooke had successfully positioned himself between
left and right on the American intellectual scene, as the consum-
mate middleman between highbrow egghead and determined
witch-hunter, in a public position of indignation at the besmirch-
ing of Hiss's reputation, while simultaneously defending the right
of Nixon and Congress to discreetly investigate his loyalty. In a
word, the perfect host for the delicate balancing act that would
have to be played by an educational television program in the anti-
Communist atmosphere of the 1950s: *Omnibus.*

As mentioned earlier, during the upheavals of the 1960s Cooke
was hosting the United Nations series *International Zone* and
preparing for his BBC history of the United States. Although present as a foreign correspondent at Robert Kennedy's assassination
in Los Angeles, Cooke was, as an English journalist, somewhat removed from direct involvement in the turmoil of the time. So when
Nixon became president, the sober, responsible, measured, reasonable, transatlantic Cooke—a man equally at home with Alger
Hiss and Richard Nixon—was precisely the voice of reason PBS
needed to fight off simultaneous criticism from both ends of the
political spectrum that the network was part of a far-left conspiracy to "get Nixon"—and on the other hand, that PBS was part of
a plot by corporate America to stifle dissent.

And if this circumstantial evidence were not enough, Cooke gave
a clear sign of his attitude towards the radicalism of the sixties in a
1970 essay he wrote for the *Guardian* entitled "The Ghastly Sixties." He began with the statement: "In thirty-seven years' experience of the United States, from the pit of the depression to the
apotheosis of Richard M. Nixon, I have known no stretch of American life so continuously disheartening as the lean years that were
so dreadfully announced by the shots in Dallas and were echoed in
Watts and Detroit and Newark, that re-echoed on the motel balcony
in Memphis and the hotel pantry in Los Angeles, and rumbled ob-
scenely on the streets of Chicago and through the stadiums of the

1968 presidential election campaign. That, to be fussy, leaves four preceding years of what may now be seen as the fool's paradise of the Kennedy era, which is what I truly believe it to have been."

Following this sobering opening, Cooke lists a litany of horrors he associates with the sixties and concludes with a warning that, "It is possible that the Negro, and the radical youth, black and white, are already too cynicised—by Vietnam, by widespread corruption in state and in municipal government, by the respectable inroads of the Mafia, by the climate of violence—to accept any longer the habit of creative compromise that is essential to effective government of the people by the people and which, in truth, has been the genius of the American system since its founding. Perhaps by now there are not enough believers left to rescue and reform the system. If this is so, what seems to be the most fearful possibility is a dogged reaction by the middle-class mass, and the arrival of fascism by popular democratic vote."[158]

Cooke went on to describe America as a "giant, writhing in its own coils, suspect, frightened, and leaderless." Given this terrifying prospect of an America Cooke had loved and admired reduced to a state of what he perceived as nightmarish anarchy, is it any wonder that Cooke began to feel more comfortable with a return to the English heritage he had fled when he moved to the United States in the thirties? Hosting *Masterpiece Theatre* represented for Cooke a welcome, reasonal, liberal alternative to the possibility of either revolution or fascism. It was the fulfillment of a lifetime of experience in the worlds of journalism and politics, radio and television, England and America.

For *Masterpiece Theatre,* Cooke was the indispensable man— acceptable to both Democrats and Republicans, aesthetes and politicos, commercial network viewers and public television snobs. And for the potential audience, Alistair Cooke *was* educational television because of his track record on *Omnibus.*[159] It is no wonder that he was the first and only choice of series producer Sarson, WGBH president Stanford Calderwood, Mobil's Herb Schmertz, and television consultant Frank Marshall. They wanted Cooke precisely because of *Omnibus,* his credibility as a journalist and foreign correspondent, and public stature as a literary celebrity. If Cooke had not agreed to host the program, Calderwood, Schmertz, and Sarson all were prepared to use "visual essays." No one else would do.[160]

Notes

1. Doug Hill and Jeff Weingrad, *Saturday Night* (New York: Vintage, 1987), 260.
2. Kay Gardella, personal interview, 12 January 1991.
3. Museum of Broadcasting, *The Museum of Broadcasting Celebrates Mobil & Masterpiece Theatre: 15 Years of Excellence* (New York: Museum of Broadcasting, 1986), 10.
4. Herb Schmertz, telephone interview, 13 February 1991.
5. The series featured 19.5 percent music and dance, 17.4 percent classical literature and drama, 17.2 percent contemporary literature and drama, 13.3 percent contemporary life and current affairs, 11.7 percent sports and light entertainment, 10.9 percent history and biography, 6 percent science and natural history, and 4 percent art and architecture. "The TV-Radio Workshop," Ford Foundation, *Annual Report* (New York: Ford Foundation, 1955).
6. "Radio & TV: The New Shows," *Time,* 24 November 1952, 85.
7. Christina Adam, "Great Shows: OMNIBUS," *Emmy,* October 1979, 42.
8. *Time,* 24 November 1952, 86.
9. Cooke, personal interview.
10. Dwight MacDonald, *The Ford Foundation* (New York: Reynal and Company, 1956), 87.
11. MacDonald, *The Ford Foundation,* 88.
12. MacDonald, *The Ford Foundation,* 88–89.
13. Alistair Cooke, PBS Press Tour, 11 January 1991.
14. MacDonald, *The Ford Foundation,* 90.
15. MacDonald, *The Ford Foundation,* 90.
16. MacDonald, *The Ford Foundation,* 90–91.
17. MacDonald, *The Ford Foundation,* 92–93.
18. MacDonald, *The Ford Foundation,* 93–94.
19. Louis Carl Saalbach, "Jack Gould: Social Critic of the Television Medium, 1947–72," University of Michigan dissertation, 1980.
20. Jack Gould, "Omnibus Evaluated: Ford Foundation's TV-Radio Workshop's Contribution to Video Is Inestimable," *New York Times,* 16 November 1952.
21. *New York Times,* 16 December 1957.
22. *Omnibus,* number 87, UCLA Film and Television Archive.
23. Schmertz says: "I didn't want to do the socially redeeming feature of changing a tire on the M5" (personal interview).
24. Daniel Blum, *A Pictorial History of Television* (Philadelphia: Chilton, 1959), 268.

25. *The Horn Blows at Midnight, Omnibus,* number 1953: 9, UCLA Film and Television Archive.

26. In that case, Cooke explained away the excision of large portions of Shakespeare's text with the promise "Peter Brook has taken the subplot and thrown it out the window, but everything that pertains to the tragedy has been kept . . . We give you *King Lear* in the hope you may learn more from Shakespeare's pessimism than from the optimism of lesser men." *Omnibus,* number 859, UCLA Film and Television Archive.

27. Schmertz, *Goodbye to the Low Profile* (Boston: Little, Brown, 1986), 229.

28. "People on Television," *New York Times,* 7 October 1956.

29. "Radio Comment: Murrow, Morgan, Swing, Cooke Give Ideas Precedence over Pictures," *New York Times,* 9 October 1960.

30. "News and Notes of TV and Radio: 'Omnibus,'" *New York Times,* 20 November 1960.

31. North American representative, memo from to D.Tel.B., "T8/742—USA Columbia b/c System. 2 1948–54," 30 November 1954, BBC Written Archives Center, Caversham.

32. Michael Gill, letter to Alistair Cooke, "Talks 2B, Cooke, Alistair, 38–62", ref. 07/NAS/MG, 18 May 1955, BBC Written Archives Center, Caversham.

33. Alistair Cooke, "A Visitor Looks at Hollywood," USIS Feature, December 1957, 5.

34. "Power among Men," *New York Times,* 29 March 1959.

35. "Radio Comment," *New York Times,* 9 October 1960. One might note, in relation to Cooke and the theme of tedium, that Richard Price, a major salesman of British productions to *Masterpiece Theatre*—including *Upstairs, Downstairs*—says: "I came into the television business in 1965, having been working in the pharmaceutical industry. You may joke about the fact that I went from one soporific to another." Personal interview, 1 August 1990.

36. "News of TV and Radio: Alistair Cooke to Host Series Designed to 'Personalize' the UN," *New York Times,* 13 November 1960.

37. "Global TV Series: *International Zone* Shows UN Work," *New York Times,* 18 February 1962.

38. *UN Dateline,* International Zone, George Movshon, executive producer, UCLA Film and Television Archive.

39. "TV Talks, Alistair Cooke, 3" Extract, Meeting, 5 February 1961, minute 243, Cooke, Alistair files, BBC Written Archives Center, Caversham.

40. Grace Wyndham Goldie, Memo to C. P. Tel, "TV Talks, Alistair Cooke, 3," 12 November 1962, BBC Written Archives, Caversham.

41. "Alistair Cooke Sends BBC 1000th Letter on U. S.," *New York Times,* 25 March 1968.

42. "Letter Writer from America," *New York Times,* 27 March 1968.

43. Alistair Cooke, *Talks about America* (London: Bodley Head, 1968).

44. "Epistles to the English," *Times Literary Supplement,* 24 October 1968.

45. Sarson, personal interview, 19 June 1990.

46. *New York Times,* 12 April 1973.

47. Alistair Cooke, *Alistair Cooke's America* (New York: Knopf, 1973).

48. *New York Times,* 25 February 1972.

49. *New York Times,* 25 February 1972.

50. *New York Times,* 15 November 1972.

51. *Who's Who* (London: A & C Black, 1990), 379.

52. Cooke had been slow to come to this point of view. In his BBC coverage of Watergate, he at first argued the incident had been blown out of proportion. Cooke, *The Americans* (New York: Knopf, 1979).

53. Alistair Cooke, "How It All Began," *The Patient Has the Floor* (New York: Knopf, 1986), 41–47.

54. Brendan Gill, *A New York Life* (New York: Poseidon, 1991).

55. Craig Unger, "House Proud," *New York,* 21 January 1991, 44–48.

56. Cooke is twice-married, a snappy dresser, and utterly charming. In addition to his "snob appeal," there is the whiff of the Edwardian dandy in the host of *Masterpiece Theatre.* His first marriage was in 1934 to Ruth Emerson, daughter of the president of the American Public Health Association. She is mother of his son, John, who dropped out of Harvard College to manage Janis Joplin's singing career. He was present when she was found dead. John Cooke, "John Cooke Tells How It Was," *The Rolling Stone Rock and Roll Reader,* Ben Fong-Torres, ed. (New York: Bantam, 1974), 395–99. Cooke remarried in 1946 to artist Jane White Hawkes, mother of his daughter, Susan. Susan Cooke graduated from the blue-blood Putney School. She worked as personal assistant to New York socialite and author Truman Capote ("Susan Cooke Will Be Married in December to Anthony Scoville," *New York Times,* 29 October 1968).

57. Ronald A. Wells, "Alistair Cooke: A Tocqueville for Our Time?" Unpublished paper presented to the European Society for American Studies, Seville, Spain, 1991.

58. Arthur Gray and Frederick Brittain, *A History of Jesus College, Cambridge* (London: Heinemann, 1979), 201–202. Jacob Bronowski, whose *Ascent of Man* was sponsored on WGBH by Mobil, was also a Jesus College man.

59. Basil Willey, *The "Q" Tradition* (Cambridge: Cambridge University Press, 1946), 10–11.

60. Willey, *The "Q" Tradition,* 25–26.

61. Willey, *The "Q" Tradition,* 35.

62. F. R. Leavis, *Mass Civilization and Minority Culture* (Cambridge: Cambridge University Press, 1930).

63. Alistair Cooke, *Masterpieces* (New York: Knopf, 1981), 213.

64. Cooke, personal interview.

65. Advertisement, *Paignton Observer,* 3 July 1931, Talks File I/32–35, Alistair Cooke, BBC Written Archives Center, Caversham.

66. Director of Programmes, BBC, Letter to Alistair Cooke, 9 July 1931, FT/JRA, Talks File I/32–33, Alistair Cooke, BBC Written Archives Center, Caversham.

67. J. R. Ackerley, Letter to Alistair Cooke, 11 May 1932, BBC Written Archives Center, Caversham.

68. Cooke, *Six Men* (New York: Knopf, 1977), 54.

69. Cooke, *Six Men,* 52.

70. Cooke, *Six Men,* 52.

71. Cooke, *Six Men,* 54.

72. Ronald Wells, "Introduction" in Alistair Cooke, *America Observed* (New York: Viking, 1988), 5.

73. Ronald Wells, "Introduction," 5–6.

74. Ronald Wells, "Introduction," 5–6.

75. The articles were published in the fall of 1933 per Wells, "Introduction," 7.

76. Cooke, *Six Men,* 22.

77. Cooke, *Six Men,* 23.

78. Cooke, *Six Men,* 24.

79. Charles Chaplin, *My Autobiography* (New York: Simon and Schuster, 1964).

80. Cooke, *Six Men,* 20.

81. Cooke, *Six Men,* 25.

82. Cooke, *Six Men,* 26–27.

83. Cooke, *Six Men,* 27.

84. Cooke, *Six Men,* 28.

85. Cooke, *Six Men,* 37.

86. David Robinson, *Chaplin: His Life and Art* (New York: McGraw-Hill, 1985).

87. Cooke, *Six Men,* 38–39.

88. Cooke, *Six Men,* 41.

89. Wells, "Introduction," 7.

90. CAS, BBC Director of Talks, Letter to Alistair Cooke, 24 April 1934, BBC Written Archives Center, Caversham.

91. M. McLaren, Letter to Cooke, 10 December 1935, BBC Written Archives Center, Caversham.

92. Cooke, *Six Men,* 57.

93. Cooke, *Six Men,* 66.

94. A. M. Sperber, *Murrow: His Life and Times* (New York: Freundlich Books, 1986), 99.

95. Cooke, *Six Men,* 68.

96. Alistair Cooke, *Garbo and the Night Watchmen* (London: Secker and Warburg, 1971).

97. Cooke, *Garbo and the Night Watchmen,* 11.

98. Cooke, *Garbo and the Night Watchmen,* 9.

99. Cooke, *Garbo and the Night Watchmen,* 268.

100. Cooke, "The Critic in Film History," *Footnotes to the Film,* Charles Davy, ed. (London: Lovat Dickson Ltd, 1938), 238–63.

101. Cooke, "The Critic in Film History," 260.

102. Cooke, "The Critic in Film History," 263.

103. Cooke, *Six Men,* 95.

104. *Who's Who* (1990), 379.

105. BBC broadcast, Wednesday, 25 May 1938, regional: 6:40 P.M., script from Written Archives Center, Caversham.

106. North American representative (FG) BBC internal memo, 10 May 1938, Memo to Miss Quigley, copies to FLO, Cooke, Alistair, Talks File 2, 1936–40, 3, BBC Written Archives Center, Caversham.

107. North American representative (FG) BBC internal memo, 10 May 1938, Memo to Miss Quigley, BBC Written Archives Center, Caversham.

108. "The Theatre: New York and London," transcript, BBC Written Archives Center, Caversham, 1.

109. Alistair Cooke, *Masterpieces* (New York: Alfred A. Knopf, 1980), 9.

110. His Paignton experience is not mentioned.

111. Cooke, *Masterpieces,* 2.

112. Cooke, *Masterpieces,* 3.

113. Cooke, *Masterpieces,* 4.

114. Cooke, *Masterpieces,* 5.

115. Cooke, *Masterpieces,* 5–6.

116. Cooke, *Masterpieces,* 7–8.

117. Cooke, *Masterpieces,* 9.

118. "Personal file, Talks, Cooke, Alistair, 1937–62," BBC Written Archives, Caversham.

119. Alistair Cooke, ed., *The Vintage Mencken* (New York: Vintage, 1990). First published in 1955.

120. "Letters," *New York Times,* 18 September 1957.

121. Cooke, *Six Men,* 95–96.

122. Cooke, *Six Men,* 98.

123. For an account, see William Stevenson's *A Man Called Intrepid* (New York: Harcourt Brace Jovanovich, 1976).

124. ADPP, BBC, Memo to: DPP, 12 February 1940, "Cooke, Alistair: Talks File 2 1936–40," BBC Written Archives Center, Caversham.

125. Mr. MacDermot, Memo to ADPP through DPP, BBC Internal Memo, "Subject: Programme Suggestions from Alistair Cooke," 16 February 1940, Talks File 2, 1936–40, BBC Written Archives Center, Caversham. Cooke writes that he felt some Americans suspected him of being a British agent.

126. Cooke, *America*, 340.

127. Alistair Cooke, *Douglas Fairbanks, The Making of a Screen Character* (New York: Museum of Modern Art, 1940).

128. Cooke, *Douglas Fairbanks*, 21.

129. Cooke, *Douglas Fairbanks*, 6.

130. Cooke, *Douglas Fairbanks*, 10.

131. Cooke, *Douglas Fairbanks*, 15.

132. Cooke, *Douglas Fairbanks*, 31.

133. Cooke, *Douglas Fairbanks*, 31.

134. Perhaps Cooke might be considered the Douglas Fairbanks of educational television.

135. Wells, "Alistair Cooke: A Tocqueville for Our Time," 6; also interview with Ned Smith in *The American Way Magazine*, Fall 1976, 23.

136. Clarence K. Streit, *Union Now with Britain* (New York: Harper & Brothers, 1941).

137. DDG, BBC, Memo to C(NC) "Private and Confidential Memo," 18 December 1941, E1/225/1 America H-H, 1939–53, BBC Written Archives Center, Caversham.

138. Cooke, *America*, 12.

139. Cooke, Alistair, "Letter to John Pringle," 5 January 1943, Talks, File II, 1941–52, BBC Written Archives Center, Caversham.

140. "Alistair Cooke," *Current Biography* (New York: H. W. Wilson, 1952), 119.

141. *Who's Who* (1990). Also see Wells, "Introduction," 6–8.

142. "Alistair Cooke," *Current Biography*, 1952, 119.

143. Basil Willey, *Cambridge and Other Memories* (London: Chatto, 1968), 140.

144. "Alistair Cooke," *Current Biography*, 1952, 119.

145. Cooke, *A Generation on Trial*, 2nd ed. (New York: Knopf, 1951), xi.

146. *Times Literary Supplement*, 1 December 1950, 759.

147. Richard Nixon, *RN: The Memoirs of Richard Nixon* (New York: Simon & Schuster, 1978), 54.

148. Richard Nixon, *RN*, 55.

149. Cooke, *A Generation on Trial,* 3.

150. Cooke, *A Generation on Trial,* 9.

151. Cooke, *Six Men,* 113.

152. Cooke, *Six Men,* 115.

153. Cooke, *Six Men,* 61.

154. Cooke, *Six Men,* 61.

155. Cooke, *Six Men,* 65.

156. Cooke, *Six Men,* 87.

157. Cooke, *Six Men,* 98.

158. Cooke, "The Ghastly Sixties," *America Observed* (New York: Knopf, 1988), 207–10.

159. Just as the Ford Foundation ceased supporting *Omnibus* in 1957, it started funding the National Association of Educational Broadcasters, preparing the way for the establishment of National Educational Television (NET). *Ford Foundation Activities in Noncommercial Broadcasting: 1951–76* (New York: Ford Foundation, 1976).

160. Schmertz, Calderwood, Sarson, personal interviews.

4

PBS and *Masterpiece Theatre*

Meanwhile, Mobil Oil and other major corporations . . . took
to sponsoring so much depoliticized culture on public television that wags took to calling it the Petroleum Broadcasting
System.

—Todd Gitlin, *Inside Prime Time*

Alistair Cooke's contract, and contact, has always been with
WGBH. He prides himself on being a part of the nonprofit and
noncommercial world of public television, a legacy of his work for
the Ford Foundation and the United Nations. While the public
identifies Cooke with *Masterpiece Theatre* and may have the impression that he chooses the programs,[1] Cooke's claim that the job
is simply "an agreeable form of moonlighting" is an entirely accurate description of his responsibilities for the series. As host,
Cooke's role, while substantial, is not decisive. Although he is permitted to make suggestions to the producer, Cooke does not select
the shows. He simply introduces them. The real creative power in
the series lies elsewhere. Where it lies was worked out in the early
years of the series in a number of decisive encounters between Mobil, WGBH, and PBS.

Cooke was first approached by producer Christopher Sarson,
representing WGBH, on October 5, 1970. Cooke did not agree
to take the job at first.[2] In his approach to Cooke, Sarson told him
he would not be required to watch the programs, that Sarson would
arrange to prepare notes that would form the basis of a script and
that Cooke could fly into Boston "and do the first 13 in a day."[3] Still,
Cooke did not accept the role. The reason, according to Sarson, was

91

Cooke "felt that his *Omnibus* image had been of a certain kind that he had cultivated." No doubt the figure Cooke fancied was that of a sophisticated, urbane New Yorker and not that of an upper-class Englishman. Sarson recalls Cooke begged off on account of the need to preserve his existing American public persona, telling Sarson, "it was now lodged in people's minds. He wanted that to be the image with which the viewers approached *America*,"[4] the Xerox-sponsored NBC-BBC series then in production. It is only natural that Cooke was apprehensive that a strongly English public personality might have made presenting the history of the United States a bit more difficult to pull off without sniping from critics.

When Sarson failed to persuade Cooke, he says "I made only what I can describe as a half-hearted attempt to find a substitute because he was so perfect that I didn't really try."[5] Without Cooke, Sarson would use "visual introductions" composed of clips and voice-overs. The first show was set to air on January 10, 1971. Writing of the segments, which were produced and directed by Sarson, began the first Monday of December without Cooke.[6] (Sarson had not heard from him since their meeting in Boston.)

On December 7, 1970, PBS announced a preview feed of *Masterpiece Theatre* through its interconnection system, for in-house viewing by station personnel. The sixty-minute presentation reel contained four clips: from *Vanity Fair, Pere Goriot, The Spoils of Poynton,* and the series opener, *The First Churchills.* The accompanying message—sent out on the PBS teletype network called the Dial Access Communications System (DACS)—banned use of the material for press screenings, explaining "a preview of episode one of *The First Churchills,* complete with *Masterpiece Theatre* titles, and introduction by a host (whose name will be announced next week) and 'fill' material, will be sent down the line on December 29 at 11:00 AM. The December 29 preview should be used for press screenings."[7] The preview, called the "Churchill Sampler," was fed to the PBS stations on December 8, 1970, with the notation on the PBS preview report: "It looks like a good series." Meanwhile, with Cooke still noncommittal, Sarson recalls phoning Antonia Fraser to see if she were interested in the hosting job.[8]

At the last minute, Cooke agreed to do the introductions. Sarson recalls that one day as he was heading out to lunch, his phone rang. It was Cooke. He told Sarson that his daughter Sarah (who had been at the meeting in Boston) had persuaded him to agree to host the series. "Although he was sure we had chosen someone else by now, he wanted me to know," Sarson recalled. "I asked him if he was still available; he said yes." Sarson taped his first introductions in mid-December. "I've never concluded a deal as quickly as I did with these gentlemen," said Sarson.[9]

Cooke came to WGBH to tape his commentary with Sarson, who, also in the role of segment director, was putting together the identifying title sequence "which of course, all had to be done very quickly." Sarson began with the British flag, "because all this stuff was going to come from Britain." He devised a "very crude" opening with the WGBH art department, consisting of a Union Jack inside the *p* of *Masterpiece Theatre*. This title card would be used until 1974, when Joan Wilson replaced Sarson as executive producer.

Sarson felt the program needed "quality" music to set the mood, to indicate to the audience that something special was to follow. He recalled enjoying very much an Italian Club Med vacation with his wife-to-be in 1962.[10] "Every morning from the plaza when they feed you, you sit at these long tables and gorge yourself silly," Sarson says. "The music that summoned you to these food events was . . . 'Music for the King's Supper' by Jean Joseph Mouret . . . it was just one of those gorgeous associations." The piece became the *Masterpiece Theatre* theme. Sarson, who read the initial voice-over identifying Mobil as an underwriter, noted that the tune was played at all the Club Meds, so anyone who had vacationed there would have found the theme familiar, but he pointed out "Club Med, in those days in America, was almost unknown. It was very much a European thing." However, Sarson did find it amusing that the tune he had chosen was of French origin, because "everything had been British" about the program. The theme has remained to this day.[11] It might be significant that the Club Med vacation appealed to European-oriented, upper-middle-class professionals on holiday, who were a part of the *Masterpiece Theatre* target demographic.[12]

Sarson also helped plan Cooke's on-air commentary. The pattern he set was followed by subsequent producers Joan Wilson and Rebecca Eaton, who provided Cooke with "producer's notes."[13] Although Cooke claims to write his own introductions, he does have help from WGBH in preparing them. Before recording his commentary, Cooke would come up to the Ritz Carlton Hotel in Boston and have dinner with Sarson. Then, the two would go over the briefing materials Sarson had put together. "I would look at the things, and all the things, and do the story continuity, what I would suggest that he would say, the meat of what he would say, at the beginning of the show as far as the next storyline went. And also points that interested me about what should be brought out in the background, many of which, in context, many of which he would include in the piece that he wrote." Although Sarson notes "if you didn't give him any suggestions, he was fine anyway."

They would rehearse the segments in Cooke's hotel the night before the taping. "He'd read it through. Timing was important," says Sarson. "He'd come in the following day and whip off . . . my memory tells me we used to do eight a day."[14] Sarson, who says his aesthetic preference is "to underproduce rather than overproduce" chose to arrange Cooke's chair on the set against a black backdrop, with one object that had been in the production and was therefore significant. For the premiere, "it was a picture of one of the *First Churchills* which was on the wall of the set . . . [and] a vase or something that was significant next to him on sort of a tasteful pedestal. And that was it."[15]

While Cooke was sitting in his chair, he would memorize the script he had written on a portable typewriter. "And then he'd sit down and memorize it in the five minutes we had before we rolled tape. And then he'd do it. And if it took 1:32 when it should take 1:28, the next time he read it for us it took 1:28. It was just uncanny that he could do that, he's a wonderful master of that."[16]

Meanwhile, as Sarson prepared *Masterpiece Theatre* for broadcast, the "sandbox kids" at WGBH threatened president Stanford Calderwood's—and the station's—new relationship with Mobil. Events came to a head when *The Ralph Nader Report* targeted the oil company in an exposé. Calderwood was upset because "I sensed, and he didn't deny, that he [the producer] had gone out of his way to get at Mobil, and wasn't about to back down . . . He made it clear he felt that WGBH, and Calderwood in particular, weren't doing Public Television any good by accepting Mobil's money. And, he insisted, his views were widely shared by the station staff, and I suspect he was relatively accurate. The nasty Mobil segment was going to stay, he made it clear. It was his claim to manhood, I suppose." Calderwood says that if he had ordered the show cut, the producer would have called a press conference and made an issue of his interference. So instead, Calderwood says he telephoned Herb Schmertz at Mobil to warn him of the upcoming attack. He recalls that Schmertz "was very gracious about it. No pressure whatsoever."

However, tension was building from the local producers and staff at WGBH. Calderwood's tenure at the station was to be short-lived. Even as production moved ahead on the premiere broadcast of *The First Churchills,* Calderwood became embroiled in a major controversy over *Say, Brother,* "a black-produced show." The program used language that Calderwood felt was endangering the station's FCC license, specifically, repeated use of the word "motherfucker." Calderwood fired the producer, leading to a storm of protest, including public demonstrations calling for his resignation. Calderwood feels "a couple of very smart activists turned the whole situation from being a matter of acceptable programming to the FCC into a matter of 'the White Man upstairs' pushing unfairly." In response to these protests, the board of the station "refused to give me adequate support," and Calderwood left the station before Christmas of 1970 to take an assignment with CPB, funded by the Ford Foundation, to travel in Europe to study other foreign programming that might be purchased by public television stations. It was three weeks before the *Masterpiece Theatre* premiere. Instead of enjoying his programming triumph, Calderwood was, in effect, in exile. With Calderwood gone, a new relationship needed to be negotiated between the partners in the production. (Calderwood soon left the world of public broadcasting for a successful career as financier.)

Calderwood was succeeded as president by David O. Ives, a Boston Brahmin and long-time WGBH "team player," who hosted the fund-raising auction program. Ives turned over day-to-day supervision of the program to station manager Bob Larsen. He and Sarson would now form WGBH's team. With Calderwood forced out, the initiative was with Mobil, in the persons of Marshall and Schmertz. And while Mobil now had satisfaction in regard to three of the elements of the package Marshall had sketched out— "theme" with the decision to focus on masterpieces of literature, "host" with the selection of Alistair Cooke, and "national network" with the agreement of PBS to give WGBH a slot—one item still remained to be worked out, the "heavy promotion and advertising." Since the series was part of Mobil's political public relations effort, clearly the promotion would be a key to Mobil's gaining the public image it desired.

From Marshall's point of view (and Marshall, like Schmertz, was a corporate public relations man), "the combination of heavy advertising and having a consistent network time was a great advantage to *Masterpiece Theatre.*" Marshall asked Mobil to request that the series be scheduled for broadcast on a high "sets in use" night, which meant a Sunday or Monday. He anticipated resistance from the local PBS stations because of the autonomy they had as members of a service set up on the principle of "localism." Marshall describes the attitude of the local PBS stations as "I don't get paid by Mobil, I don't get paid by PBS, and I don't get paid by WGBH, thank you. So it takes a lot of persuasion."[17]

Mobil left it to WGBH to exercise "persuasion" on PBS and the local stations. Part of the leverage in their agreement with WGBH was Mobil's decision to keep control over advertising and promotion within the corporation. This arrangement actually increased WGBH's influence within the PBS system to obtain a national broadcast time slot, in the case of *Masterpiece Theatre,* at 9:00 P.M. on Sunday nights, a prime spot.

For the first broadcast, scheduled for January 10, 1971, Mobil placed eleven major print advertisements in the following publications: *Time, New Yorker, Saturday Review,* the *New York Times* op-ed page, the *Los Angeles Times,* the *Boston Globe,* the *San Francisco Chronicle,* the *Philadelphia Bulletin,* the *Washington Post,* and the *Chicago Tribune.*[18] The ad was headlined: "Winston Churchill's Great Great Great Great Grandmother."

Marshall and Bloom were serving as the press agents for the series at the time, with Frank Marshall working closely with Mobil and Phil Bloom handling the reporters. They put together a public relations campaign featuring public appearances by Susan Hampshire and reminding the public of the legacy of *The Forsyte Saga.* So, by 9:00 P.M. on January 10, 1971, the package making up *Masterpiece Theatre* was fully formed. Marshall's checklist of theme, host, regular national time slot, and promotion and advertising had been completed.

But the series included an element Marshall did not have in mind. The fifty-minute shows had ten-minute fillers inserted by WGBH, which had been obtained by the now departed Calderwood from the BBC. This series of BBC archaeology shorts was entitled *And Another Thing.* The first four episodes were: *Water, Wine, and Wisdom,* featuring Greek pottery; *Hub of Two Worlds,* about a Chinese bowl; *A Little Hippo Goes a Long Way,* which compared an Egyptian to a faience hippo; and *Fashionable Frolic,* the story of ancient Egyptian fashion.[19] Classic English literature would be accompanied by relics of classic civilizations.

Immediately after the broadcast, strains began to show in the relationship between PBS and the local stations on the one hand, and Mobil and WGBH on the other. Local stations were making a move for independence. On January 11, Sam Holt of PBS received a letter from Ward Chamberlin of WNET (later head of WETA in Washington, DC) complaining about Mobil's and WGBH's inclusion of a twenty-second announcement at the end of the first episode of *The First Churchills* that asked viewers to write to a New York City post office box for a free pamphlet giving background program information about *Masterpiece Theatre.*

Chamberlin said: "I have since discussed the announcement with Bob Larsen [of WGBH] and have been persuaded that it should be aired in New York City because it is important to the underwriter and to WGBH, the producer. So we will cooperate. However, I am concerned about the way this matter was handled by both WGBH and PBS. In general, I do not believe that anything other than program material should be included in any program without approval of PBS and without adequate notice being given to the stations. This applies to plugs, promotions, box numbers, underwriting statements—the entire gamut of possibilities. PBS should first of all evaluate the material and make its best judgment about the advisability of including it. Having decided to permit its inclusion PBS should notify each station promptly so that each station may decide for itself whether the material is suitable for air.

"Specifically in the case of the *Masterpiece Theatre* box number, a more leisurely consideration might have produced a way to get the desired effect without the possible detriments. We, for instance, feel that it is important that our community of viewers associate Channel 13 with everything we do, and we do not like the confusion that a separate, non-Channel 13 address causes. This might have been overcome by inserting our own message with our own special box number. (This could still be done.) Again, we plan to use the paperback edition of the Churchill series as a premium offer, and we are concerned about the confusion the additional box number message will cause. I would be interested in knowing your feelings on this matter because I wonder if the box number was noticed when the program was previewed by the PBS personnel and why it wasn't considered necessary to call the inclusion to the attention of the stations at that time or yesterday when it was brought to your attention by EEN [Eastern Educational Network]."[20]

Sam Holt took two weeks to reply to the complaint from WNET, perhaps reflecting a crisis atmosphere at PBS headquarters. He noted in his answer to Chamberlin that "your concern over offering of the brochure on *Masterpiece Theatre* was shared by some other stations in the system," and concluded—after pleading ignorance of the offensive announcement until it was too late to stop—"I feel you are right that efforts of this sort are best handled through local stations when possible and that course, if somewhat more expensive, is one which should be considered first in the offering of any premium or support material in a national series."[21]

This small conflict was an outgrowth of the larger PBS-WGBH struggle over who would control the public relations and advertising for the series. It was a power struggle, a money struggle, and a struggle of personalities. Frank Marshall, whose firm of Marshall and Bloom handled all aspects of promotion until Frank Goodman took over in 1973, recalls that "PBS was giving WGBH probably a hard time because they wanted to control promotion. I met the new head of promotion for PBS who was lobbying that Mobil give them money, so that they could promote Mobil's program. Over dinner, she told me that although she had never done anything in television before, she thought she could bring real objectivity to her job because she had never owned even a television set. And that kind of inverse logic struck me as so disastrous, that I dug my heels in with Schmertz and said, 'No, we'll control the promotion, we'll control the advertising.'" Mobil was determined to keep the control it had over the money for these accounts. According to Marshall, PBS originally asked for the entire promotion budget to be transferred to its jurisdiction. Marshall kept control of the money with Mobil.

Marshall and Schmertz gave PBS only one concession in regard to promotion and advertising, promising "it will be in good taste, we will consult with you when necessary, but we'll pick the markets, and we'll promote it our way. It's that simple. So to this day, I don't believe there is any promotion budget that goes from Mobil to the public television system. All the promotion is done by the in-house staff at Mobil, and Frank Goodman."[22]

Schmertz agreed with Marshall, and defended the logic of Mobil's position. "Nobody was going to spend Mobil's money but me," he says. "I had a fiduciary responsibility for the expenditure of Mobil's money and I felt that the only way I could carry out that fiduciary responsibility was to be involved. That simple."[23]

PBS tried to go around Mobil for the next season's shows, making an offer directly to the BBC in the person of executive Sean Sutton to purchase rights to *Elizabeth R*. In the name of the CPB (for some technical reason not explained in the telegram), Sam Holt of PBS offered £5,000 for an option against £7,000 per episode in a telegram dated January 29, 1971. A note indicated the CPB was trying to make the offer "a returnable advance."[24] Apparently Schmertz got wind of this move, and decided to test Mobil's influence on the system. Shortly thereafter, Sam Holt received a phone call from Herb Schmertz indicating Mobil was not planning to pay for a third season unless *Masterpiece Theatre* would broadcast *The Six Wives of Henry VIII* (selections for the second season were already made). The series had already been shown on CBS, and PBS executives did not like the idea of becoming a dumping ground for network reruns. Yet the Tudor series had been extremely well received, and Mobil wanted the tie-in to *Elizabeth R*. On February 3, Calderwood, now at CPB as a consultant—and still involved in the politics of the series—wrote Schmertz a conciliatory three-page letter (perhaps reflecting the result of negotiations among PBS, CPB, and Mobil) giving his "evaluation of what I think can be done if Mobil decides to extend its underwriting by 26 weeks." Apparently there were also strains forming with the BBC, and Calderwood told Schmertz he had reminded Robeck "that Public Broadcasting was not married to the BBC." This was a threat to use material from British Independent Television (ITV) suppliers to keep BBC prices competitive.

Calderwood reassured Schmertz that Bob Larsen of WGBH "will push hard to get you a deal that will merit extension of your underwriting" by getting Mobil summer reruns and the same low prices. In return, Calderwood asked Schmertz to give CPB a decision by April 1, 1971. Calderwood attached a list of BBC shows for Schmertz to consider on his trip to London.

Mobil had committed itself to only one year at first, not even signing a formal contract, but rather an amended standard Time-Life program distribution agreement. Calderwood, at CPB, wanted Mobil and *Masterpiece Theatre* back on PBS. Calderwood presumably wanted the series he had worked hard to realize during his brief time at WGBH to continue as a broadcasting institution.

Calderwood concluded his letter saying, "So I leave Herb by telling you that everyone in Public Broadcasting—CPB, PBS, and WGBH—is hard at work to make Mobil's extension of its under-writing for another 26 weeks very attractive. I predict what is finally offered will be acceptable to you. As I fade off into the Egyptian sunset [Calderwood had resigned from CPB to travel down the Nile], let me tell you again how delightful it has been working with you. I'm pleased that *Masterpiece Theatre* is finding such warm public reception and that Mobil is getting its money's worth. That is enough to make any conscientious peddler sleep well at night."[25]

Copies of Calderwood's appeal were sent to John Macy, chairman of the CPB, Thaddeus Holt, secretary of the CPB, Bob Larsen and Chris Sarson at WGBH, and Frank Marshall. That same day, Calderwood sent another letter to Peter Robeck at Time-Life. "I thought you might appreciate sharing this man's personal view of the situation," he wrote. "The gun is still at our head. Mobil is not that hot to extend its underwriting unless they get summer reruns . . . The people going to London have lists of other programs to preview that can easily go into the *Masterpiece Theater* [sic] slot. The prices are right. And, they can have a decent rerun policy. In short, Public Broadcasting has in its hands an alternative that can help it win the Mobil underwriting extension. . . . If BBC holds out too long, they may very well find that Public Broadcasting goes ahead with other programs in its efforts to win the Mobil extension. . . . The partnership I'd like to see win the Mobil extension is Public Broadcasting and the BBC. I feel it would be a shame if the partnership was Public Broadcasting and some other production house."[26] Already, as Calderwood informed Schmertz earlier, the BBC was being threatened by competition from ITV companies.

This was the last negotiation Calderwood undertook on behalf of the series he helped create. While Calderwood had turned over affairs at WGBH to Bob Larsen, Sam Holt at PBS was trying to assert authority over *Masterpiece Theatre,* probably taking advantage of a presumed power vacuum. On March 1, 1971, he sent a strongly worded memo—ostensibly a report on a viewing trip to London—to Hartford Gunn at PBS, asking that the agreement with Mobil be "renegotiated." Sam Holt complained that Mobil was accusing PBS of breach of contract, noting "they use this as a club

two or three times in discussions." Sam Holt says he told Schmertz
and Marshall "some points in the agreement could not be met due
to the nature of public broadcasting, e.g., assurances that all stations would clear programming offered by PBS, assurances that
the time for carriage for clearing stations would be the same
throughout the country."

Sam Holt pointed out his suspicions about the Mobil operation,
writing "I think that the day-to-day operation of this set up is one
in which Frank Marshall has the dominant hand. He and Schmertz
work together, and Marshall apparently consults Mobil on a variety of things beyond merely the package here." Sam Holt also complained about the conduct of the London bargaining sessions: "The
formal negotiation was between WGBH, Shmertz [sic], and Marshall on the one side and Roebeck [sic] on the other. I was not a direct party to the negotiations. Rightly or wrongly I felt that under
the precedent we have, it was WGBH's formal acquisition and
merely, as in the case of a normal production, PBS's role to accept
or not the individual components of the series as offered. I should
note here that this entire experience is one which makes me think
that the precedent should be changed." Clearly, Sam Holt, as PBS's
representative, was extremely uncomfortable at being unable to
participate in the talks over the future of a major PBS series.

Later, Sam Holt asked Gunn to consider setting up a "single acquisition officer" and a "single underwriting officer" for all of public broadcasting. He complained that the *Masterpiece Theatre* sessions involved too many "problems of playing off parties." His
only good words were for Sarson, with whom he felt PBS was "in
reasonably good hands." Holt opposed showing *The Six Wives of
Henry VIII* because the episodes were ninety minutes long, and because, as the PBS official responsible for scheduling, he had not
been given proper notice. Holt suggested that PBS could work
with Schmertz, but faced "problems" in dealing with the team of
Schmertz and Marshall, although noting "Marshall is ultimately
the key on a regular basis." Then Holt revived the problem of publicity and advertising for the series. He asked that Gunn and Slater
"get PBS, CPB, WGBH, Mobil and Marshall all together and go
through the promotion problems. . . . We should eliminate friction
among the parties here as any kind of excuse." Holt also asked for
"a meeting of the involved parties . . . to iron out the arrangements
made in the letter of agreement for last season. Many of them are

onerous and I don't feel that I can get any fully satisfactory resolution on some that I would like (such as time of run) unless there
is a different kind of understanding. . . . I think it is imperative that
we remove the kinds of negative grounds for dissatisfaction which
Mobil and Marshall use against us in this. Also, we should eliminate any arrangements we cannot make." Holt's final suggestion
was for "formal and consistent procedure for acquisition and underwriting such that there is at least one agency for each, if not one
for both . . . until this happens, the confusion and overlay which
this deal has shown will be repeated."[27] But Sam Holt's pleas
would not result in the type of arrangement he was seeking. He,
and PBS, were being pushed out of the loop.

Sam Holt had his meeting with Schmertz and Marshall to "rene-
gotiate" the deal with PBS on March 18, 1971. In another memo
to Gunn and Slater, he reported, "The deal which came out differed
in no major extent from the one that went in." It called for a rerun
of *The First Churchills* and the screenings of *Elizabeth R* and *The
Six Wives of Henry VIII* , as well as *The Last of the Mohicans.* The
result was fifty-eight new shows and thirteen repeats. Combined
with the repeat of the *Churchills,* the deal agreed came to eighty-
four weeks for $800,000. Holt was still unhappy that *Elizabeth* and
Henry were ninety minutes per episode. He also was unhappy with
the promise of a specific time-slot for the shows. But he said he
could live with those aspects. However, Holt was not willing to
recommend a "more-than-one-year commitment." "Are we opening a Pandora's box here? Will it rebound to cause trouble with
other production centers (e.g., NET's three-year film package)?
We need network policy. The best would be a guaranteed option,
exercised next spring or summer-fall. It may be impossible. Rights
are as this year. They weaken the overall position. Are we willing
to make it a major fight?"[28] Attached to the memo was a draft of
the "CPB/PBS/WGBH position on *Masterpiece Theatre.*" This
statement was the result of a March 22 meeting of the public
broadcasters, including Sarson of WGBH. It listed an agreed-upon
broadcast schedule for July 1971 to September 1972 of: *Churchills*
reruns followed by *Jude the Obscure, Maisie, Resurrection, Henry
VIII, Elizabeth R, Point Counterpoint, Vanity Fair, Cold Comfort
Farm, Spoils of Poynton,* and *Jude the Obscure* reruns.[29] This was
apparently not the final word on the subject. The actual running order for the broadcasts in 1971–72, after the repeat of *Churchills,*

was *Jude the Obscure, The Gambler, Resurrection, Cold Comfort Farm, Henry VIII, Elizabeth R,* and *The Last of the Mohicans.*[30]

In an attempt to exercise some leverage over Mobil and the running of *Masterpiece Theatre,* the public television executives wanted to regain control over their time-slot. The joint public broadcasting position changed the promised broadcast hour from 9:00 Sunday nights to "between 8:00 P.M. and 10:00 P.M." with a provision that PBS could move the show to another night in the summer of 1972. PBS would also cancel its second weekly satellite feed of the show. PBS would have the right to edit the programs and to supplement them with new filler material. There was a clause with a new price of $385,000 through September of 1972, with the costs of framing and filler "additional." Finally, the joint agreement would only promise to keep the series on the air until September 1972. It concluded with the statement "Public broadcasting is more than willing, however, to express its sincere expectation of continuing *Masterpiece Theatre* for at least one further year so long as 1) BBC product is available in sufficient quality and quantity at acceptable prices and with acceptable rights and 2) Mobil is willing to finance the full cost of acquisition and adaptation of the BBC programs for network broadcast under conditions set by PBS."[31] This attempt to introduce itself into decision-making about the future of *Masterpiece Theatre* was accompanied by requests for more money from Mobil. A cynical observer might be tempted to characterize PBS's operations as an arrangement of sorts, whereby hassles might be reduced in exchange for a monetary payment. An idealistic observer might see in the efforts of public television executives the attempt to rein in corporate control of a public television system. But even an idealist would have questions as to whether these public television executives were arguing over principle or over price. Mobil's position seems consistently a matter of preserving its corporate self-interest and keeping expenses to a minimum.

A follow-up memo was sent to Hartford Gunn by Norm Sinel of PBS on March 23. It noted all the public television staffers who had been at the meeting, and added the costs of framing and filler, in the amounts of $100,000 and $115,000 respectively. This pushed the PBS budget from $385,000 to $600,000. In other words, public television was proposing that 56 percent of the cost of acquiring the programs be spent on introducing them and filling the holes in the schedule—and this was a calculation that excluded twelve weeks of filler, when there was "no filler necessary for Elizabeth or Henry." This memo concluded, "PBS must be prepared to justify the following: 1) Decision not to commit for two years; 2) Decision not to run *Elizabeth* and *Henry* in fall of 1971 . . . ; [and] 3) Decision not to use *Last of Mohicans*."[32]

Soon the CPB was in the act, as the factions fought for control of one of the major successes on the PBS schedule. On March 24, 1971, Thaddeus Holt of the CPB (not to be confused with Sam Holt of PBS) made his memo for "the record" regarding the state of the negotiations with Mobil. Here he detailed the public broadcasting planning session, and a subsequent meeting with Schmertz and Marshall, held on March 23, in which "Mr. Gunn appropriately took the laboring oar." The involvement of the president of PBS showed the importance of the stakes. Thaddeus Holt noted, "The Mobil side appeared quite serious of underwriting a two-year package, and pointed out various supposed advantages of doing so. Mr. Gunn made such points as the increased supply of quality domestic programming which he anticipated, and the fact that even from the BBC superior programming to the run of these classic serials might become available." Perhaps Gunn was angling for coproductions, or for the importation of contemporary BBC kitchen-sink drama not favored by the *Masterpiece Theatre* slot. Gunn was raising a specter of alternatives that would reduce the role of the oil company.

However, Gunn's gambit gave Mobil an opportunity to flex its corporate financial muscle, and its own "special relationship" with the BBC, where they could subsidize the British image in America while the BBC helped polish Mobil's image as well. Thaddeus Holt recorded the discussion as follows: "This diverted the subject to a general discussion of improving direct relationships with the BBC, and to the very emphatic discussion by Schmertz that Mobil would like to underwrite coproduction with the BBC. In particular, the forthcoming 26-part *History of the English-Speaking Peoples,* based on Sir Winston Churchill's books, is said to be available for coproduction now. Mr. S. Holt will investigate. . . . They brought up yet again the undertakings that they felt were embodied in the exchange of correspondence of September 15 and October 12, 1970. It was pointed out to them that the person who negotiated the original deal on behalf of public broadcasting regrettably promised a number of things that CPB and PBS simply were in no position to undertake to deliver. All sides understand the necessity of issuing a new letter in proper form that will replace the former exchange of letters and clarify the activities of public broadcasting that are underwritten for the future. . . . Meanwhile, Mr. S. Holt will ascertain as much as possible about future BBC plans. Since the BBC has expressed great confusion as to whether Calderwood, Marshall, Schmertz, or somebody else speaks for American public broadcasting in the program selection area, they will be informed that Mr. S. Holt is the sole representative of American public broadcasting for that purpose."[33] While public television was telling the BBC that Sam Holt spoke for America, apparently Schmertz, Calderwood, and Marshall had been advising the BBC to deal directly with Herb Schmertz and Mobil. Two sets of tracks had been put down for the *Masterpiece Theatre* train to traverse. Soon, the PBS tracks would become a disused siding and Mobil would have the control it claimed by right of financial investment.

On April 8, a videotape of *Pere Goriot* was shipped to Sam Holt for viewing at PBS. Perhaps reflecting the confusion surrounding the status of the series, and the conflicts over controlling renewal of the series between Mobil, CPB, PBS and WGBH, the DACS accompanying the tape had a handwritten note from Sarson to Holt that read, "Sam—The program with Cooke won't be finished until we know what Cooke should say at the end of the program."[34] In other words, they were waiting for the conflict between public television executives and Mobil to be resolved.

Meanwhile, Thaddeus Holt of the CPB was now negotiating directly with Schmertz and Marshall, making another memo to "the record" with copies to Hartford Gunn and John Witherspoon, respectively president and vice president of PBS, and John Macy, chairman of the CPB. By now, it was clear that Mobil was getting its will. Thaddeus Holt said Mobil "continues very, very pleased with *Masterpiece Theatre*." Schmertz still wanted a two-year renewal, "particularly since Schmertz and Marshall's visit last week to London, where they explored forthcoming BBC product and are certain that PBS will be able to secure quality material for the third year." Mobil still wanted *The Six Wives of Henry VIII* for the series. And Mobil was also making noises about the objections to their role from public broadcasting executives (probably PBS's Sam Holt). Thaddeus Holt recorded that "Schmertz seemed a little concerned lest public broadcasting regard Mobil as too much of a nuisance." Speaking on behalf of CPB and PBS, Holt responded to Schmertz's comment: "I assured him that on the contrary we are extremely appreciative of what Mobil has done and particularly of the good taste they demonstrated throughout the operation." Schmertz then made Holt an offer, which he hoped CPB would not refuse, "to give CTW [Children's Television Workshop, producers of *Sesame Street*] some more money to underwrite something." In other words, Mobil would facilitate matters with PBS by making a donation to a favorite charity: *Sesame Street*. In exchange, Thaddeus Holt apparently agreed to leave the series alone.

Then, Schmertz and Marshall told Holt of their plans for the coming year's run. "He and Marshall have several new promotional and marketing ideas for next season. One is that during the period *Henry* and *Elizabeth* are running, BOAC and the organization that promotes British tourism (BHTA) would run a major campaign on the theme 'Visit the land of Henry and Elizabeth.' Another is an extension of the books idea which we worked on earlier. They have discovered that all the books in next season's likely schedule have been printed in paperback editions in England with illustrations from BBC dramatizations—exactly what we explored here last fall. They envisage an arrangement under which an American publisher would utilize these plates to print up a boxed set of these books called 'Masterpiece Library.'" Thus was the tie-in introduced, which lives on in the book-tag announcement at the end of many shows, promoting the sale of "the companion volume, available at libraries and bookstores everywhere."

Mobil also held out a financial carrot that would be of interest to public television executives. The oil company would seek to encourage others to follow its example in supporting public television. Schmertz told Thaddeus Holt "at least two other oil companies have approached Time-Life looking for BBC material that might make public broadcasting underwriting." Holt concluded that the meeting with Mobil was "all in all, a fruitful session which may have clarified several matters."[35] Mobil's suggestion of even more corporate support clearly pleased Thaddeus Holt, and CPB was effectively "on board" with Mobil.

Already, in the initial 1971 negotiations with CPB for control, the foundation for the so-called "petroleum broadcasting system" (which Gitlin mentioned in the quotation at the start of this chapter) was present. Far from rejecting Mobil's offers—just saying "no" to corporate money—CPB's Holt instead encouraged them to bring more oil companies into the public television family. CPB's Thaddeus Holt—in a direct contrast to PBS's Sam Holt— eagerly sought to smooth the relations that PBS's Holt had upset. The CPB mission was apparently successful, and talks were back on track for an extension of the *Masterpiece Theatre* run for an additional *two years,* on precisely the terms Mobil had wanted.

One of Mobil's particular concerns was checking WGBH's attempt to increase the charges for framing and filling each episode of the series. In response to Schmertz's request, station general manager Robert Larsen had sent Schmertz a detailed accounting of costs related to packaging the BBC productions. He noted sending a carbon copy to Frank Marshall, and sent "blind" copies to Gunn, Sam Holt, and Gerry Slater at PBS. Significantly, no copies were sent to CPB. One can hypothesize that WGBH may not have wanted CPB to see which costs were being billed to Mobil that might already have been covered by other grants from CPB.

Larsen's letter asked more money from Mobil in order for WGBH to continue with *Masterpiece Theatre.* Since WGBH was (and is) a nonprofit corporation, one source of revenue was to be found in overhead charges. The higher the overhead, the more money for WGBH to use as it saw fit—on productions such as *The Nader Report,* for example. Larsen's letter was conciliatory in tone, with an opening reference to the future of the series "as we hope and expect it will develop next season." Larsen then went on to claim that although Mobil had paid $110,000 for "packaging and filling" thirty-nine programs (approximately 28 percent of the cost of acquiring the programs themselves), "that budget was completely misestimated." After Stanford Calderwood's departure from WGBH, Larsen and the staff of the station "sat down and figured out what our actual budget would be, and calculated it out to $154,434. . . . and we've had to sustain a considerable loss." That figure represented packaging costs of almost 40 percent of the cost of program acquisition.

Larsen meant to enforce this price increase for carrying the show. "We're already on record that we cannot repeat the folly next season, and that budgets for any further work will be based on our actual experience of this year. But as Chris [Sarson] has said to you many times, we don't intend to be punitive in the new budget, either." Larsen then pointed out that the original fillers were not of sufficiently high quality. Erskine's lectures on ancient pottery "fell on the stations like a lead balloon. PBS has received innumerable complaints from the stations and they have taken the position that we must provide a full hour with decent fill to lead into the next show." Then, Larsen put forth an itemized list of expenditures for the coming season. To prepare a new opening for the *First Churchills* reruns, $6,782. To frame *Henry* and *Elizabeth,* "no additional cost." Since the shows were running a half hour longer than the normal schedule, this was not much of a concession, since no filler was necessary. Total cost of assembling twenty-seven new programs and filler, $221,305. This figure was equal to approximately three-quarters of the cost of acquiring the new programs from the BBC. Larsen broke down the numbers, citing Sarson's analysis, as follows: assembly, $44,658; Cooke, $42,832; miscellaneous, $35,400; fills, $98,415. Then Larsen asked for a meeting with Frank Marshall and Schmertz to discuss the figures "when and if we get sorted out with Time-Life."[36] Clearly, Larsen did not like the idea that Time Inc., a profit-making publishing company, might be earning as much money from *Masterpiece Theatre* as nonprofit WGBH. It is rather obvious from the correspondence that WGBH was in effect upping its price to Mobil for being in the oil company's camp in confrontations with PBS over who would control the series.

Schmertz was not happy with the high overhead WGBH tried to charge his company, seemingly in exchange for switching sides in the power struggle from the public television service to the corporate sponsor. He remembers "We had a lot, not a lot, we had some fights over money. The money in the contracts. It was simply straight commercial negotiations. They wanted more overhead and I was trying to keep the budget down. That simple. I don't think we ever fought about anything substantive relating to *Masterpiece.* I think it was all over money. I'm positive it was just money."[37]

Frank Marshall, who would go over budgets for Schmertz, defends Mobil's hard line on overhead as well, saying, "If you're doing business say with Warner Brothers, for all I know they charge their country club dues to productions, I don't know. That's why I want to examine it and figure out what's a fair amount to put in that will end up on the screen instead of paying the chairman of the board's salary."[38] But still, Mobil needed the cooperation of both WGBH and CPB to win its bureaucratic battle with PBS. In a sense all sides were translating the "public service" mission of public broadcasting to mean "what's in it for me?"

Negotiations continued through late spring. On May 23, Sarson sent a DACS to PBS and CPB stating his terms for an agreement with Mobil.[39] Gerry Slater, PBS executive vice president, sent copies to Sam Holt, who penciled in his objections to Sarson's terms on the contract proposal. Where Sarson agreed to Mobil's request that "PBS will use their best efforts to secure the same Sunday evening time slot for October 1972-June 1973," Slater differed, writing "nonsense, our choice." In the next clause Sarson agreed that "PBS will use their best efforts to get their affiliated stations to broadcast each program three times during the seven day period following the network feed—twice during prime time evening hours and once before 4:00 P.M. local time." To this Slater simply replied, "No." The next clause called for PBS not to preempt the program except for news specials, and if preempted, that the show would be broadcast the next week. Again, Slater wrote, "No." On the clause reading, "PBS will provide a network feed of one 60 second and one 30 second on air promotion of each episode of *Masterpiece Theatre*. PBS will use their best efforts with their affiliated stations to ensure that these promotions are broadcast each week in prime-time," again the reply was "No." The following clause, "Final choice and sequencing of programming will be made by the program producer assigned by WGBH in conjunction with the program coordinator of PBS. Mobil will have the right to consult with both on program choice and sequencing," again was written "No." Slater demanded that PBS be consulted on Mobil's promotion and declined to promise that PBS stations would credit Mobil for its support. He objected to the inclusion of Time-Life in the final clause, which called for a joint announcement of the new agreement to be shared by Mobil, CPB, PBS, and the distributor. Negotiations continued for three weeks between the various parties.

How exactly Schmertz and Marshall handled themselves is not fully documented. But by June 11, 1971, a new program agreement had finally been drafted. The battle and bidding war were over. Copies of the contract between WGBH and Time-Life Films called for WGBH to have exclusive rights to the BBC films sold to the series, granted WGBH the rights for all noncommercial educational stations in the United States, limited rights to two reruns (one at night and one in the afternoon), permitted network broadcast of *The*

Six Wives of Henry VIII prior to the WGBH showing, permitted commercial sales of that program and *Elizabeth R* after the WGBH broadcast, and let Time-Life Films retain other rights to the shows, with the exception of cable sales, for which WGBH would need to give permission.

In the deal, WGBH paid $795,000 to Time-Life, which Time-Life acknowledged was "being furnished to WGBH by the Corporation for Public Broadcasting, and agrees to abide by and comply with all financial requirements and other governmental regulations to public broadcast programs financed by the Corporation for Public Broadcasting." Thus, in the written record, there was no mention of Mobil's involvement with Time-Life, the BBC, or WGBH. Officially, the agreement was between public television and the BBC distributor and the money came from the CPB.

In exchange for this payment by WGBH, the station was given the right to "add new American titles" to the shows, "and to supplement each BBC program as desired with an introduction and commentary as well as such other related or nonrelated program material . . . to achieve standard American public television length." The contract also gave the Boston station "the right to cut or edit any BBC program WGBH may deem necessary or desirable to achieve American public broadcasting standards."[40] Thus, the power to censor BBC programs was incorporated in the original contract with WGBH.

On June 23, 1971, Thaddeus Holt of the CPB sent a letter to Frank Marshall, addressed to his Lexington Avenue office at Marshall and Bloom Associates, specifying the arrangement between Mobil, CPB, and WGBH. That Marshall, as consultant, was sent the initial agreement gives some indication of his crucial importance to the future of the series. CPB's Holt noted sending copies to Slater at PBS and Larsen at WGBH. He also sent "blind" copies to Chairman Macy and three other public broadcasting executives. Slater's cover memorandum to Hartford Gunn, dated June 28, 1971, read "Attached is the Mobil letter that was agreed on by all parties." It had taken six months from the season premiere of *The First Churchills* in January until the agreement covering the future of the series was approved.

The CPB letter gave Mobil almost everything it asked for. The agreement also in effect provided $340,000 for WGBH overhead, an amount equal to 42 percent of the $795,000 program acquisition fees paid to Time-Life. Curiously, although Mobil paid WGBH directly, the letter to Frank Marshall refers to Mobil's grant to the Corporation for Public Broadcasting, and implies a channeling of the money through the CPB. To see how Mobil won the battle for control of the series against PBS by building its alliance with WGBH and CPB, it is helpful to quote the entire letter. It reads:

Dear Frank,

This is to confirm our understanding with respect to the Mobil grant to the Corporation for Public Broadcasting for continuation of the "*MASTERPIECE THEATRE*" series produced by Station WGBH and carried on the Public Broadcasting Service.

Description of Series:

1. "*MASTERPIECE THEATRE*" will continue as a weekly dramatic series for at least two years beginning this June. As before, the series will consist of dramas produced and made available by the BBC along the lines of the attached network schedule developed jointly by Station WGBH and PBS.

2. Exclusive American broadcasting rights for all of the BBC programs in the series are being acquired by Station WGBH through Time/Life Films, the BBC's American representative. Under the WGBH-Time/Life arrangements, acceptable American-standard broadcast videotapes will be required for the BBC programs, which will be accompanied by introduction and commentary by Alistair Cooke recorded at Station WGBH.

3. Station WGBH, in consultation with PBS, will make the choice of programs to be included in the series, as well as the sequence of program presentation, repeat programs, etc. All artistic, creative and technical elements will be the responsibility of Station WGBH; network broadcast scheduling and distribution will be the responsibility of PBS.

The current PBS network schedule provides for continuation of consecutive weekly release of the series until June, 1973. Original network broadcast will continue on Sunday nights at 9:00 P.M. for the 1971–72 season, but may be moved in September, 1972 to another starting time between 8:00 P.M. and 10:00 PM. on that or another night. All network stations will have the right to rebroadcast locally once at night and once during school hours within the succeeding six-day period after original network interconnection.

In accordance with standard public broadcasting practice, PBS will not interrupt any series program except for important news announcements, station identification requirements or similar matters called for in FCC rules and regulations. If any network program pre-emption is made for a special timely program of national importance, the preempted program will be rescheduled for the next week in the series. PBS does not intend to preempt any series program for non-timely substitution, nor to mix other network programs into this series on an individual or group basis.

4. Maximum audience is of important interest to the "*MASTER-PIECE THEATRE*" series. To this end, PBS is committed to delivering at least one 60-second and one 30-second on-air promotional announcement for each program, which will be made available to all network stations for use in 10-second on-air promotional announcements. The on-air promotional announcements will be prepared for PBS by Station WGBH in connection with series production.

Conditions of Grant:

1. Mobil's grant will be in the amount of $1,135,000 to cover the new rights-acquisition and program-production costs of Station WGBH. Payment of the grant to CPB will be in two stages upon request: $563,000 in January, 1972, and $572,000 in January, 1973, and will be additional to the balance of $245,000 still payable to CPB in January, 1972, for the past Mobil grants for "*MASTER-PIECE THEATRE.*"

2. All series broadcasts and rebroadcasts will carry appropriate Mobil underwriting announcements in the same form and position in the program as have appeared on "*MASTERPIECE THEATRE*" in 1970–71. Promotional materials distributed by PBS will similarly contain a reference to the fact that the series was made possible by the Mobil grant.

3. Mobil's assistance in audience-promotional efforts will be welcomed—especially with respect to print and other media supplemental to public television on-air publicity. It is expected that PBS and Mobil will cooperate closely in all their respective promotional activities to assure maximum effectiveness and acceptability. Mobil has undertaken to see that whatever print promotion is prepared and distributed under its auspices will be aimed solely at increased appreciation of "*MASTERPIECE THEATRE,*" will be appropriate and tasteful in nature, and will be in keeping with American public broadcasting practice.

4. PBS and WGBH will keep Mobil advised of all project decisions on program selection and scheduling for "*MASTERPIECE THEATRE.*" PBS will also make available to Mobil all PBS-assembled information on station use of the series during the initial network release, as well as any audience estimates that PBS and its member stations may be able to make from time to time.

5. PBS does not presently know whether it will wish to continue *"MASTERPIECE THEATRE"* beyond June 30, 1973. If Mobil should desire to underwrite a further continuation of the series beyond that date, PBS will advise Mobil of its intentions in this regard by January 31, 1973.

The foregoing arrangements have been expressly agreed to between CPB, PBS and Station WGBH in anticipation of the proposed grant from Mobil for continuation of this series—and are, of course, subject to all applicable FCC and other laws and regulations.[41]

Attached to Thaddeus Holt's CPB letter was a network schedule for *Masterpiece Theatre*'s next two years. It shows clearly that Mobil had won what it wanted. Frank Marshall had his shows scheduled precisely where he had asked for them, including *Cold Comfort Farm* and *The Last of the Mohicans*.

The arrangement worked out between Mobil and public broadcasting in 1971 endured until 1973, when a disagreement over the scheduling of a Mobil-favored British miniseries once again sparked opposition from the American public broadcasters. They decided once more to regroup to face Mobil down. They would come together to take a stand against the attempt by a major corporation to bring British commercial serial melodrama onto PBS. The producer of the show PBS and WGBH did not want was London Weekend Television, and the title was *Upstairs, Downstairs*. The result of the struggle resulted in a permanent change in the relationship of Mobil to the series, not only on the American side of the Atlantic, but even more importantly in England. After 1973, Mobil would no longer be content to merely buy "off the shelf." In order to maintain its control over source of supply, Mobil would organize the television operation like it operated its oil business: Mobil would prebuy, coproduce, and commission English programs from both ITV and BBC sources, transforming the international television market as well as American public television. That is the subject of the next chapter.

Notes

1. At a Los Angeles press conference on 11 January 1991, Cooke surprised television journalists when he revealed that he did not pick the shows.

2. Alistair Cooke, personal interview, 19 June 1990.

3. Christopher Sarson, personal interview.

4. Sarson, personal interview. Sarson also says he had hoped the fact that his grandfather (Arnold Sarson) had been headmaster of Blackpool grammar school might have helped convince Cooke to do *Masterpiece Theatre*. "My mistaken impression was that he had been a pupil at my grandfather's high school. I hoped this would convince him to do *Masterpiece Theatre*. Cooke put me right; he had been to the Blackpool grammar school." Letter to author, 15 February 1998.

5. Sarson, personal interview.

6. Sarson, personal interview.

7. "To: All Stations, From: Bill Oxley, Re: Change in Preview Schedule," DACS no. 1182, 7 December 1970.

8. Sarson, personal interview.

9. Letter to the author, 15 February 1998.

10. It was in the Palermo Club Med, according to a later press release. In the same release, Sarson says he was not forthcoming about the source of the music at first. "Almost immediately, people began calling and writing and asking 'What is it and where can I get the rest of it?' That's when the cover-up began. Sarson now chuckles as he admits 'I used to say it was just an old piece I'd found in the library.'" "Former TV Producer Confesses to Masterly Cover-Up," 3 December 1990.

11. Sarson, personal interview.

12. In 1991, callers to Sarson's home phone heard a recorded message for educational package tours put together by a firm doing business as "Travel and Learn." Personal phone call, 15 May 1991.

13. Program files, *Masterpiece Theatre,* WGBH, Boston.

14. Sarson, personal interview.

15. Sarson, personal interview.

16. Sarson, personal interview.

17. Marshall, personal interview.

18. Joan Larson, PBS, "Memo to: All PI directors, Re: Mobil *Masterpiece Theatre* ad," 23 December 1970.

19. Christopher Sarson, WGBH, DACS, to Sam Holt, PBS, 4 January 1971.

20. Ward B. Chamberlin Jr., executive vice president, WNET, letter to Samuel C. O. Holt, PBS, 11 January 1971.

21. Samuel C. O. Holt, PBS, letter to Ward Chamberlin, WNET, 25 January 1971.

22. Frank Marshall, personal interview.

23. Schmertz, personal interview.

24. Samuel Holt, PBS, "Memo to: Marlene, Re: Telegram to Sean Sutton, BBC," 29 January 1971.

25. Stanford Calderwood, CPB, letter to Herb Schmertz, Mobil, 3 February 1971.

26. Calderwood, letter to Peter Robeck, 3 February 1971.

27. Samuel Holt, memo to Hartford Gunn, PBS, 1 March 1971.

28. Sam Holt, memo to Hartford Gunn, PBS, 19 March 1971.

29. "CPB/PBS/WGBH position on *Masterpiece Theatre*," 22 March 1971.

30. Gregory Vitello, ed., *Twenty Seasons of Mobil Masterpiece Theatre : 1971–1991* (Fairfax: Mobil, 1991), 18–24.

31. "CPB/PBS/WGBH position on *Masterpiece Theatre*," 22 March 1971.

32. Norm Sinel, PBS, "Memo to Hartford Gunn, PBS, Re: *Masterpiece Theatre*—Work Sheet," 23 March 1971.

33. Thaddeus Holt, CPB, "Memorandum, To: The Record, Subject: Programs—*Masterpiece Theatre*," 24 March 1971.

34. Ralph Schuetz, DACS, to Gay Luddington, PBS, 8 April 1971.

35. Thaddeus Holt, "Memo to The Record, Subject: Corporations—Mobil Oil," CPB, 9 April 1971.

36. Robert L. Larsen, WGBH, letter to Herb Schmertz, Mobil, 23 April 1971. This is the only figure for Cooke's salary available, although sources have said during the first year he was paid $30,000.

37. Schmertz, personal interview.

38. Marshall, personal interview.

39. Christopher Sarson, DACS, to G. Slater, PBS; T. Holt, CPB; G. Aleinikoff, CPB, "Re: *Masterpiece Theatre*—New Contract," 21 May 1971.

40. Eugene Aleinikoff, letter to Richard Barovick, Esq., with attached agreement between WGBH Educational Foundation and Time-Life, 11 June 1971.

41. Thaddeus Holt, CPB, letter to Frank Marshall, 23 June 1971.

5

British Television and *Masterpiece Theatre*

The BBC has always resisted with fervour the notion that it should concentrate its resources on providing high-quality programmes to the educated middle class, leaving the popular lower ground to the commercial companies. It calls that 'ghetto television,' the ghetto being the living-rooms of the highly cultured minority. As a dreadful warning, it points to the Public Broadcasting Service in the United States, funded partly by the administration and partly through appeals to the public. Because of its chronic poverty, it can afford to make few programmes of its own, buying instead from the BBC (and to some extent from the British commercial companies).
    —Michael Leapman, *The Last Days of the Beeb*

Britain is the Taiwan of television, producing a high-quality, low-cost product.
    —Peter McKay, *Mail on Sunday*

The report might have gone on to say that what Section 4(6) of the Act expressly precluded was the appearance of sponsorship, whether sponsorship was being exercised or not.
    —Bernard Sendall, *Independent Television in Britain*

Mobil bought programs made in England for *Masterpiece Theatre*. The corporation also commissioned the production of shows for the series, yet private sponsorship of television drama is banned on both the BBC and ITV networks in England. How can this apparent paradox be explained? Clause 12 of the BBC License and

Agreement specifically prohibits corporate sponsorship and "in effect forbids the BBC to obtain revenue (or any consideration in kind) from the broadcasting of advertisements or from commercial sponsorship of programmes."[1] Independent Broadcasting Authority (IBA) programming guidelines forbid corporate sponsorship for "Drama, including films." But the IBA rules do permit sponsorship of certain types of broadcasts, such as the weather and sporting events. In the case of these sorts of shows the name of the sponsor must be displayed prominently. The rules state, in the exceptional cases, "Any sponsored programme must have either a front credit or an end credit for five seconds duration, in vision only."[2] There is another clause in the IBA guidelines, which seems to be of special relevance to *Masterpiece Theatre* and to the relationship developed by Mobil through WGBH with the ITV companies. Section 26 notes that "IBA guidelines apply to programmes made for UK transmission. Programmes which have been made for overseas use and which have already been shown abroad under different sponsorship regulation may be acceptable. They should not, however, retain any sponsor credits which would not be acceptable under IBA Guidelines. And any branding or product placement (which is prohibited for UK productions) must wherever possible be stripped out."

In other words, this language is a possible loophole that results in a situation where "All sponsorship (except as noted under 26) must be declared."[3] Which means sponsorship is prohibited in English commercial television, unless the programs are made for export. In this case, it is in fact permitted, as long as the credit for sponsorship is concealed from the British audience. This sort of provision, and the view that Mobil was simply purchasing, prebuying, or coproducing shows through WGBH, allowed the oil company to, in practice, at least partially sponsor not only the broadcast of drama series on American public television, but also the production of series by British television companies as *Masterpiece Theatre* developed during the 1970s.

Yet, even in the case of permissible sponsored programs, IBA guidelines state "the funder must not influence the editorial content of a programme, nor may the appearance be given, whether by reason of the funder's commercial activities or otherwise, that such influence has been exerted."[4] Despite this restriction, by the end of the 1970s Mobil would have script, cast, and key personnel approval for many of the shows it funded on ITV and the BBC, through its relationship with WGBH. Herb Schmertz, sponsoring several series on both commercial and public television, would come to be known as "the most powerful man in English television" because his "green light" could assure funding of a project.[5] Schmertz's valuation of his own reputation is that it was "true to the extent that I had an impact on British television because I had money . . . I mean, I was an important player, but I don't know whether they say that with kindness or with malice."[6]

Schmertz maintains that, despite his approval rights for cast, script, producer, director, and finance, Mobil "would not interfere with their productions." He says, "the reason, basically, I wanted approval was to be sure they weren't doing what they [the British] shouldn't be doing, which is trying to make stuff for the American [market]. I wanted to keep the American content out. Whereas the others who wanted approval want to get it in. And so I had to always restrain Marshall, GBH, etc. not to muck up the process that was producing quality television. . . . So if I had script approval, it was only to be sure that they weren't screwing that up to make it for me, trying to think what would make me happy."[7]

However, Schmertz acknowledges that Frank Marshall and Joan Wilson (Sarson's successor as *Masterpiece Theatre* producer) "on a number of shows made significant contributions to the scripts, and I think on occasion we made some significant contributions on the casting. I don't want to overstate that, but we did help them on the casting. But again, even with the British we tried to develop a collegial kind of relationship that wasn't a them and us kind of thing, it was an attempt to really be, you know . . . a team." Schmertz says the British wanted a collegial working relationship with Mobil because of "money."[8]

Marshall agrees with Schmertz, stating that Mobil worked closely with British producers, maintaining approval over script, producers, directors, and casting. He comments, "We all acted in concert to get the best product we possibly could. And that meant we all read the scripts, we all talked about them. We all discussed what problems we saw with them. We all gave input back to the producers. So, if you're looking for a nice, neat organization chart with defined tasks, it just wasn't there. I know job descriptions are convenient, but we never had any."[9]

Marshall says that he and Schmertz at Mobil had approval of

script, key production personnel, and casting on projects, including *Dickens of London, Disraeli, Edward and Mrs. Simpson, I Remember Nelson, Churchill: The Wilderness Years, Sons and Lovers, Nancy Astor, The Jewel in the Crown, The Last Place on Earth, Mountbatten: The Last Viceroy, By the Sword Divided, Paradise Postponed, Lost Empires, Star Quality, The Bretts, Fortunes of War, A Piece of Cake, Scoop,* and *By the Sword Divided II.*[10]

In the early 1970s, although Mobil had come to play a dominant role in the politics of American public television surrounding *Masterpiece Theatre,* the oil company had yet to find its place in the world of British broadcasting. When *Masterpiece Theatre* first came looking for programming and bought it off-the-shelf, British television was a still a cozy duopoly of the BBC and ITV companies. At the time, the commercial companies in Britain were selling programming primarily to the American commercial networks and independent stations in the United States.[11] Naturally, the BBC, which also sold programs to commercial networks, assumed that as a noncommercial public service broadcaster, it would maintain a special relationship with PBS. It was presumed this unique relationship would carry over to *Masterpiece Theatre.*

Within the first few years of the series, Mobil began purchasing ITV programs for *Masterpiece Theatre.* In 1973–74, *Masterpiece Theatre* broadcast *Upstairs, Downstairs,* produced by London Weekend Television (LWT). The series had originally been shown on LWT with commercial breaks and advertising. Its purchase by Mobil was to set a benchmark. The move to ITV changed the character of *Masterpiece Theatre* from its original format (featuring BBC adaptations of literary works) to one that included a mix of popular mysteries—foreshadowing *Mystery!,* which spun off in 1980—and original serial melodramas for television. In time, these original ITV miniseries would come to represent part of a new franchise for *Masterpiece Theatre.* Yet no matter how predestined the selection might seem in hindsight, *Upstairs, Downstairs* was not a natural first choice for *Masterpiece Theatre.* It was a popular commercial television series in England, and was opposed by PBS executives, the CPB, and WGBH producer Christopher Sarson, who left his job shortly after it was acquired.[12]

Frank Marshall says that the importance of *Upstairs, Downstairs* to *Masterpiece Theatre* cannot be overemphasized. He comments, "The occurrence of *Upstairs, Downstairs* made it [*Master-piece Theatre*] more than successful, made it a cult program . . . it became like *Roots* or *Twin Peaks,* people stopping to watch it. And that was lucky. And any series that wins the best series Emmy four years in a row and then is precluded from doing it again because the rules change, you've got to be happy with that."[13]

    Upstairs, Downstairs did more than make Mobil happy, however. It established a framework for the politics of relations among WGBH, Mobil, and the independent British companies, who came to rival the BBC as suppliers to *Masterpiece Theatre.* The deal to buy the series also set a pattern for Mobil. The oil company would now find itself dealing directly with British producers. This system endured at least until Schmertz's departure from Mobil in 1988, if not to this date. The late Pete Spina, Schmertz's successor at Mobil, said he was less involved in programming decisions, although he was still given cassettes to preview.[14] Rebecca Eaton, the WGBH producer who succeeded Sarson's replacement Joan Wilson after her death in 1985, said that WGBH kept Spina fully informed. Eaton called Spina's attitude quite different from Schmertz's, and said he expected WGBH to program the series independently of him.[15]

    In the early days of *Masterpiece Theatre,* because Mobil was the source of finance and was also purchasing programs for its commercial Mobil Showcase Network, British production companies preferred dealing with Mobil directly, sometimes entering into side agreements not recorded by WGBH. This practice began with the purchase of *Upstairs, Downstairs.*[16]

    Mobil bought *Upstairs, Downstairs* after chairman Rawleigh Warner—to whom the series was reportedly personally recommended by the Duchess of Bedford at a dinner party in London—suggested to Herb Schmertz that he consider the series for *Masterpiece Theatre.*[17] Schmertz looked at it, liked it, and wanted to put in on the air. Frank Marshall, in his role as television consultant, also screened the series. He recalls recommending the series as "brilliant." Yet, Marshall says that getting the program broadcast on PBS was "a lot of work" because public television executives "had no confidence in the program."[18] Richard Price—the salesman who represented London Weekend Television—said he had trouble because "CPB and PBS were extremely worried about the situation that commercial television programming was going to go into *Masterpiece Theatre.* "[19] Christopher Sarson of WGBH was one of the doubters. When WGBH balked, Mobil dealt directly with Price and London Weekend Television to get around opposition within the Boston station.

Herb Schmertz remembers WGBH refused "on principle"—because it would drive up the cost of other imports—to pay LWT salesman Richard Price's asking price of $25,000 an episode. "I took care of Richard," he says. "GBH didn't know that. I took care of Richard because I thought he was getting screwed. That's true. I was willing to pay 25 [thousand], and GBH balked and said 'We can't. That'll screw up a lot of things.' For them. Not me. So I said, 'OK.' But then I took care of Richard. I made a side deal with him."[20]

One of the reasons Schmertz "took care" of Price, aside from the enthusiasm of Mobil's chairman Rawleigh Warner for *Upstairs, Downstairs,* was that Price had been dealing directly with Mobil from the beginning of his sales campaign. "I had been in contact in my regular visitations to America, with Herb," says Price, adding that in the early days of his business he spent one week out of four in New York. "I was looking for outlets for British programs." Price says he had made eleven presentations of *Upstairs, Downstairs* to various broadcasters in the U.S., including National Educational Television and Group W stations, before he visited Schmertz. "I know the last presentation, which got the deal, was number twelve. One of the previous ones was to Herb and to Mobil, because I tackled it with Mobil. . . . Herb's situation and Herb's relationship was a very strong one. He was the man who was the gentleman who was paying the piper."[21] That is, Price sold the program directly to Schmertz, who placed it on *Masterpiece Theatre.*

Vivien Wallace worked at the New York office of Granada Television International in the 1980s, and had a similar experience. She recalls "one of the jobs of the director of that office was to maintain the relationships with Mobil and with Exxon, who were really the only people then who were specifically interested in the types of programs that we made."[22] Following Mobil's example, Exxon had established *Great Performances* in 1974, creating another market for English cultural programming on public television. Wallace, like Price, sold her productions first to the commercial sponsors, who placed the programs on their PBS (and other) series.

Mobil's role in dealing directly with British companies, ostensibly unknown to WGBH, was not secret from the English newspaper-reading public. For example, the *Evening Standard* reported in 1978 that London Weekend Television's production of *Lillie* "has been bought by the Mobil Oil Corporation."[23] Readers of American trade publications were aware, too, of the oil company's direct contacts with English producers. A headline from a 1984 *Variety* read: "Mobil Greases Its BBC Program Link: 17 Hours Annually."[24] British broadcasters were certainly cognizant of Mobil's importance, and knew how to go about working with the American oil company in a diplomatic fashion. Mobil's Herb Schmertz said he had a good relationship with BBC head of drama Shaun Sutton, who ran the department from 1969 until 1981 (when he left to produce the BBC/Time-Life Shakespeare series).[25] Mark Shivas, a later BBC head of drama, explains that Schmertz used social occasions to facilitate his business endeavors. "Herb would come by London yearly, at least once, and give a party, and sometimes drag in everybody who was making the kind of stuff he would like to buy, or they [Mobil] liked to buy. He would tour around with the *Masterpiece Theatre* people, difficult to say which was the dog and which was the tail and who was wagging what. I think it's true to say that he got very excited about a series that I was the executive producer [at Southern Pictures] that was called *Churchill: The Wilderness Years*. Probably more excited about that than I'd ever seen him about anything else. And he put more money into that than he normally ever put into anything."[26]

Roger Laughton, one time head of coproductions at BBC Enterprises, said of Schmertz "he may socially have met people . . . it would be naive not to agree with you that Schmertz knew people at the BBC."[27] Still, Laughton emphasized that the BBC contracts were all with WGBH, and only through that channel "the BBC gets indirect benefit from WGBH's relationship with Mobil . . . but that doesn't mean we have a direct relationship with Mobil. It means that WGBH has a relationship with Mobil."[28] It also meant, in a sense, that the Boston station was serving as a financial conduit between Mobil and the BBC.[29]

With the American money came influence on productions, as Jonathan Powell, a controller of BBC-1 (and producer of numerous *Masterpiece Theatre* shows), diplomatically admits. He recalls that the American input evolved slowly over the years, saying, "There was a time, and I think I started producing roughly round the end of it, when you could do these programs on relatively low budgets and with enough money to make them in bulk, so actually you could have a conversation with Joan Wilson [WGBH's producer of *Masterpiece Theatre*] that went, 'This year we're going to make eight classic serials or two classic serials.' She would say, 'Oh that looks really interesting. I'm not interested in your remake of *Rebecca,* which they weren't, but I am interested in *Crime and Punishment* and anything else, and frankly you're going to do the Sartre books *The Road to War,* that's not right for my audience, but I will have *Germinal.*' Then you'd say, 'Fine, that's great.'

"You'd still make them. It wasn't critical whether they put them on the air or not. And over, as time went on, . . . one year it would be two, next year it would be three and so on, I can't remember the contractual details at the time and what guarantees and all that sort of thing, but then what happened was that costs went up and there wasn't so much money, for us and for anybody throughout the world. It's not, the development of the relationship is merely a mirror in microcosm of, and in fact its a relationship that's survived better than most other relationships in broadcasting, but its simply a microcosm of the costs of production and the difficulty of achieving the kind of budget that you need to make top class drama. And so as the cost went up, well, we would ask them for money. They would say, completely understandably, 'Well you want more money, sure, we want a bit more input. Not just going to take two. We'd like to discuss the titles with you before you get to them.' And its all been completely reasonable, but it's just the kind of development of the relationships you have when you want to do something and you go to somebody else. And you're not saying, I think nobody put it in terms of the budget, but they've got well, fine, that's 20 grand and now you're [saying to WGBH] 'So, O.K. you want us to do this program? Cough up. Do you have 200 thousand? This is what the budget's going to be, you know.' But that's the development. The development has merely gone on in a more civilized and amicable fashion, because there remains at the heart of it a mutual need. And so that preserves the relationship. That's all it is, I think."[30]

Powell characterizes WGBH as "a benign and forgiving and supportive organization, in the sense that whilst we have discussions about scripts, writers, projects, and stars and so on and so forth, they've always, I think, been generous enough to appreciate that what makes these programs distinctive and therefore work for them is the fact that they're made by the program makers."[31] Although Powell points out he worked primarily with *Masterpiece Theatre* producer Joan Wilson of WGBH and did not deal directly with Mobil, he admits to knowing Herb Schmertz. "He's great," said Powell, "Smashing. I've met him a few times. He was an admirer, and above all, as far as I remember, I didn't know him that well, he was just really committed to this idea that, I suppose, that Mobil should back *Masterpiece Theatre,* obviously for the benefit of Mobil in terms of their corporate identity, but it wasn't just that. It was a real commitment to try to demonstrate, I think, that television was an important medium."[32]

Not all Britons welcomed American buyers with open arms when Mobil and WGBH appeared, checkbooks ready, in the 1970s. Peter Fiddick (who would later contribute a testimonial essay to a Mobil-sponsored catalog tribute to *Masterpiece Theatre*)[33] complained in the *Guardian* about American marketing considerations influencing the BBC. As one example, he cited the decision to have writer Simon Raven extend the length of *The Pallisers* from forty-five minutes an episode to fifty-two minutes to better match American program lengths. This, he felt, was an indication of the dangers American money posed to the integrity and independence of British broadcasting (in any event, *The Pallisers* was not shown on *Masterpiece Theatre*).[34]

To better understand American financing for BBC and ITV productions and its subsequent impact on both sides of the Atlantic, it is necessary to trace the origins of the Anglo-American television trade. When Mobil gave life to *Masterpiece Theatre* in 1971, the idea behind the series was not actually a new one to the British. Just as WGBH and public television had maintained a longstanding policy of corporate sponsorship prior to *Masterpiece Theatre,* so too American public television—in its previous incarnations of the National Association of Educational Broadcasters (NAEB), the National Educational Radio and Television Center (NERTC), and National Educational Television (NET)—also had its own long-standing tradition of using inexpensive BBC product to fill up broadcasting schedules.

The BBC had a history of trying to sell product to American educational television, and went to elaborate lengths to do so. This trade was an outgrowth of British transcription sales to educational radio, from which educational television grew. Nineteen years before the debut of *Masterpiece Theatre,* a delegation of American educational broadcasters had visited the BBC on a well-documented program buying trip. It was an expedition very much like those taken by Schmertz, Marshall, and Sarson on behalf of *Masterpiece Theatre.* Just as they did with the Mobil and WGBH people, the BBC had given its 1952 visitors from the National Association of Educational Broadcasters the best possible treatment, no doubt hoping to make a good impression on potential customers. To the BBC, American educational television at that time represented a newly opening market, a target of opportunity not to be missed.

In a preparatory letter from New York to London, the head of the North American Service, Basil Thornton, asked his superiors: "Can we get them into the Dorchester or an equally good hotel? . . . On money, DSW [director of the spoken word] is of the opinion that we should treat this like the Commonwealth Conference; that is to say, that the delegates would be responsible for their own hotel rooms, but that otherwise, in a general way, the BBC would be financially responsible for their visit here."[35]

The NAEB delegates were George Probst, director of radio and television at the University of Chicago, Seymour Siegel, head of WNYC and president of the NAEB, and William Harley of the University of Wisconsin (Parker Wheatley of WGBH was at one point on the list, but he did not make it to London). They came to England on September 8, 1952. The BBC representative said their travel was financed by a generous grant from the Ford Foundation, and jokingly dubbed the travelling trio "the three Wise Men of Gotham."[36] The BBC had put together a full ten-day schedule of meetings and entertainment. The NAEB appointments included conferences with Harman Grisewood (director of the spoken word), J. B. Clark (director of external broadcasting), Rooney Pelletier (North American service organizer), B. E. Nicolls (acting director-general), Gregory Bridson (assistant head of features department), J. Warren McAlpine (controller, overseas services), Hugh Carleton Greene (the legendary broadcaster was, at the time, assistant controller of overseas English services), and various producers.

Their visit was full of what are now called "heritage experiences." In addition to conducting business meetings, the Americans were wined and dined—at BBC expense—at the Cafe Royal, The Ivy, Rules, and the Savile Club, among other historically posh London venues. The NAEB travellers were also taken to the Royal Opera, Covent Garden for a performance of Delibes's *Sylvia*. They were given tours of the BBC studios at Lime Grove, and a sherry party was held in their honor. Seymour Siegel, as president of the NAEB, was given a national television broadcast slot where he could address the British people on the BBC. He was put on the air at 9:15 on September 11, 1952, "televising in 'Speaking Personally.'" The group was taken on a sightseeing tour to Oxford the next day, where they lunched with Isaiah Berlin.[37] During World War II, Berlin had been in charge of Weekly Political Summaries for the British Embassy in Washington, where he monitored "changing attitudes and movements of opinion in the USA on issues considered to be important to Anglo-American relations."[38]

After lunch the BBC transported the Americans to Stratford, stopping for a brief visit at Blenheim Palace, Churchill's birthplace. Arriving in Shakespeare's hometown, they were introduced to the controller of the BBC Midland Region and the general manager of the Memorial Theatre. Here, the BBC sponsored a dinner in their honor. Then, all adjourned to see a production of *The Tempest* before settling down for the night in the Welcombe Hotel. The weekend was near Manchester, with Lord Simon at his home in Broomcroft, Didsbury. Returning to London the following Monday, there was another round of meetings with BBC executives, followed by a dinner with George Barnes, director of television broadcasting. On Tuesday, they met with Val Gielgud, head of drama, and lunched with the acting director-general, Nicholls, and Lord Tedder. Then they visited Brian George, head of central program operations, before adjourning to Sir John Hodsal's home.

Money was clearly on everyone's mind, since a handwritten notation on the schedule of their visit reads "millionairess" (although perhaps this referred to the title of a Shaw play, as well). The next day, the delegation met with J. Scupham, the head of schools broadcasting, and Kenneth Adam, controller of light programmes. The BBC then held a photo session, a press conference, and a cocktail party in the Council Chamber before bringing the group to Waterloo Station the next morning.[39]

What were the results of this extensive and, no doubt for the BBC's hospitality fund, expensive visit? The BBC prepared an official report, which was circulated widely within the bureaucracy. It noted that "since its inception, the NAEB has been in contact with the BBC" and that "rebroadcasting of British material by NAEB has become an important item in the activities of the North American Service." The objectives of the meeting were to "a) show the NAEB officials as much of the BBC operation as possible; b) discuss all possible methods of mutual cooperation."

These objectives were met, according to the report. The NAEB purchased a film on Henry Moore by John Read. They also accepted "a telefilm of the interview of Siegel by Robert Mackenzie." They wanted the "Andy Pandy films." And most important, they wanted a series of BBC telefilms dealing with "BRITISH WORTHIES" (emphasis theirs).[40] This proposed series was a direct ancestor of *Masterpiece Theatre*. The report concluded "as a result of these discussions NAEB's hand will be immensely strengthened in their attempts to get increasing sums of money for the rebroadcasting in the United States of the kind of programmes that the BBC would wish to be heard there."[41]

In the case of the "British Worthies," the NAEB representatives had suggested funding a series of thirteen half-hour programs "dealing with famous figures in British history and literature." This set of shows was originally intended to be done in the documentary form, "to search for the traces left by these figures on present-day British life." However, there was room for "acted scenes" if "existing difficulties with the artists' unions are overcome." Greene sent Probst a list of names from which to choose: Johnson and Boswell, Disraeli and Gladstone, Trollope, Wordsworth, Jane Austen, the Brontës, Darwin, Cromwell, Marlborough, Constable, Wedgwood, Wren, Swift, Walter Scott, Cobbett, Florence Nightingale, Thomas Arnold of Rugby, and Benjamin Jowett of Balliol. The BBC was negotiating the specifics of the project, which also included renting thirteen existing films to the NAEB for a total of £684. The costs given for the production of the new programs in 1952 "should not exceed $250,000 for 13 half-hour films." Greene later headed the BBC.[42] The price of $250,000 was almost twice what Mobil paid per hour for the first year's run of "British Worthies" on *Masterpiece Theatre* many years later. A comparison of this list with the list of *Masterpiece Theatre* programs shows a significant parallel, although of course the biographical and documentary treatment of the stories is different. Yet, the precedent for *Masterpiece Theatre* is clearly apparent.

During its visit, the NAEB delegation also proposed that the BBC make a special series of radio broadcasts for America. The BBC's director of external broadcasts told the director of the spoken word, "We said categorically that if they could contribute $100,000 a year we would 'tailor' two hours of output a week specially for them . . . on bidding farewell to them at lunch on September 16th the visitors jointly and severally made it clear that they fully understood our position and left me with the impression that they were going back to the United Sates to look for dollars."[43] Here, then, is a precedent for the preproduction and coproduction deals found in *Masterpiece Theatre*.

Dollars were important enough for the BBC to note that the NAEB contract should not affect other commercial deals with American networks. "The NAEB delegates were fully informed of our commercial television aspirations and our current commercial commitments to the William Morris Agency."[44] What were the agents at William Morris planning? "Programmes which, it was thought, would earn good money in the USA included a series on great trials which have influenced the development of the common law as a joint Anglo-American heritage . . . and readings from English literature of the type popularized by Charles Laughton and Emlyn Williams."[45]

American dollars were also important enough for the BBC to follow up the NAEB meeting in 1953, when the North American representative met with "a Mr. Sweeney, the head of the Harvard Poetry Library, who is connected with WGBH" and obtained a promise of "a financial contribution towards increasing the number of poetry programmes . . . I suggest the best way of making use of this offer would be to send a sample costing of some suitable programmes which might not otherwise be taken for transcription." This is further evidence that the BBC was willing to make programs for export very early on.

Thornton also went to see Robert Maynard Hutchins at the Ford Foundation about the expected grant for the NAEB series. "Mr. Hutchins immediately said that there was no reason for delay and that I could inform Sy Siegel that he could go right ahead and 'purchase the whole BBC output' if he wanted to. I asked him to repeat this surprising statement, which he did. On my return to New

York I informed Sy Siegel who soon had the wires humming . . .
to decide, it was hoped, on a grant to the BBC of $56,000 a year."[46]
So, at the time the Ford Foundation was willing, in principle, to
buy *everything* the BBC had to offer. When Mobil did the same
sort of thing (actually following through on the offer, although
buying selectively), it was not an exception, but rather the rule for
American noncommercial television.

There is, therefore, clear evidence of an identifiable market for
British programming in American educational broadcasting almost two decades before the establishment of *Masterpiece Theatre*. The BBC wanted to exploit this market for reasons of publicity, prestige, and profit. The BBC was attempting to do so for
years prior to the establishment of the Mobil series, using contacts
with the local stations, the NAEB, and the Ford Foundation. This
history certainly is evidence that the British were trying to market
their "heritage" to American audiences long before *Masterpiece
Theatre*. Clearly, the perception of Britain given by the series is
one that the British have very much wanted the Americans to have,
for at least two decades.

Basil Thornton, the BBC's North American representative, attended the annual NAEB meetings in the United States to sell his
wares. He sent reports to London on the excellent market for BBC
programs on educational stations. The reason the market was so
rich was, Thornton thought, that the Americans making up the
NAEB were incompetent and naive. Thornton characterized them
as "idealistic amateurs. In fact, taking a degree in education and
communications and working two or three years in a small station,
acquiring an MA and then returning to some University to
teach the same unrealistic stuff, seems to have been all too common . . ."[47] In polite language, the BBC's man in New York was
in effect calling American educational broadcasters "suckers" who
would buy whatever the BBC had to offer. Years later, English
broadcaster Jeremy Isaacs expressed a similarly condescending
view in his memoirs. Writing in 1989, he said, "The American
public broadcasting system, PBS, will show anything in a British
accent and in crinolines—many Americans think life here is like
Upstairs, Downstairs or *The Pallisers.* "[48]

However, most of Thornton's report was devoted not to evaluations of American broadcasters, but to money matters, specifying
possible BBC funding sources such as the Kellogg Fund, the Ford

Foundation, and the Lowell Institute, Boston (parent foundation for WGBH). Thornton noted "more than 50% of our features are perfectly suitable for use with NAEB. The question is how do we get them. I am having more communication with Parker Wheatley [station manager of WGBH] and others on the subject and will finally send you a list."[49]

Thornton was more than just a salesman. He was gathering intelligence for the BBC, reporting on the possible role of educational television in American politics. In one report he wrote: "The NAEB is very interested in the prospects of educational television and look forward to policing, to a certain extent, the standards of commercial television, to acquiring time for themselves on commercial television, and to running their own television station. Finance, of course, is the big problem, but as the medium seems to be more picturesque, and to have captured the dismay of responsible people more than radio, money may be found in the Foundations. Given money, equipment is no problem. All of this, however, is sufficiently far ahead for us to occupy ourselves with the sound aspect of NAEB only for the time being."[50]

But by 1954, Aubrey Singer (then U.S. television officer for the BBC) reported on proposed legislation that would set up a U.S. government study on "transatlantic television" linking England and the United States. The group studying the proposal would include two senators appointed by Vice President Richard Nixon, and the purpose would be "to encourage development and use of radio-tv in fostering cooperation and mutual understanding among the free nations of the world."[51] Nixon's long-standing interest in Anglo-American television, seen in this proposal, perhaps also partially explains the birth of *Masterpiece Theatre* during his watch as president.

In 1955, Thornton attended the NAEB convention in Chicago to accept a citation honoring the BBC. Thornton reported on the new facilities for educational television in the windy city and compared them with WGBH, adding that "A number of the TV programming staff on WGBH, Boston, was enquiring once again what BBC TV material was available. He said they had been extremely grateful for the fairly large quantity of documentaries they had been able to obtain from BIS [British Information Services, the propaganda arm of the government]. These had now come to an end, and they urgently required more material."[52] WGBH continues to use

British documentaries to this day in its series such as *Frontline* and *Nova*.

By 1956, Barrie Thorne had replaced Thornton—who had gone to work for the Americans (as NET program buyer)—at the annual NAEB convention. Thorne still kept up the BBC interest in American educational broadcasters. He noted in his report "BBC programmes can, therefore, play a greater part in conveying British cultural views and opinion to a small but potentially important thinking audience . . . The BBC built up a unique reputation for itself in radio, but there is, one fears, a danger of its losing this if it does not start building television programmes of quality and integrity designed for the American noncommercial market."[53] The key here is the phrasing "designed for the American noncommercial market." The push for an export-oriented BBC is nothing new.

In 1960, the North American representative, Derek Russell, filed his report on "Promoting the BBC in the USA." He said, "The convention [of the NAEB] underlined the desirability of sustained and imaginative promotion of all aspects of the BBC in the U.S. Though there were many friendly references to the BBC (I was on the panel in one discussion) there was also much ignorance of the range and scope of BBC operations, both external and domestic, sound and TV. Moreover, as noted above, ITV promotion is aggressive and effective. ITV's profits have given it economic prestige and its programme quality was demonstrated. As regards the Home Services, there was respect for BBC drama, features and children's programs, and for BBC production technique, but little up-to-date knowledge."[54]

In the 1961 broadcast of a BBC dramatic series, one can see the precedent for the form and content of *Masterpiece Theatre,* including the rough division of the grant between educational television station overhead and British program costs. In 1961, the BBC, through Peter Robeck, sold a set of Shakespeare plays to NET, entitled *An Age of Kings*. Humble Oil and Refining Company (Standard Oil of New Jersey, now Exxon) granted the National Educational TV and Radio Center $150,000 to package and distribute the programs. The grant was broken into a payment of $60,000 to NETRC to pay for promotional, advertising, and instructional expenses, and $90,000 to the BBC for North American rights. The program was to be sponsored by Humble on commercial channels in New York and Washington, DC, as well. The NET broadcast featured opening and closing remarks by Dr. Frank Baxter (a University of Southern California English professor who hosted *Telephone Time,* a dramatic anthology series aired by CBS and ABC during the late 1950s). These wrap-around segments were paid for by a separate Humble Oil grant.[55] Here was the precise format used by Mobil in the 1970s: oil company sponsorship, intellectual introduction, BBC series, noncommercial television broadcast with commercial television spin-offs.

Yet, while the BBC was friendly to American educational television when trying to place programs, internal memos also reveal a sense of threat from the newly formed NET, which was seen as a possible rival in the international export field. In 1963, for example, Aubrey Singer sent a memorandum complaining that not only were the Americans sending "a large entry" to the Tokyo Television Festival, but also "at the same time I learn that NET is trying to force an entry into the South American market. In view of our wish to sell our educational programmes abroad, I thought this information might be of value to you."[56]

Meanwhile, the BBC was limiting the amount of American programming to a quota of approximately 12 percent. The ITV had a quota of 14 percent. In 1967, when Jack Valenti requested the quota be raised, the English responded by proposing to cut it to 10 percent.[57] On the other hand, the introduction of color television was seen as a major opportunity for exporting color shows to the United States, because it was seen to make obsolete the rerun libraries holding black and white material. Michael Style, writing in the *Financial Times,* urged British broadcasters to exploit this opportunity. He pointed out the peculiarities of the American market British producers faced. There was seen to be no market for documentary sale in America. However, this left "variety, drama and high-quality film series such as *Danger Man* and *The Avengers.*" Style noted that the average network sale could yield between $100,000 and $250,000 per hour, and that "production costs are underwritten by the fact that a broadcaster can get most of his money back by a British transmission." His final advice was "when contemplating international television, it is important to adopt the right frame of mind. If you are selling to America, you must act like an American, think like an American and practically be an American. Sales to America are not made in London, they are made in New York."[58]

At this time, the BBC was not competing directly for cash with the ITV companies, because it had the luxury of confidence in the license fee to fall back upon, as well as its accepted role as a public service broadcaster. In 1969, for instance, while the commercial broadcasters set up shop in Cannes, the BBC stayed away, saying that they had BBC offices around the world and did not need to attend the market. A newspaper article reported that BBC gross sales totalled £1,500,000 for 13,800 programs, compared to far larger sums earned by the competition. One private company alone, Lew Grade's ATV, earned £10,000,000.[59] Perhaps responding to the press accounts, the BBC announced that it had sold a record number of programs, 16,180, to eighty-eight countries. However, the BBC did not release price figures. They did claim sales to America for 1968–69 of 3,255 programs.[60] The BBC was also proud to announce that *The Forsyte Saga* would be showing simultaneously in the United States and in the Soviet Union.[61] A related column in the *Daily Telegraph* complained that the BBC was lagging badly behind ITV in exporting to the United States. In the article, L. Marsland Gander explained "the reason is that BBC productions appeal more to the impoverished educational stations in America than to the opulent commercial networks."[62]

The issue of exports was widely reported on, because increasing them seemed to be a logical revenue source that could supplement the license fee. The BBC was under domestic political pressure to match the success of the ITV companies in selling to American markets. This political atmosphere is reflected in Milton Shulman's newspaper column from the *Evening Standard,* reprinted in the *Liverpool Daily Post,* in which he explained: "Considering the size of the BBC operation, and the glories that have been heaped upon so much of its product, its penetration into foreign markets has been relatively disappointing. Although something like a quarter of its overseas sales have been in the American market, they are rarely seen on the major networks and most of its programmes are transmitted by NET, the public service network with about 2 percent of the total American viewing audience. Its revenue from this source is commensurately small. The Corporation, indeed, seems to have a very unsure and uncertain touch when it comes to producing shows that might conceivably find markets overseas after they have been seen here."[63]

Shulman then picked out what he saw as the most outrageous

example of BBC incompetence, a historical costume drama that he felt was among the worst ever broadcast and that Shulman thought would hurt the BBC's international reputation. "It will, however, amaze me very much if this slow, stiff, involved, pompously written, tedious series—so far—will earn us much foreign currency. I have watched the first four episodes with a growing and mounting incomprehension and bewilderment. As a costume piece, it reminds me of those early J. Arthur Rank epics when Denis Price used to be got up as Lord Byron and Fredric March was Christopher Columbus with a permanent wave. Veering from moments of dubious romantic fiction to the most intricate minutiae of political intrigue at the court of Charles II, it is like trying to digest some unholy collaboration between Baroness Orczy and the historian G. M. Trevelyan . . . It is a real pity that with the large American market now increasingly open to us because of our venture into colour that there was no one at the BBC who could recognise that expensive programmes like *The First Churchills* would inevitably do us neither any good at home—nor abroad."[64] In his attack on BBC incompetence, Shulman had fixed on the very series that provided the opening program for *Masterpiece Theatre.*

Meanwhile, Kenneth Adam was presenting the BBC's side of things in his own newspaper column. He was triumphantly crowing over the conquest of the United States by British television. "Just as in the fifties British actors conquered Hollywood, and in the sixties British playwrights took over Broadway, so in the seventies British television may at last show up bright on America's screens in the way which, quite frankly, it merits, because for most of the time it is so much better."[65]

By 1970, the BBC was at the Cannes television market with two representatives.[66] Then, BBC followed up with an announcement of the one-million-dollar sale of *Civilization* to Xerox for NET.[67] A few days later the trade journal *Television Today* followed up with an editorial attack on Lew Grade's American-style program exports entitled "End of Road for Money-Conscious Packagers?"[68] Then, on October 22, British newspapers reported "An American oil company is paying 235,000 pounds to sponsor the screening of BBC serials in the United States. Most are dramatisations of classical literature, starting in January with '*The First Churchill*' [sic] starring Susan Hampshire and John Neville. The programs will be shown for 39 weeks by the 200 stations controlled by the Public Broadcasting

Corporation. A grant to the corporation by Mobil Oil was announced in New York yesterday."[69] So it is clear that, from the British side at least, the American sales to *Masterpiece Theatre* by the BBC were the culmination of years of effort at penetrating the American marketplace, and that the educational broadcasters were targeted as more open to BBC product than their commercial counterparts. Indeed, it was naturally assumed that the ITV companies would sell to American networks.

In March 1972, Hartford Gunn, president of PBS, received a letter from Robert Larsen, WGBH general manager, following up on a previous discussion with Gunn about the future of *Masterpiece Theatre*. One might note that the existence of this correspondence indicates interest at the highest level of PBS about the future of the series (carbon copies were sent to Samuel Holt and Gerald Slater). The inquiry through Larsen is evidence that the communications with Mobil were established by the PBS bureaucracy as traveling via the WGBH conduit. Larsen told Gunn that he had written to Schmertz at Mobil and told him "that Public Television couldn't afford to drop a winner if there were any chance of continuing." As noted earlier, Schmertz had indicated that there might not be enough material at the BBC suitable for programming on the series. Larsen reassured him that if the BBC did not have the type of shows Mobil wanted "we could always look to Granada and other foreign producers who were very eager to get airtime and revenue from the States." Then Larsen suggested a veiled threat to Mobil, telling Gunn that "if Mobil had no plans to continue, we would want to start looking for another underwriter very soon so as not to lose the momentum of the series."

Larsen followed up his letter with a phone call, and reported to Gunn that Schmertz was delighted with the ratings for *Elizabeth R* and had said "that Mobil wasn't planning on going out of Public Television and that we ought to get together in New York within a few months for a relaxed evening and talk about the possibilities." Then Larsen warned Gunn that the wind was changing, that Mobil wanted to take a new tack with the series. "He's not sure that Mobil wants to continue *Masterpiece Theatre* as it has been. There might be entirely different kinds of programs they'd like to subsidize," Larsen cautioned. Apparently, Schmertz told Larsen "about Mobil, on its own going into coproduction with BBC,

Granada, and Harlech, controlling all the American rights of the programs, releasing them first on Public Television, and then syndicating them in the States. With revenues from syndication, they might roll back more money into coproductions which would again appear first on Public Television."

In this opening to the private sector in Britain, Mobil was responding to an acrimonious campaign being waged by the English advertising industry against the BBC Time-Life deal. *Campaign* (Britain's answer to *Advertising Age*) had criticized the BBC's arrangements for foreign sales, questioning two aspects. "One is whether the increasingly international character of television is forcing the BBC to conform more and more to the norms of the international rather than the British audience. Time-Life is, after all, the BBC's distributor in the States . . . by far the largest television market in the world. The second question is whether the BBC is now in the joint venture business or not. Why should Time-Life (except for its position as the BBC's U. S. sales agency) be privileged to be the only business partner for the BBC, gaining the enormous boost of, in effect, free publicity on the BBC? For the plain fact is that the BBC has now gone in for a type of promotion-cum-advertising of a commercial company's wares . . . that must surely set a precedent for other ventures. It is not, of course, the same as 'spot' advertising. Rather, it comes closer to that even more feared form of advertising (in traditional BBC terms, that is) namely sponsorship . . . The BBC may, as some maintain, have stepped outside the bounds of its charter in allowing this thinly veiled form of advertising."[70]

While British advertisers were warning the BBC that it was treading on their toes, WGBH was warning PBS about Mobil's moves toward dealing directly with the English. In his letter to Gunn, Larsen tried to downplay the importance of Mobil's threat—which would have the effect of eliminating the WGBH middleman in its relations with British broadcasters. He joked to Gunn that "this is only the latest Schmertz scheme—there will undoubtedly be more." But then Larsen seemed to be taking Schmertz seriously himself, and he strongly urged Gunn to make a decision as to whether PBS wanted the series renewed, saying "we don't have a lot of time to lose in deciding the future of *Masterpiece Theatre,* and one of the first things Herb says he needs is to hear from PBS whether they want to continue."[71] In other words, Larsen was apparently serving as Schmertz's errand boy to keep Gunn in line.

The somewhat dry tone of Larsen's letter to PBS was belied, however, by an extremely emotional internal WGBH staff memorandum revealing the importance of *Masterpiece Theatre* to the Boston station. It was prepared for Michael Rice, WGBH program manager, and analyzed the impact of showing *Elizabeth R.* The memo began with a reference to a Broadway musical that was seen as representing the spirit of the Kennedy New Frontier during the 1960s (presumably the highest praise a Boston television executive could hope to read). It began, "There is a line in the closing scenes of *Camelot* which goes something like 'And lest it be forgot for one brief moment, there was a place called Camelot.'

"*Elizabeth R* is public television's *Camelot.* Top quality, first run drama on public television in Boston is overwhelmingly popular with the audience . . . the TV audience in the metropolitan area . . . preferred it over several commercial network movies." The memo went on to note that the broadcast had enjoyed a rating of 14 and a share of 19, and that the third episode came in second for its time slot, beaten only by a network comedy special. The conclusion to be drawn: "Public television has arrived. *Camelot* is here."

Overall, WGBH had increased its cumulative prime time audience 50 percent over the previous year, from 22 percent of all households in 1971 to 33 percent in 1972. Some 49 percent of all households were watching WGBH at least once a week.[72] Clearly, this report would suggest WGBH now needed *Masterpiece Theatre,* as much, if not more, than Mobil did. Indeed, the series was so successful that the Ford Foundation now wanted to tag along. In June 1972, David M. Davis, the Ford Foundation officer in charge of Public Broadcasting, wrote to Samuel Holt asking that the fill time after the dramas be made available to "our station independence project." He suggested "a 45-second pitch, a minute for people to get to the phones, and perhaps two pledges per operator." Davis wanted Holt to talk the WGBH people into a new format, saying, "This then is a plea for the producers of film material to make them in two parts, so that the stations that need to fundraise could opt for dropping just the first one, which would be three and one half minutes long, and take the second one to fill the hour; or drop the entire fill during special pledge nights or pledge weeks. Is there any way that you could work with the producers and program suppliers to help with this problem?"[73] Holt promised to discuss the matter. As this memo shows, *Masterpiece Theatre* was clearly seen early on as a potential cash cow for public television.[74]

The success of the series was a major factor in the negotiations for renewal, and the threat of alternative types of programs and program suppliers mentioned by Larsen in his letter to Gunn was still in effect. In late June, Frank Marshall weighed in, with a memo to Gerry Slater, executive vice president of PBS, giving his views for the future of *Masterpice Theatre*.[75] The memo was carefully worded, with the admonition that its views were "of course, very unofficial and represent basically my own thinking, rather than that of Mobil. However, I hope it will be helpful in giving you some idea of the direction of our thinking." Despite the disclaimer, there could be little doubt in the minds of those familiar with the Mobil-Marshall relationship that Marshall was speaking for Schmertz as well as himself.

Marshall began by noting that, in his personal opinion, *Masterpiece Theatre* was a success and "that success makes it very difficult, if not impossible, to abandon after the 1972–73 season." However, Marshall, like Schmertz, did not think that the BBC would be able to supply the full needs of the series in the future. "The probability of broadcasting a full 34-week season of classic serials from the BBC, after the coming season, is very slight," he wrote. "In effect, in less than two seasons, we have already skimmed the best of BBC serials and are now into serials that were made for children (*Last of the Mohicans, Tom Brown's Schooldays, Moonstone,* etc.). In addition, the direction of the classic serials department seems to be more and more toward what I would call abstract novels. Books like *Road to Freedom, Man of Straw,* and *Eyeless in Gaza* just don't seem to me suitable for an American audience."

Marshall was not simply concerned with the content of the programs being unsuitable. As a businessman, he was also worried about the rising prices of BBC material. He noted: "Our access on favorable economic terms to large productions like *Elizabeth R* will in the future be heavily limited. Having proven the viability of shows like the *Henry*s and the *Elizabeth*s, Time-Life can realize a much greater return through commercial sales at substantially higher prices."

Marshall also felt that *Masterpiece Theatre* must break away from showing repeats of commercial broadcasts, a precedent set by the prior showing of *The Six Wives of Henry VIII* on CBS that summer:

"I doubt whether it is in the best long term interests of public television to take replay rights to such properties after they have already appeared on commercial television." Because of the shortage of BBC material, increased prices, and competition from commercial broadcasters, Marshall predicted that the BBC would be able to supply only fifteen hours of programming from their serials department per year. This shortage of material meant that "the concept of *Masterpiece Theatre* will probably have to be revised in some form."

Already in June of 1972, Marshall was setting out the position that *Masterpiece Theatre* would be transformed because of the nature of its dependence on the output of the BBC. The original concept of showing classic adaptations had been improvised. It had depended on the flow of a certain sort of material, BBC classic serials. With the source of supply in question, Marshall would consider alternatives. He was not specific about the precise nature of the change, musing, "I wish I knew what that form would be." Yet he did put forward three options for the program: the series might show "great motion pictures," "short plays," or "old black-and-white serials from the BBC."

Although undecided about the future course, which depended on how he could "figure out availabilities," Marshall was certain of one thing: he wanted to stop paying production costs for WGBH's filler material, "regardless of which direction *Masterpiece Theatre* itself takes. There seems to be enough evidence that the filler in the past two years has been unacceptable to a number of stations, while also being quite expensive. As I told you at lunch, it would take a magnificent proposal for filler material for me to even get slightly excited about its potential. It seems to me that the $330,000 spent for filler in our last grant might have been extremely well spent in other ways."

Two days after Marshall's memo was written, Gerry Slater of PBS sent a letter to Herb Schmertz and Frank Marshall at Mobil, and to Robert Larsen and Chris Sarson at WGBH. They were invited to attend a meeting on Tuesday, July 18 at 2:00 P.M. in the Washington headquarters of PBS "to discuss plans for the fourth and fifth seasons of *Masterpiece Theatre*. Attending this meeting will be representatives from Mobil Oil Corporation, Marshall and Bloom, WGBH, and PBS."[76] However, there is no record of any agreement for a shared future vision of the series growing out of that meeting (or even of the meeting taking place).

In February of 1973, negotiations on the future of the series were still continuing directly between WGBH and Mobil. However, Michael Rice at WGBH was keeping PBS advised of the progress of their talks. On February 5, Rice called Sam Holt and told him a deal was "close." Sam Holt—although not personally involved—made a memo of the conversation and sent copies to Hartford Gunn and Gerry Slater, among others.[77] There would be thirty serial episodes over two years, with summer reruns. And there would be an important addition: a strand of British mysteries would be added to the *Masterpiece Theatre* slot—the Lord Peter Wimsey novels of Dorothy Sayers. At the same meeting, Mobil offered to pay for one-third to one-half of the cost of putting on *War and Peace* in a separate slot, "if someone noncommercial like the National Endowment for the Humanities picks up the rest of it." WGBH was doing the negotiating for this series directly with Time-Life salesmen Lee Heffner and Wynn Nathan, and Sam Holt noted "WGBH finds them somewhat saner to deal with than the Robeck-Schmertz-Marshall axis (apparently Mobil is letting WGBH do more negotiating [on the *War and Peace* deal])." Holt then noted he would go with the NEH people to the New York screenings of *War and Peace,* no doubt to help them decide to fund it. WGBH also wanted to show the BBC series *Onedin Line* (a BBC dramatization about the Cunard Line). Holt recorded that *War and Peace* would cost $450,000 for an eighteen-part series, and that *Onedin Line* would also cost $25,000 per hour. He then noted that *Masterpiece Theatre* was budgeted at $15,000 per hour by WGBH. Rice asked Holt if the prices were "out of line" and Holt replied that "they were not bad" and "represented a relatively consistent movement in per hour costs as we become more and more noticeable."

Then Holt's remarks encapsulated the relationship between Mobil-WGBH-PBS vis-à-vis the British. On February 12, Herb Schmertz was going to London and WGBH found out about his trip. "Rice himself may have to go along 'to assure that Mobil does nothing separate,' though he is assured it is only for screening and checking out options," Sam Holt recorded in his memo. "He was kind enough to offer PBS the chance to go; WGBH 'doesn't need you, but you can feel free to tag along if you wish.'"

On February 9, Wynn Nathan of Time-Life sent Michael Rice at WGBH a deal memo that would serve as the basis for future programming.[78] It confirmed the selection of the Lord Peter Wimsey and Somerset Maugham programs as additions to the "serialized dramas" available at the cost of $15,000 per episode. In addition, Nathan listed a number of programs that had been rejected by WGBH:

The Way We Live Now	*Daniel Deronda*
Middlemarch	*Sense and Sensibility*
The Spanish Farm	*Portrait of a Lady*
Germinal	*Sentimental Education*
Roads to Freedom	*Villette*
Nana	*Sinister Street*
Christ Recrucified	*Imperial Palace*
Emma	*Shadow of the Tower*
Visitors	*Man of Straw*
What Maisie Knew	*Eyeless in Gaza*

At this point, as his memo shows, Marshall clearly wanted a change in the focus of the program, and the trip to London, no doubt, was another exploration trip searching for new veins to exploit. Nathan presumably thought so, for he reminded WGBH of their contractual obligations to Time-Life. "When you are going to London on Monday, February 12, 1973, to commence screening, it is understood that on this screening mission as well as other future programs of serialized dramas, you will evaluate and accept or reject those programs within 60 days of notification by us of their availability," wrote Nathan. The letter also mentioned the WGBH deal for *War and Peace* and *The Onedin Line*. A copy of the letter was sent to Herb Schmertz at Mobil.

What happened in London? The visit confirmed what Marshall had predicted. Sarson wrote a report for Michael Rice at WGBH. "My outstanding impression is one of disappointment in the BBC Classic Serials we were shown," he stated. Sarson then commented on each show that was offered. He categorized them as "Standard Classic Serials." *Cranford* suffered "the absence of any quality that makes the series noteworthy." *Wives and Daughters* was "adequate, but no more" and, sitting through the second episode with Schmertz, Sarson felt it was "even duller than episode one." *Love and Mr. Lewisham* (based on an H. G. Wells story) was described as "Forebodings of doom! Another so-so series." *Fathers and Sons* provoked Sarson's ire: "Ten minutes of this reminded me that we had rejected the serial last year. And rightfully so. It's boring." *Wood-stock* seemed "so promising that I decided to see it with Schmertz on Wednesday." However, it was not good enough. "The serial had the elements of a Classic Serials Reunion party. Flashman played Charles II (he was dreadful). . . . The second [episode] . . . was awful—melodrama poorly acted." *Silver Sword,* also screened with Schmertz for the "promising first episode," was found to be a "good story" but "poorly acted and staged . . . Monotonous, unbelievable and eventually boring." *Hole in the Wall* was "tediously slow . . . oh so slow!" *The Passenger* was simply "no good."[79]

However, there were some programs the American contingent did enjoy. Among them were *The Man Who Was Hunting Himself,* which was characterized as a "beautifully written, well acted taut modern mystery . . . it's a masterpiece of its kind." Also, *The Unpleasantness at the Bellona Club,* about which Sarson wrote "the first episode is better than that of *Clouds of Witness* . . . my hunch is that the other episodes of *Belona* [sic] are good, too." The result of their expedition was obvious, as Sarson recorded the views of Marshall, Schmertz, and himself. "It's quite clear that there's a 'Masterpiece Mystery Theatre' series of twelve episodes (*Belona* [sic] *Club* (4), *Witness* (5) and *Man Hunting* (3)." Marshall and Schmertz discussed with Sarson the possibility of "another host." Sarson personally felt "Cooke admittedly would be out of place in *Man Hunting,* which is very trendy; but very much at home with the Wimsey novels. If he were not to host, who would? I have few ideas, all of them bad (Alfred Hitchcock, James Mason, that sort of person). . . . My (conservative) instinct is to stay with Cooke!"

But even with the twelve weeks of mysteries, the show had a problem filling the rest of the season. Sarson suggested *Onedin Line* and, as a "fall-back position," *Cranford, Wives and Daughters, Love and Mr. Lewisham,* and *Hole in the Wall.* He also recommended forcing Time-Life to find some other material for the series. He listed *The Weir of Hermiston* and *The Regiment,* which had been produced independently from Shaun Sutton and which were therefore not represented by the Time-Life agreement. Sarson also urged that the series consider doing "unconnected plays," such as a P. G. Wodehouse series that Cooke recommended to him [no doubt *Wodehouse Playhouse*]. Sarson's summary of the situation at the BBC was:

1. Have a mystery theatre, 12 episodes in 1973–74.
2. Try to negotiate *Onedin Line* at a cheaper price as a substitute for standard classics (I don't think Time-Life will buy this).
3. Reject all unsuitable material now and expand *Masterpiece Theatre* in 1974–75 to include Maughm [sic], Wodehouse, etc.
4. *GET A LIST OF KNOWN UPCOMING AND AVAILABLE TITLES FROM TIME-LIFE* [emphasis in original].[80]

The *Masterpiece Theatre* group also met with Granada and London Weekend Television while in London. Sarson was seeking to obtain *Joseph and His Amazing Technicolor Dreamcoat* and *Coronation Street* for WGBH. But Schmertz and Marshall also wanted a Granada product for *Masterpiece Theatre*. They looked at *Country Matters*. All agreed it was "well-staged and very well-acted." Sarson recorded "I was impressed. On Wednesday afternoon Herb offered to take five plays at $15,000 each. Barry Heads [Granada's salesman] said privately afterwards that he thought that was 'a lot of money.' Thursday morning he presented the offer to the Granada International Board. Thursday afternoon he reported back that the Board would not take less than $30,000. Herb had made it clear on Wednesday that $15,000 was a firm price (i.e., no negotiating) so officially the deal was off. Heads and I had dinner on Friday and I'll report that conversation verbally. Cooke happens to be an old personal friend of Sidney Bernstein [owner of Granada]. I told him the story and he promised to try to get to Bernstein on Monday in New York to change his mind."[81]

It is apparent that Mobil was seeking to find other sources of supply to compete with the BBC. It is also clear that Herb Schmertz was doing the buying, not Sarson, who seemed more of an advisor representing WGBH's interests in the negotiations, that is, with the station seeking to purchase other Granada programs, Sarson would not want the price to rise too high on those sold to *Masterpiece Theatre*. Instead, he would be more naturally inclined to seek a price reduction as a personal favor, through Cooke's relationship with Bernstein.

The American group also met with London Weekend Television salesman Richard Price, who showed them three episodes of *Upstairs, Downstairs*. Sarson did not feel the series should be shown as a regular part of *Masterpiece Theatre*; instead, he recommended "we show it from start to finish without host and without break." However, Sarson agreed with Marshall and Schmertz that "the writing is always good and sometimes exceptional. . . . Comparison with the *Forsyte Saga* is inevitable. I think *Upstairs, Downstairs* will hold up well."

Sarson wanted Rice's opinion on *Upstairs, Downstairs*. He made arrangements for Rice and the CPB/PBS people to view episodes. He reported that the major obstacle to acquiring the shows was price. Marshall was prepared to pay $20,000 to $25,000 an episode while Sarson thought $17,500 was the top. Finally they agreed on offering $20,000 for the first thirteen programs, with an option on eight more at $20,000 and a further thirteen at $26,000, for six releases over three years on PBS. The deal was for two separate runs of three plays per week and guaranteed exclusivity for the first set of shows, thereafter permitting them to run in syndication while PBS aired further episodes. As mentioned earlier, Schmertz made a side deal for the price difference with Richard Price of which Sarson remained ignorant. Unknown to Sarson, his stubborn role in the negotiations with London Weekend Television (detailed later) would eventually be side-stepped.

Sarson made clear his reluctance towards paying the high price of the series. He wrote Rice, "my own feeling is that the shows are worth a little more than BBC 'standard' serial which we are getting for $15,000. Under no circumstances (in my book) are they worth $26,000 (the price of the second option). I made this very clear very eloquently twice during the talk and said that it was doubtful whether CPB would approve a cost as high as the last offer on two grounds: 1) It set a precedent for future acquisitions 2) With such limited rights and at such a high price, the cost per hour was nearly comparable to the cost of home-produced drama (which could be amortized over a large number of broadcasts), so CPB might encourage underwriters to invest in production rather than acquisition."[82]

Here Sarson was invoking the alliance between CPB and WGBH, which had enabled Mobil to enlarge its role in the series during the first year. Sarson also was referring to his earlier understanding that WGBH would begin producing domestic drama. It was a very subtle threat that he might ask the CPB to arrange its guidelines so that Mobil's acquisition of foreign programming would no longer be tolerated, that he would perhaps make Mobil look bad and threaten the corporate image Mobil was trying to improve. In a sense, however, it was also a bluff. At that point, it seemed PBS needed Mobil more than Mobil needed PBS.

Sarson reported that in response to his argument "Marshall and Price listened attentively. Marshall said he would, of course, have to clear the offer with Mobil and CPB. Price said he would have to clear it with London Weekend. Marshall said afterwards that the price was justified because: 1) Production costs have gone up, 2) The dollar has been devalued, [and] 3) Compared with *Onedin Line* it was a better and cheaper serial (Touché!)."[83]

While in London, Mobil also took steps to fight the high cost of fillers WGBH was providing on *Masterpiece Theatre*. Sarson reported to Rice that Marshall and Schmertz had viewed tapes of the LWT show *Aquarius,* an arts magazine program that had ten-minute segments. Although admitting that the program was "good," Sarson cautioned Rice not to fall for what he saw as a trick by Mobil. "I'll bet that at some stage we'll be asked to accept a package deal with some of these bits thrown in 'free.' The main reason not to is that it will take production out of WGBH. The pieces themselves I'm sure would be O.K."[84] Here we see Sarson's determination to protect WGBH's overhead, which was billed as filler and framing costs. He submitted with his report a budget of $1,081,000. Sarson's explanation for the figure was that "any time we came to a total of much more than $1,000,000 Herb would shout 'too much' and we'd start refiguring."[85] Schmertz was clearly calling the tune for *Masterpiece Theatre* during the trip.

Two weeks later, after the London viewings, Chris Sarson talked to Schmertz on the phone to plan the upcoming season of *Masterpiece Theatre*. The change in emphasis Marshall had first suggested some months prior had finally been decided upon. Mobil would sponsor fifteen mystery programs and, despite Sarson's warnings, eleven hours of *Upstairs, Downstairs.* [86] It would not fund *The Onedin Line*. Mobil would also pay for only one-third the cost of *War and Peace.* [87]

Mobil had come to this point based on what had transpired in the London screening sessions, using Sarson's official evaluations as evidence. Sarson had categorized the results of the trip in three ways: First, there were programs "not to be included in *Masterpiece Theatre*," for reasons recorded by Sarson. They were:

Fathers and Sons	Boring.
Silver Sword	Good story, inadequately produced.

Woodstock	Good first episode, then agonizingly inept production.
Cranford	Incredibly slow, meticulously mannered piece, unlikely to hold our audience through the first episode.
Wives and Daughters	[same]
Love and Mr. Lewisham	Same as Cranford.
Hole in the Wall	[same]
Onedin Line	Good at $17,500; not worth $25,000.
Passenger	A not-very-well-expounded mystery serial.
Anne of Green Gables	U.S.A. rights not available.
Woodlanders	[same]
Tenant of Wildfell Hall	Wiped.

Sarson listed a second program classification as "upcoming and unknown." Presumably, these were not available for screening at the time of the London visit. These shows were *Little Princess, Denotti Conspiracy* (a mystery serial), *Cheri, Song of Songs, Two Women,* and *Pin to See a Peepshow.* Sarson also noted that there were others yet to come but "who the hell has a list?"

The final category was of those projects labeled "good, and to be considered." These were listed by program source as follows:

BBC	*Clouds of Witness* (5 episodes)
BBC	*Unpleasantness at the Bellona Club* (4 episodes)

BBC	*The Man Who Was Hunting Himself* (3 episodes)
BBC	*Somerset Maugham* (Must be re-viewed. Perhaps 5 hours?)
BBC	*Onedin Line* (Up to 30 episodes, but not worth the selling price)
London Weekend	*Upstairs, Downstairs* (Up to 34 episodes, but expensive)
Granada	*Country Matters* (Up to 13 episodes, but too expensive).[88]

Given this documented tabulation, Mobil felt it wanted to go with the strongly rated programs from London Weekend and Granada. Sarson and WGBH didn't want to pay more, because of the bad precedent for their other deals. Mobil and WGBH were at odds. Therefore, on February 20, Michael Rice notified PBS that "We have agreed to agree only on the limited continuation of *Masterpiece Theatre*."[89] Perhaps at the urging of WGBH, Time-Life's Wynn Nathan wrote Herb Schmertz to suggest additional programs, recommended by BBC drama chief Shaun Sutton, that might fit *Masterpiece Theatre*. He concluded "from what I can gather, of the various programs we have available for you, there should be no trouble picking upwards of forty shows of the same quality that 'Mobil *Masterpiece Theatre*' has had over the past two years."[90] A copy of the letter and the list of films was sent to Sam Holt's office at PBS.[91]

Negotiations dragged on between Mobil and WGBH over the inclusion of the Granada and LWT shows. Presumably, Sarson had made good on his threat to involve the CPB in the opposition to Mobil, because his next memorandum was sent to David Stewart at the Corporation for Public Broadcasting as well as to Sam Holt at PBS. He informed them both that WGBH would acquire the mystery serials "*Mystery at the Bologna Club* [sic], *The Man Who Was Hunting Himself,* and *Clouds of Witness*" for *Masterpiece Theatre*. Then Sarson went on to discuss *Upstairs, Downstairs,* "the famous Edwardian drama of which you have heard so much." Apparently Sarson and Mobil had come to a compromise where WGBH would acquire the first and second series for $17,500 an episode, and obtain rights "slightly more generous than current *Masterpiece Theatre* rights from the BBC." Sarson was not told that Schmertz had agreed to pay Richard Price $7,500 an episode in a separate agreement. One should note here that Sarson refers to *Upstairs, Downstairs* as a different series from the shows making up *Masterpiece Theatre*. In Sarson's compromise version, as sent to CPB and PBS, the LWT drama would run as a separate entity "in the *Masterpiece Theatre* time slot." Sarson put together this table representing his plans for the 1973–75 seasons:

The 1973–4 Season

October–December 73	*MASTERPIECE THEATRE* Mysteries
January–March 74	UPSTAIRS, DOWNSTAIRS "first" series
April–June 74	12 *MASTERPIECE THEATRE* repeats (Classic Serials or Mysteries)

Then, if UPSTAIRS, DOWNSTAIRS is badly received:

July 74	4 more *MASTERPIECE THEATRE* repeats; and 73–74 series ends

If UPSTAIRS, DOWNSTAIRS is well received:

July –September 74	UPSTAIRS, DOWNSTAIRS "first" series repeat.

Options for 1974–75

October–December 74	UPSTAIRS, DOWNSTAIRS "second" series premiere
January–mid May 75	18 *MASTERPIECE THEATRE* Classic Serials, Mysteries (to be selected)
Mid May–September 75	up to 21 *MASTERPIECE THEATRE* repeats
or	
	UPSTAIRS, DOWNSTAIRS "second" series repeat [92]

Sarson mentioned what he called "one thorn" about the package of programs. "London Weekend wishes to include in a commercial syndication package five episodes of our UPSTAIRS, DOWN-STAIRS option (our 'second' series)." This condition meant that the programs might be running on commercial television before PBS had repeated them, and Sarson wanted to warn his colleagues.

However, he refrained from asking them to kill the deal, noting "this strikes me as not too much of a problem and I propose that we accept this condition along with the package." Finally, Sarson commented that "Mobil has agreed to pay for the acquisition and the framing of all the above material."[93]

On the same day, Sarson sent a letter to Richard Price in London setting out the agreement for purchasing the series. Among the clauses in the agreement, it specified a price of $17,500 per episode with the option to purchase further episodes, and also that LWT would provide actors and/or TV executives to come to the United States on publicity tours, their expenses to be reimbursed by WGBH.[94]

This clause would become crucial to the success of the series, when Jean Marsh's national tour became a legendary public relations coup. Schmertz described why Mobil wanted to do a national tour for *Upstairs, Downstairs*. "It provides an opportunity for journalists around the country to have good interviews to use at various times, and so provides an unending stream of good stories that focus on the shows."[95] The tour started shortly after Sarson's letter, with a press preview of the 1973–74 *Masterpiece Theatre* season in the Terrace Room of New York's Plaza Hotel at 11:30 A.M. on June 26. A buffet lunch and cocktails were served. The event featured Jean Marsh, "familiar to you for her movie roles, most recently in Hitchcock's *Frenzy*. People from Mobil (whose grants make this series possible), Public Broadcasting Service, and the Corporation for Public Broadcasting will also be on hand to answer questions."[96]

For *Upstairs, Downstairs,* Schmertz sponsored what was at that time an unprecedented media blitz for a PBS series. The idea was that of newly hired press agent Frank Goodman, who—at Schmertz's urging—had replaced former Marshall partner Phil Bloom as *Masterpiece Theatre* press agent. Goodman says "what we literally did was the same thing we would do in the theatre, and we would do in motion pictures, and commercial television. And since I had been in that [commercial television], practically all my working life, we applied some of the same things. So we took *Upstairs, Downstairs* as an example." The distinctive public relations campaigns of Frank Goodman's firm would mark *Masterpiece Theatre* from then on. The series would be known for its showmanship, a reputation provided in part by Frank Goodman's own background on Broadway, with Hollywood, and as a press agent for NET.

The hiring of Frank Goodman was of enormous importance to the future success of the series, because Goodman could work with all the elements of the *Masterpiece Theatre* package with equal skill: the corporate sponsor, the critics and television press, and the public television bureaucracy. Because he was well respected and had a track record at PBS, Frank Goodman was therefore a key "player" for the bureaucratic diplomacy involved in the making of *Masterpiece Theatre* into a PBS institution, as well as for the daily dealings with the press. Once Goodman was hired, Marshall (by that time a partner in a new public relations firm called Visualscope) reported directly to Schmertz on questions of program selection and policy, no longer meeting with PBS. Goodman and his associates were responsible for the public image of *Masterpiece Theatre,* reporting directly to Schmertz.

Goodman knew his way around the competing interests of the local stations and the national programmers in a way that would prove invaluable to *Masterpiece Theatre.* "Each PBS station, I don't know that this makes sense, was very jealous of its territorial rights," he recalls. Goodman knew how to package national programming, taking account of PBS's legal obligation to serve the individual needs of local stations and their communities. "They didn't want somebody working on a national level to come into their territory . . . and soon it became apparent that this was another national venture. OK, I'm used to that, because aside from all this we had done *The Great American Dream Machine . . .* Channel Thirteen [WNET in New York] hired me because they wanted national, and [I] don't want to mention it, but they wanted to bury the fact that they were looking into national."[97] That is to say, Goodman was a trusted diplomat who knew, like Henry Kissinger, how to keep a secret to accomplish a long-term goal. He was accepted as a public television "insider." Goodman had also worked for Los Angeles's KCET and for WNET as press agent for the Ford Foundation's *Hollywood Television Theater.*

Frank Marshall says he had first recommended Goodman to Schmertz after his work with Xerox on Kenneth Clark's *Civilization* and Alistair Cooke's *America.* Marshall recalls, "I knew him from Xerox, when he was doing all of the promotion for Xerox."[98] Goodman explains that the thinking behind Mobil's decision to use his firm was simple. "Xerox was getting credit for a lot of television programming. Mobil wanted to get similar credit."[99] Marshall adds that Goodman had a unique personal network of contacts. "Frank had been in the business for a long, long time. He knew everybody in the business. He knew every editor. He knew every writer. He was tenacious."[100] According to Schmertz, he hired Frank Goodman as Mobil's press agent for *Masterpiece Theatre* because "he gets better results than anyone."[101]

At the time his firm was hired, Frank Goodman's public relations practice included theater, film, and television. In addition to NET and Xerox, in television he had represented *GE Theater* (hosted by Ronald Reagan), *Producer's Showcase, Max Liebman Spectaculars,* and *Your Show of Shows.* His film work included *Last Tango in Paris, Tom Jones,* and *Judgement at Nuremberg.* He had worked for Rodgers and Hammerstein, David Merrick, and George Abbott on Broadway shows including *The Sound of Music, South Pacific, The King and I, Funny Girl, Gypsy,* and *Gigi.* Goodman had started his career as publicist in 1935, working for the WPA Federal Theatre press department, including the Orson Welles and John Houseman projects. He followed Houseman and Welles to the Mercury Theatre, and subsequently represented (on an individual basis or as part of shows) Jose Ferrer, Paul Muni, Otto Preminger, John Barrymore, Joan Blondell, Laurence Olivier and Vivien Leigh, Peter Ustinov, and Henry Fonda, among others. Goodman also had been Marilyn Monroe's personal press agent for *The Seven Year Itch.* It was no understatement to say Goodman was one of the most prominent theatrical press agents in New York, and that he represented a direct personal link to the showmanship of the most prestigious names on Broadway and in Hollywood. Such ties could only enhance the reputation of *Masterpiece Theatre.*

Frank Goodman recalls his philosophy of promoting *Masterpiece Theatre* as that of any legendary showman. "We tried to convince Mobil that we should treat it as if we were trying to get the biggest audience in the world, rather than be content with the tune-in we normally would get with PBS."[102]

Goodman worked closely with his wife Arlene Goodman, a former AP reporter who also wrote many of the press kits for *Masterpiece Theatre.* She recalls "an editor could take our copy and use it as it was. He didn't have to *patschke* around with it. Ever." Arlene Goodman recalls that even the *New York Times* had faith in their credibility. "I would call Les [Brown, television editor] up and would say to him thus and so, there was never any checking. Never anything. Because my reputation as a journalist stood me in good stead. I always said that I never wrote a story I wouldn't have written if I was still at the AP . . . there was no baloney." Her husband and partner concurs, saying that their principle was "no puff stuff."[103] He attributes their success at getting good publicity for Mobil to the fact that "We had a track record. And credibility as well."[104] As the next chapter will show, *Masterpiece Theatre* enjoyed excellent press coverage, especially from the *New York Times*.

Frank and Arlene Goodman made their own trips to London, where they would conduct research for their public relations work on location with the various productions. They worked intensively. "Arlene and I went over for *I, Claudius*. We saw *I, Claudius* in two takes, all the episodes on Saturday and Sunday. We went over and she [Arlene] interviewed twelve to fourteen actors, directors, script assistants in two days . . . If you read the *I, Claudius* press kit, it shows." This attention to detail, original research, and first-hand knowledge of the productions gave the Goodmans credibility with the actors, the press, and the production companies.[105] Goodman says he considers his public relations company "to be, literally, agents *for* the press, as well as press agents [emphasis original]."[106] While in London, the Goodmans were also the eyes and ears for Schmertz and Mobil.

They found that their work affected the British way of conducting public relations. "We even taught the English," says Frank. "*Masterpiece Theatre* convinced the BBC and a lot of other people how to promote a show in England." He says their work introduced the use of press books and client advertising. Arlene Goodman recalls, "You used to go to the BBC on a show that they had done that was coming up on *Masterpiece Theatre* and say, 'So, where are all the bios? Where are the press cuttings? Where are the reviews?' And all you would get would be something like oaktag in colors and it had one picture, and the cast—sometimes. Sometimes not."[107] Goodman says that Jonathan Powell introduced "tune-in" promotion at the BBC because of his experience with *Masterpiece Theatre*, and that Michael Grade (later to head Channel Four) also was closely involved in learning American public relations techniques when he worked with the Goodmans at London Weekend Television.

The Goodmans' national press tours directly affected the careers of British stars who would travel to the United States at Mobil's expense. Many careers benefitted from the exposure provided by the press agents. "It's Jean Marsh during *Upstairs, Downstairs* who went back and talked about us. It's the agents who found out all about the success. It was the fact that Nicola Pagett got a movie job out of being booked on the *Today* show." Other stars who gave the Goodmans "a good press, metaphorically speaking" were Jane Seymour, Bryan Brown, Bob Hoskins, Derek Jacobi, Ian Richardson, and John Hurt. "So after a while we got to know the English actors, and the English actors then passed the word . . . 'Hey, John Hurt went here and there . . . We got a credit rating.' " That is to say, the English stars recognized the work the Goodmans had done to help their careers.

Meanwhile, as the Goodmans were promoting the series in America, in London Richard Price announced the sale of *Upstairs, Downstairs* to the press, and the general manager of LWT said, "This is the first sale to the United States of a London Weekend drama series following successful exposure of our comedy programmes and it is only a beginning."[108]

But there were still some dissenting voices in England who disapproved of American sales. James Thomas, a columnist for the *Daily Express,* opined, "I cannot think of anything worse than the British producers revising their standards for the sake of American cash and quick sale abroad."[109]

Despite the considerable publicity for *Upstairs, Downstairs,* in fact no new contract for *Masterpiece Theatre* had been signed between WGBH and Mobil. And WGBH had not yet agreed that *Upstairs, Downstairs* would appear in the series, were it renewed. Two days after the splashy Plaza Hotel press event in New York, PBS issued an angry response to Mobil's promotion efforts. A DACS message was sent to all local PBS stations warning them about the unauthorized publicity for the coming season of *Masterpiece Theatre.* PBS would stand up to Mobil, it seemed, and seize back control of public relations, which they rightly saw as a crucial element for control of the series itself.

The PBS message read: "In the past few days you may have received a *Masterpiece Theatre* press kit from Marshall & Bloom prepared by them under contract with Mobil Oil. Please take careful note of the following inaccuracies in that press kit: 1) The PBS boards have approved *Masterpiece Theatre* in the fall schedule, and the PBS program department says that the program will remain on Sunday nights, but that the 9 P.M. time announced in the kit cannot be confirmed until a final schedule is announced. 2) *Masterpiece Theatre* is beginning its fourth, not third, season on PBS, as stated in a feature release in the kit. 3) PBS has 237, not 234 stations. 4) Mobil Oil has been one of the primary underwriters of *The Electric Company,* not one of the charter sponsors of *The Electric Circus.* We suggest that if you intend to use the materials in this press kit, you remove the 9 P.M. time and make the other changes noted above. In addition, we have been notified that this same press kit has been sent by Marshall & Bloom directly to TV editors of newspapers in the top 300 markets. We suggest you contact your local TV editors and inform them of the inaccuracies listed above as soon as possible."[110]

This embarrassing communication, which reflected as poorly on PBS as it did on its intended victims, was probably designed to shame Mobil into going through PBS for its publicity. It was soon followed by a phone call and personal letter to Phil Bloom of Marshall & Bloom from PBS public relations executive George Page (later host of the PBS television series *Nature*). Enclosed with the letter was a copy of the DACS message. In explaining his response to their public relations work, Page said, "as you can see, the release contained several mistakes which we felt necessary to point out to the stations." Bloom was at the time on his way out, replaced by the Goodmans.

Page maintained that Bloom agreed in the phone call "to clear with PBS prior to release all future publicity materials regarding MASTERPIECE THEATRE, UPSTAIRS, DOWNSTAIRS, and WAR AND PEACE [emphasis in original]." Page insisted that this was necessary "to protect the interests of our member stations." Then he offered some conciliatory remarks: "We at PBS are delighted with the fine promotional support you and Mobile [sic] plan for these programs and sincerely appreciate your efforts. I believe the PBS Public Information department can enhance the effectiveness of your work if we cooperate and coordinate the publicity planned for the outstanding series being underwritten by Mobil Oil." Page sent copies of the letter to Schmertz and Sarson, among others.

He soon received his reply. It was a handwritten note on Page's letter, short and pointed, reading simply: "To George Page: 1) We were a charter underwriter of *The Electric Company.* 2) Mobil has no 'e'. Herb Schmertz."[111] Bloom was out, Goodman was in, and Mobil was not going to be intimidated by the pressure tactics of

George Page and PBS. With PBS taken care of, Mobil was going to make WGBH an offer it didn't think it could refuse.

Sarson recalls the conclusion to the controversy surrounding *Upstairs, Downstairs* with some ambivalence, saying, "I mean my decision as producer was final. It's always a giggle when somebody says that in public television, as we'll find out with *Upstairs, Downstairs*. Especially to the guy who's got the money. . . . I guess we all take the credit and I take the blame, at least that's the way it worked. . . . I saw it and thought it was commercial. And that was the reason it shouldn't be on public television. This, when I say we're all responsible for the decisions, this is where Mobil, who has the money, says, 'OK, we have no problem with you not wanting to run *Upstairs, Downstairs*. Come up with something else.' Strangely enough, everything else I came up with they didn't want to put money in. They didn't mind putting it on *Masterpiece Theatre,* as long as we could get the money from somewhere else to put it on. I mean it's a kind of political squeeze, so we ended up with *Upstairs, Downstairs*.

"The story that's got out is that I hated *Upstairs, Downstairs* and felt it didn't belong on the series. That's a convoluted sentence that's more concisely explained in the way that I just did. But it doesn't make as good copy."[112]

Frank Marshall recalls stepping in personally to break the stalemate with WGBH over *Upstairs, Downstairs*. "The argument, simply, was that they simply refused to broadcast *Upstairs, Downstairs*. And I threatened to kill *Masterpiece Theatre*. They told me I had no such right. And I said, 'I do, too. Because I own the name.' And they were shocked. And they accused me of blackmail. And I said, 'Yes, that's what I'm doing. That's how strongly I feel about these programs. And you are very concerned about the integrity of your system. This will test it.' Eventually, somehow, they agreed to broadcast."[113]

Schmertz says that he was personally involved in the negotiations as well. He recalls, "I just said that Mobil is going to buy this show, and 'if you people don't want to run it, we'll find other ways to distribute it.' I said, 'I mean it's your decision, I'm not trying to pressure you into anything. I'm not threatening you in any way. I just want you to know that we're going to buy it because we think it's a good show. And if you don't want it, that's fine. We'll take the risk of it. And maybe you're right. Maybe it's no good. And we'll get egg on our face. But we're willing to take that risk. It's that simple.' And they said we're trying to pressure, we're trying to bamboozle, we're trying to dictate to them. We didn't try to dictate anything. I just said we're going to take the decision, that this is a show the American public should see and will enjoy. And maybe our judgment is right and maybe it's wrong, but we're willing to put our money up to find out. That's the whole story. Now they characterized that in negative terms of threats and everything else. But I merely said that I could syndicate this with public television stations around the country. Without PBS and GBH. Which I'm sure we could. But that's just a practical statement of the truth."[114]

On August 2, Michael Rice reported that an agreement had finally been reached by WGBH and Mobil as to the future of *Masterpiece Theatre* in relation to *Upstairs, Downstairs*. Rice said "The question of whether *Upstairs, Downstairs* will be presented as part of *MASTERPIECE THEATRE* or separately under its own title has been resolved: it *will* be a part of *MASTERPIECE THEATRE* [original emphasis]." Rice went on to announce that Alistair Cooke would be remaining with the series as host, and that he would present "a short essay (about 4½ minutes) on some feature of the period portrayed in the series. . . . Each *Upstairs, Downstairs* program will be, therefore, an integral whole. There will be no need for fillers." Frank Marshall and Herb Schmertz had clearly gotten their way. Not only would *Upstairs, Downstairs* be shown, WGBH would not even get funds to make filler material.

As far as WGBH was concerned "the only questions still outstanding . . . is whether *Upstairs, Downstairs* will begin on December 30 . . . or . . . January 6." Rice concluded "since this is a PBS scheduling matter that must be resolved within the terms of the agreement signed by CPB, PBS, Mobil, and WGBH, or otherwise especially agreed to by those parties, let me simplify the resolution by saying that WGBH will abide by whichever of these options PBS proposes, provided it either falls within the existing agreement or is specially accepted by Mobil."[115] This was a very small bone indeed to throw the growling PBS dog. And PBS was to find that this bone was also Mobil's. After receiving the memo, Sam Holt of PBS had talked with Schmertz on the phone and asked Sarson to resolve the scheduling issue directly with Schmertz.[116]

With the conflict over *Upstairs, Downstairs* concluded, Rice announced an important personnel change in his memo. "While Chris

Sarson will continue to be available for advice and background, the producer for WGBH's presentation of *Upstairs, Downstairs* on *Masterpiece Theatre* will be Joan Sullivan." (Sarson had announced his resignation from WGBH—both *Masterpiece Theatre* and *Zoom*—before Rice wrote this memorandum.)[117] Joan Sullivan, later known as Joan Wilson, would remain in her job as executive producer for the series until her death from cancer in 1986. She would also produce *Classic Theatre: The Humanities in Drama, Piccadilly Circus,* and *Mystery!*—all WGBH British acquisition anthologies made possible by grants from Mobil.

Importantly, according to Arlene Goodman, Joan Wilson had liked *Upstairs, Downstairs*. Goodman considered Joan Wilson to be "her friend . . . wonderful to work with . . . [Joan] kept us constantly and thoroughly informed . . . I mean we would hash over even things like, I mean she and Frank, more than I, whether you should put on show A before show B, or show B before show A, and how it fit into the schedule in terms of variety."[118]

The conflict over *Upstairs, Downstairs* resulted from a shortage of BBC material, as perceived by Frank Marshall and Herb Schmertz. They took the initiative of acquiring ITV material from Granada as well as London Weekend Television, and fought and overcame WGBH resistance to this programming. The aftermath of this battle resulted in a reconfiguration of the arrangements surrounding *Masterpiece Theatre* on both sides of the Atlantic. Mobil had a new press agent in Frank Goodman. Now Mobil would deal directly with ITV companies to assure a steady supply of programs suitable for its series. With multiple sources of British supply competing for Mobil's dollars, and with an executive producer in Joan Wilson who was more cooperative with Mobil, the series could branch out in directions unanticipated at its inception. Fifty-five hours of *Upstairs, Downstairs* would run for four years on *Masterpiece Theatre*.

The new relationship between Mobil and WGBH in the person of Joan Wilson can be seen in her 1980 memo to WGBH president Henry Becton and Herb Schmertz about the tenth anniversary of the series. As previously noted, Wilson worked closely with the Goodmans. Schmertz and Wilson also worked together, with Schmertz frequently making suggestions for scheduling. For example, in one memo Wilson wrote "Attached is my suggested program and order of broadcast for the 1980–1981 season. Most of this we have already discussed, Herb, as you suggested when we met that we hold *Testament* later in the season and we both felt there should be a goodly space between the two "darker" series, *Crime and Punishment* and *Therese Raquin.*"[119]

Mobil continued to deal directly with the English to secure programming. On April 7, 1983, for instance, Wilson wrote a memo to Henry Becton to inform him that Paul Gerken of Mobil had executed a license agreement on *By the Sword Divided.*[120] Mobil also took to running programs acquired for its commercially syndicated *Mobil Showcase* slot in *Masterpiece Theatre.* Herb Schmertz said the reason was "quality." He remarked, "By and large Mobil Showcase had material that was better than was in *Masterpiece Theatre.* There was not nearly as much of it, but what there was, was better."[121] An example was *Edward and Mrs. Simpson.* This sort of arrangement further increased the corporation's leverage over both English suppliers and WGBH. For example, in regard to a dispute over charges for use of *Edward and Mrs. Simpson* on *Masterpiece Theatre,* Wilson wrote that she told Thames television "I only said that since the original contract was made with you, Herb, that he would have to work it out directly with you."[122] In a later memo from Wilson to WGBH production coordinator Pauline Mercer about *Winston Churchill: The Wilderness Years,* the total cost to Mobil of $1.6 million was designated at a cost to WGBH of only $800,000 because of the *Mobil Showcase* connection.[123] The pattern of side deals directly with the British established with the negotiations for *Upstairs, Downstairs* was still in evidence.

Notes

1. BBC, *Guide to the BBC: 1990* (London: BBC, 1990), 2.
2. IBA, "A User's Guide to Television Sponsorship for programs on ITV, Channel 4, BSB," London, IBA, 1988.
3. IBA, "A User's Guide."
4. IBA, "Sponsorship and Indirect Advertising," number 12.2, London: IBA, 1988.
5. Several English television producers used this phrase, on condition of anonymity.
6. Herb Schmertz, personal interview.
7. Schmertz, personal interview.
8. Schmertz, personal interview.

9. Frank Marshall, personal interview. Marshall says the first major pre-production deal was *Dickens of London,* produced by Yorkshire Television.

10. Marshall, personal interview, 4 January 1991, 16.

11. For an excellent account of the ITV program trade with the U.S., see Jonathan David Tankel, *The ITV Thriller: The Interaction of Media Systems and Popular Culture,* University of Wisconsin dissertation, Madison, 1984.

12. Sam Holt represented PBS. Marshall says the CPB executive was named David Stewart, and Schmertz commented that "Stewart was legally blind. He could see, but he was legally blind." Marshall, personal interview; Schmertz, telephone interview.

13. Marshall, personal interview, 4 January 1991.

14. Peter Spina, personal interview, 17 April 1991.

15. Rebecca Eaton, personal interview, 9 January 1991.

16. Schmertz, personal interview, 15 March 1991.

17. Schmertz, *Goodbye to the Low Profile,* 226. This was confirmed by Warner's secretary, although Jean Marsh says it was the Duchess of Argyll in an interview with Karen Goodman and Kirk Simon of Frank Goodman Associates.

18. Marshall, personal interview.

19. Richard Price, personal interview, 1 August 1990.

20. Schmertz, personal interview, 15 March 1991.

21. Price, personal interview, 17 August 1990.

22. Vivien Wallace, personal interview, 17 August 1990.

23. "U. S. Snaps Up Edwardian Drama," *Evening Standard,* 22 May 1978.

24. *Daily Variety,* 10 January 1984.

25. Schmertz, telephone interview, 13 February 1991.

26. Mark Shivas, personal interview, 14 August 1990.

27. Roger Laughton, personal interview, 15 August 1990.

28. Laughton, personal interview.

29. Andrew Ferguson wrote about the PBS financial system in a different context, "In other businesses this circuitous routing of funds would be called money-laundering. Within the cloisters of PBS, it's business as usual—and, of course, perfectly legal." "The Power of Myth," the *New Republic,* 19–26 August 1991, 22–25.

30. Jonathan Powell, personal interview, 23 August 1990.

31. Powell, personal interview.

32. Powell, personal interview.

33. Peter Fiddick, "A British Perspective," *The Museum of Broadcasting Celebrates Mobil & Masterpiece Theatre: 15 Years of Excellence* (New York: Museum of Broadcasting, 1986), 26–35.

34. Fiddick, *Guardian,* 2 April 1974.

35. H. Rooney Pelletier, letter to F. B. Thornton, 31 July 1952,

"E1/194/NAEB Visit May–August 1952," BBC Written Archives Center, Caversham.

36. Basil Thornton, "Three Wise Men of Gotham: A Progress Report on the NAEB Visit to London in September," letter to NASO, 1/194 NAEB Visit May–August 1952, 22 July 1952, BBC Written Archives, Caversham.

37. "Agenda: National Association of Educational Broadcasters, Visit to the United Kingdom, 8–18 September 1952," D. S. W.'s office, E1/194 NAEB Visit May–August 1952, BBC Written Archives Center, Caversham.

38. Isaiah Berlin, *Washington Despatches: 1941–45* (Chicago: University of Chicago Press, 1981), vii.

39. "Agenda: National Association of Educational Broadcasters, Visit to the United Kingdom, 8–18 September 1952."

40. H. Rooney Pelletier, "Report on the Visit of the National Association of Education Broadcasting to Britain," E1/194/2 NAEB Visit August–November 1952, 14 November 1952, BBC Written Archives, Caversham.

41. H. Rooney Pelletier, "Report on the Visit."

42. Hugh Greene, letter to George Probst, E1/193 NAEB, 1950–53, 26 September 1952, BBC Written Archives Center, Caversham.

43. J. B. Clark, "Memo to D. S. W. Re NAEB," E1/194/2 NAEB Visit August–November, 26 September 1952, BBC Written Archives, Caversham.

44. H. Rooney Pelletier, "Report on the Visit."

45. "TV Foreign Countries. USA TV Development, File 3, 1953–54," T8/88/3, BBC Written Archives Center, Caversham.

46. "TV Foreign Countries. USA TV Development."

47. Basil Thornton, "NAEB Conference, Biloxi, Mississippi," 6 November 1951, BBC Written Archives Center, Caversham.

48. Jeremy Isaacs, *Storm over Four: A Personal Account* (London: Weidenfeld and Nicolson, 1989), 156.

49. Thornton, "NAEB Conference."

50. Thornton, "NAEB Conference."

51. Aubrey Singer, letter to Barbara Halpern (Intelligence and Research), E1/277/6 America TV 4, 1952–54, 29 July 1954, BBC Written Archives Center, Caversham.

52. Basil Thornton, "Report on NAEB Convention, October 31, 1955," E1/1565/1 NAEB 1955–66, BBC Written Archives Center, Caversham.

53. Barrie Thorne, "NAEB Convention at Atlanta: October 1956," E1/1565/1 NAEB 1955–66, 24 October 1956, BBC Written Archives Center, Caversham.

54. Derek Russell, "Report on 30th Anniversary Institute for Education by Radio-TV," E1/1565/1 NAEB 1955–66, 4–7 May 1960, BBC Written Archives Center, Caversham.

55. "Educational Television in the U.S.," E1/1555 America Intelligence Bulletins, BBC Written Archives Center, Caversham.
56. Aubrey Singer, Memorandum to CP Tel, "NETRC 1," 6 November 1963, BBC Written Archives Center, Caversham.
57. London *Times,* 5 January 1967.
58. Michael Style, "Programmes for Export," *Financial Times,* 21 August 1967.
59. *Mirror,* 14 April 1969.
60. *Financial Times,* 22 April 1969.
61. Norman Hare, "The World Buys from Britain," *Daily Telegraph,* 28 April 1969.
62. L. Marsland Gander, "BBC Finance: The Exports Factor," *Daily Telegraph,* 18 August 1969.
63. Milton Shulman, "Inside TV: These Churchills Won't Help Our Exports," *Liverpool Daily Post,* 25 October 1969.
64. Shulman, "Inside TV."
65. Kenneth Adam, "Kenneth Adam's View: British Is Best on U.S. Screens," *Evening News,* 13 December 1969.
66. Norman Hare, "British TV sales drive at Cannes festival," *Daily Telegraph,* 13 April 1970.
67. *TV Today,* 21 May 1970.
68. *TV Today,* 28 May 1970.
69. *Daily Telegraph,* 22 October 1970.
70. *Campaign,* 14 April 1972.
71. Robert L. Larsen, WGBH, letter to Hartford Gunn, PBS, 22 March 1972.
72. WGBH, Mark [no surname], "Memorandum to Michael Rice, Re: An exuberant and somewhat illiterate draft of public information from the February–March 1972 Boston Nielsen Viewers-in-Profile Report," 29 March 1972.
73. David M. Davis, Ford Foundation, letter to Samuel C. O. Holt, PBS, 14 June 1972.
74. Samuel C. O. Holt, PBS, letter to David M. Davis, Ford Foundation, 26 June 1972.
75. Frank Marshall, "Re: *Masterpiece Theatre*'s Future," memo to Gerry Slater, PBS, 27 June 1972.
76. Gerry Slater, PBS, note to Sam Holt "Re: letter to Robert L. Larsen, et al.," 29 June 1972.
77. Samuel Holt (SCOH), PBS, "Memo to the Files Subject: Call from Michael Rice at WGBH," 5 February 1973.
78. Wynn Nathan, Time-Life, letter to Michael Rice, WGBH, 9 February 1973.
79. Chris Sarson, "Memo to Michael Rice, Re: Update on *Master-*

piece Theatre 1973–75 based on London viewing last week," 20 February 1973.

80. Sarson, "Memo to Michael Rice."
81. Sarson, "Memo to Michael Rice."
82. Sarson, "Memo to Michael Rice."
83. Sarson, "Memo to Michael Rice."
84. Sarson, "Memo to Michael Rice."
85. Sarson, "Memo to Michael Rice."
86. *Masterpiece Theatre* did not purchase all of the original *Upstairs, Downstairs* episodes. Thirteen of the first twenty-six shows were eliminated during the negotiations between Richard Price and *Masterpiece Theatre* because of objections by PBS and CPB staff (Sam Holt and David Stewart, respectively). Five of these omitted episodes were in black and white, due to a strike by technicians at London Weekend Television. Richard Price, personal interview.
87. Christopher Sarson, "Memorandum to Michael Rice, Re: Conversation with Schmertz—February 20, 10:45 A.M." Photocopy in author's collection.
88. Sarson, "Memorandum to Michael Rice."
89. Michael Rice, WGBH, memo to Sam Holt, PBS, 20 February 1973.
90. Wynn Nathan, Time-Life, letter to Herb Schmertz, Mobil, 19 March 1973.
91. Dean Patterson, Time-Life, letter to Sam Holt, 26 March 1973.
92. Christopher Sarson, "Memorandum to David Stewart, CPB, and Sam Holt, PBS, Re: *Masterpiece Theatre:* 1973–75," 1 May 1973.
93. Sarson, "Memorandum to David Stewart."
94. Christopher Sarson, WGBH, letter to Richard Price and Arthur Marmor, RPTA, 3 May 1973.
95. Schmertz, personal interview.
96. Press release, Marshall and Bloom, 19 June 1973.
97. Frank Goodman, personal interview, 14 March 1991.
98. Marshall, personal interview.
99. Goodman, personal interview.
100. Marshall, personal interview.
101. Schmertz, personal interview.
102. Goodman, personal interview.
103. Goodman, personal interview.
104. Goodman, personal interview.
105. Goodman, personal interview.
106. Frank and Arlene Goodman, "Memorandum to Peter A. Spina and Fran Michelman," Mobil, 6 June 1988.
107. Goodman, personal interview.
108. *Stage & TV Today,* 28 June 1973.

109. James Thomas, "Boost for British Viewers as U.S. Foots the Bill," *Daily Express,* 30 June 1973.

110. Lance Webster, PBS, "TO: All Station Promotion Directors, RE: Masterpiece Theatre press kits," DACS number 17144, 28 June 1973.

111. George H. Page, PBS, letter to Phil Bloom, Marshall & Bloom, 29 June 1973.

112. Sarson, personal interview.

113. Marshall, personal interview.

114. Schmertz, personal interview.

115. Michael Rice, WGBH, "Memo to PBS, CPB, & Mobil," 2 August 1973.

116. Sam Holt, PBS, "Memo to Gerry Slater, Re: *Masterpiece Theatre,*" 7 August 1973.

117. Christopher Sarson, letter to author, 15 February 1998.

118. Frank Goodman, personal interview.

119. Joan Wilson, "Confidential Memo to Becton and Schmertz, Re: M. T. 1980–81 Season," n.d., 6.

120. Joan Wilson, "Memo to Henry Becton, Re: Call from Bob Shay, New York," 7 April 1983.

121. Schmertz, personal interview.

122. Joan Wilson, "Memo to Henry Becton."

123. Joan Wilson, "Confidential Memo to Pauline Mercer, Re: *Wilderness Years,* 'Note on Telephone Conversation with Paul Gerken [Mobil],'" 11 May 1982.

6

Mobil Masterpiece Theatre

My dying words—like those of, I hope, millions of Americans—will request that the hearse bearing my remains to burial be powered by Mobil, as thanks for Mobil's support of *Masterpiece Theatre* on public television.

—George Will, the *Washington Post*

It's not the shows that are important. It's exploiting it with the American public that's important. I don't care whether anybody watches the shows. I want them to feel socially pressured so they have to lie and say they watch the shows. It's the cartoons in the *New Yorker* and all the ancillary stuff that are important.

—Herb Schmertz, telephone interview

When *Masterpiece Theatre* premiered on PBS in January 1971, it was a harbinger of a new presence in public television that would come to replace the Ford Foundation as the largest single contributor to the system. Mobil's initial grant of $390,000 to cover thirty-nine weeks of programming for WGBH would end up a $12 million a year commitment by 1990. Mobil's move into public television was soon followed by other oil companies, and led to the popular joke that PBS was the "petroleum broadcasting service."[1] Herb Schmertz has said the most significant thing about *Masterpiece Theatre,* from the corporate point of view, was his complete autonomy to run Mobil's public relations efforts as he saw fit. He comments, "It never happened before that such a vast amount of money and total discretion to do what he wanted were given to one person. Decisions were not subjected to committees. For once in corporate America, they did it the way it ought to be done."[2] In its advertising and public relations material, Mobil Corporation refers to the PBS program the company supports at WGBH as *Mobil Masterpiece Theatre*.[3]

Stanford Calderwood, WGBH president at the time of the Mobil deal, felt Schmertz's—and therefore Mobil's—role was central to the creation of the series. He said, "Obviously, without his convictions and money, there would have been no program." Calderwood noted the corporate public relations man "either initiated or went along gladly with all the subsidiary aspects to the show: the Cooke contract, ads on TV pages in key markets, I think posters for schools, and so on. In short, once I had a handshake deal from Herb, he was the key element."[4]

Herb Schmertz has said straightforwardly that Mobil's interest in *Masterpiece Theatre* was primarily political. He described his approach as a unified one, with PBS as one element in a complex approach to putting across Mobil's public image. Schmertz notes, "everything we did was organized as if it was one big political campaign. And any of the things that you focus on are simply part of the overall campaign. It's impossible and would be misleading to isolate any of the ingredients and try to evaluate them as a stand-alone program. Because as a stand-alone program they are probably not worth it. It's the belief that the sum is more than the total of the parts. So you have to take all of the parts and look at the sum total, and just to take *Masterpiece Theatre,* or any other piece of it is, it may be interesting, but it's not an accurate way to look at things." Schmertz concluded, "My political campaign was to win elections also, on public policy issues."[5]

In his memoirs, Schmertz made explicit eight philosophical reasons that applied to Mobil's "affinity-of-purpose" *Masterpiece Theatre* campaign: 1) cultural excellence indicates corporate excellence; 2) cultural projects present top managers as "corporate statesmen . . . intellectually entitled to be listened to on vital public-policy issues"; 3) such projects improve employee morale and loyalty; 4) corporations that support the arts "usually find themselves in a position to play an influential role in the community's political affairs"; 5) arts sponsorship is important for networking because it "allows you to entertain important customers at openings, special tours and similar events, where you have the opportunity to introduce important people to other important people"; 6) since politicians have "favorite projects, your sponsorship of similar projects and causes provides the opportunity to form useful alliances and valuable contacts"; 7) arts support helps in recruiting intelligent and talented employees; and 8) it refutes the criticism that corporations are antisocial, since "participation in cultural or arts programs can present excellent opportunities to be involved in constructive social action."[6]

Pete Spina, Schmertz's successor as vice president for public affairs at Mobil, said that the various relationships begun by Mobil with *Masterpiece Theatre* in the 1970s have proven themselves over time. For example, when the Iraqi Army invaded Kuwait in 1990 and there was fear of another oil shortage, the oil company found itself attacked in the press. Spina recalls, "We're being beat up again as an industry, as we were in the '70s. Immediately prices went up, and we were 'gouging' and so forth. Now we have this new found relation with stations [the local PBS stations through a Spina-initiated local unrestricted grants program for *Masterpiece Theatre* publicity, begun in 1988]. So we wrote a letter to all the stations, managers and so forth . . . and said, 'You have such a close identification with Mobil. I just can imagine you're getting some heat with all these claims of gouging. Now, here's an ad we just ran in the *New York Times,* and here's our explanation of the crisis. We are not gouging, in fact we're losing money, etc., etc.' Some of these stations even put it in their [program] guides. . . . You talk about credibility!"[7]

Herb Schmertz's style, and his vision of *Masterpiece Theatre,* were very much in tune with the corporate identity Mobil was forging for itself in the late 1960s as it sought to establish a new name for itself—as a corporation different from its predecessor, Socony-Vacuum. The television series *Masterpiece Theatre,* in one sense, gives a picture of how Mobil executives would like to see themselves. It combines a tough, modern public relations campaign to improve the image of the oil company with an acknowledgment of the socially and culturally prominent history of the firm's previous generation of company executives, many of whom were from families listed in the *Social Register.* Mobil Corporation had been formed from Socony and Vacuum Oil Company, two Standard Oil units created in 1932, after the divestiture of Standard Oil Company under court order. Socony had previously been the Standard Oil Company of New York, headquartered in the heart of John D. Rockefeller's empire at 26 Wall Street. It had concentrated its efforts on refining and marketing in New York and New England, as well as the export of petroleum products. Vacuum Oil was a specialist in lubrication and Mobil had been a trade name for marketing lubricants. The merger of the two formed Socony-Vacuum, later Mobil Oil when the corporate name changed officially in 1956, to exploit the reputation for quality of the Mobil products. In 1976 the company name became Mobil Corporation, after the purchase of Montgomery Ward. Mobil is a partner in Aramco, the Saudi Arabian oil company.[8]

The reorganization of Mobil began in 1958, when post-Suez profits had declined from $270 to $157 million. Until then, a socially elite, blue-blooded, conservative old guard had traditionally made up the corps of Mobil executives. This group gave the corporation an identity as a "good, gray, Republican company."[9] The older generation of Mobil corporate loyalists, now on their way out as a result of a management shakeup, had been described as one with "a policy of hiring and promoting their own kind, a policy which filled the ranks with men whose conservatism substituted for ability. There was a distinct snobbery within the company which was to play a role in shaping the policies to come. Whatever else they were, progressive they were not. The departure of 12,000 of their ranks to join the unemployed, as a consequence of the reorganization, occasioned a glut in the antique markets of John D. Rockefeller roll-top desks and cuspidors which were removed upon their departure."[10] As discussed earlier, snob appeal and antiques (though not necessarily roll-top desks and cuspidors) are two important elements in the aura of *Masterpiece Theatre*. When CPB gave Alistair Cooke the Lowell Award for public broadcasting at its 1991 annual meeting in Orlando (held at Walt Disney World), WGBH president David O. Ives simultaneously presented Mobil vice president Pete Spina with an antique clock.[11] But unlike the private splendor of the old oil company, the new Mobil made an aggressive public display of its corporate taste through its support of the arts, education, and culture.

The problems Mobil faced when it downsized after the Suez crisis were described as "elitism and social prejudice; intelligence not rewarded; managers who were not long on brains."[12] After a McKinsey & Company management study, the old guard was replaced by a young team of aggressive and intelligent new managers.[13] Among them were Rawleigh Warner and William Tavoulareas, respectively assuming the posts of chairman and president of Mobil, in 1969. As William N. Greene comments: "Management decided the company would become 'long on brains' even if it remained short on crude. The realization that they were not Standard Oil, that the time of gentlemanly competition was over, plus the vigor of new men and ideas, launched the company on a quest for a new identity: to be scrappy, aggressive, and intelligent. It would get the best of competitors, not just live with them."[14]

Part of Mobil's aggressiveness would be in public relations and vigorous advertising on behalf of both its products and its political interests. *Masterpiece Theatre* grew out of these efforts. In a study of Mobil's advocacy campaigns, Janice Anderson said "Mobil's ads clearly reflect the personal styles of Mobil's top executives, Chairman Rawleigh Warner and President William P. Tavoulareas (Tav). As one executive who is familiar with both individuals remarked, 'Tav has imbued the company with its bare-knuckled style, from Warner it has absorbed its implacable self-assurance—the sense that we're Mobil and we'll do it our way.' Mobil's advocacy advertising certainly contributes to the company's corporate image as 'tough minded, hardheaded, contrary, self-assured.' As another analyst commented: 'This is really a company speaking as a person in its ads.'"[15]

Anderson criticizes Mobil for its tough public relations stance, remarking "while Bill Tavoulareas might legitimately think of himself as an underdog who must continually struggle against uneven odds, the organization he represents is one of the largest in the world. For this organization with its vast resources to similarly cast itself in the role of underdog stretches the bounds of credibility." She feels that studies by leading academics show Mobil's strategy may not have actually been as effective as the corporation had hoped.[16] Another scholar of Mobil's public relations work, Patricia Davis, argues that although Mobil *feels* that its support of cultural activities had a positive effect on the corporate image, "research available to the public suggest that neither government nor populace has been positively influenced by Mobil's advocacy advertising."[17]

This is not a view shared by Herbert Schmertz, as the designer of the overall Mobil multimedia effort to spruce up its image, of which *Masterpiece Theatre* was a part. Schmertz had joined Mobil in 1966 in the labor relations department, and rose to the position of vice president for public affairs in 1969. He was promoted to president of the Mobil Shipping and Transportation Company in 1973, and returned to his public relations job in 1974, joining the board of directors of Mobil Oil Corporation in 1976. He was elected to the parent board of Mobil Corporation in 1979. Schmertz is a Democrat and a labor lawyer specializing in arbitration and mediation.[18]

In addition to his corporate assignments, Schmertz had extensive experience in national political campaigns, working as an advance man and advisor for John F. Kennedy in 1960, Robert Kennedy in 1968, and Edward Kennedy in 1979.[19] In 1970 Schmertz, Tavoulareas, and Warner developed a new public relations strategy for the company, dubbed by Schmertz as "goodbye to the low profile."[20] They determined to put forward a provocative and combative public image to counteract what they saw as "powerful adverse external events" resulting from the actions of environmentalists and politicians.[21] As a prominent Democrat, Schmertz's high profile would help change the image of the company from its previous incarnation as a good, gray, Republican institution. Yet, *Masterpiece Theatre* would, through its appeal to historically established elites, balance, in a way, the pushy populism of the new Mobil public relations strategy of issue-oriented newspaper advertising, *Fable for Now* television commercials featuring cartoons and animals, simulated newsroom broadcasts from the "Mobil Information Center," and defiant testimony before investigating committees of Congress.

Schmertz disagrees with Anderson, Davis, and other scholars who hold the view that a tough, aggressive, bare-knuckled image is bad or ineffective for a company's public relations. Schmertz believed that the oil industry was starting with the worst possible reputation, and nothing he did could make it worse. From Schmertz's point of view, the bad image could only stand to be improved through determined public relations efforts. And if Mobil were taking a bare-knuckled approach, the combination of op-ed advertising and underwriting of *Masterpiece Theatre* could be seen as a one-two punch.

Mobil was hitting back at the antibusiness environment of the 1960s. Bombs had exploded in front of Mobil's headquarters on at least two occasions.[22] In his response to industry critics, Schmertz was committed to giving Mobil a reputation as a good corporate citizen. The reason was his view, "if you consciously set out to choose an industry whose public image had all of the ingredients of the perfect villain, Big Oil would be the ideal choice. To begin with, crude oil is an essentially dirty product . . . the major companies in our industry are extremely large, which by itself leads to hostility from the public. In addition, we do business with foreign nations that are not always popular in this country. To make matters worse, there is considerable confusion as to our real identity. In the mind of the public, we are often confused with the Texas oil entrepreneurs, the world of *Dallas*. In actual fact, there's very little connection between Big Oil and the Texas entrepreneurs . . . In case all of these problems weren't enough to deal with, our industry has experienced two major international crises during the past twelve years."[23]

Schmertz's analysis, which was shared by Mobil's chairman, Rawleigh Warner, held that the challenge to the oil industry's public image called for an unorthodox public relations program. "Conventional public relations has generally been concerned with how to get people to see you in mythic terms, rather than how you really are. Our problem is the reverse: we want people to see past the myths so they can understand who we really are and how we operate. That's why we require a visible and articulate presence, not only in the economic marketplace, but also in the marketplace of politics and ideas."[24] In the American marketplace of ideas, two stalls with prime locations for reaching influential customers were the *New York Times* and PBS.

Mobil's chairman, Rawleigh Warner, noted that in 1970, "for the first time, a powerful environmental lobby had emerged. Politicians and the press could not leap on that bandwagon fast enough. Clean air and clean water became paramount. . . . Coupled with this was the emergence of consumerism dramatized by the anointment of Ralph Nader as its patron saint. As never before, business institutions were under critical review, scrutiny and attack. The very social utility of the private economic system was being questioned in many unexpected quarters. Coupled with this was the growing awareness on the part of executives in this company that in the very near future, this nation and the world would start to experience energy shortages. And insofar as the U.S. was concerned, rapidly depleting domestic crude availability would very quickly lead to an escalating reliance on foreign crude oil supplies. The economic, political and social consequences, leaving aside all other emerging external problems, of tremendous dependence on foreign oil supplies and the uncertainties attendant thereto probably alone would have justified a change in our public affairs strategy."[25] And change strategies Mobil did.

Under Warner's leadership, Mobil developed plans for promoting policies to decontrol natural gas, permit more offshore drilling, restrict environmental regulations, and encourage nuclear power-plant construction. However, instead of confining itself to behind-the-scenes lobbying, Mobil went public with an advocacy campaign that, in Warner's own words, "broke all the rules of traditional public relations. We undertook a program that was more highly visible, more controversial, and more intense than had ever been attempted by any company. We affirmatively committed ourselves to the long haul."[26] Warner felt it was important to reject traditional image advertising, which he described as "conclusatory in nature, all things to all people."[27] Mobil felt that, instead, it was vital to participate directly in political debates "at very high intellectual levels on a number of issues which, when resolved, would directly affect the course of our business, our industry and our nation."[28]

American society in 1970 was still reeling from the shocks of the 1960s. Mobil was frightened by what it saw as a threat to the American system and the danger of, if not revolution, at least an attack on, capitalism as an economic system. The company was afraid of the possibility of nationalization or strict governmental control. As late as 1979, Herb Schmertz, by then a director of Mobil, appeared as a guest on a panel entitled "Will Capitalism Survive?" to argue the unpopular view that "capitalism does indeed have a future."[29] In 1970, Mobil also took the decision that the threat was not only to the corporation and to capitalism as an economic system, but to all the institutions of American society. Warner gave the reason for this move from self-interest to selflessness as being part of Mobil's corporate personality, saying "it has long been our view that America, as a pluralistic society, is composed of a number of free, private institutions: religion, the press, academia, business, labor, etc. The history of the world is that if any of these institutions falter or collapse, the other institutions are in jeopardy. We therefore undertook to escalate our support where we could for some of these other institutions, particularly education and culture."[30] That is, the threat to one organization would be perceived as a threat to all of them. A bomb at a university campus was, in this view, equivalent to a bomb at Mobil. Mobil would actively promote art and learning through its advertising and public relations efforts, tying the survival of Mobil to the survival of other established American institutions. One such pillar of the civilized establishment, in the view of Mobil, was PBS.

Mobil saw its participation in PBS as a mutually beneficial arrangement. Warner credits Mobil's support with creating a larger audience for PBS, as well as increased contributions and "a large influx of corporate support." He also notes that support of PBS "has provided a tremendous increase in the public's favorable awareness of Mobil."[31] But the original climate of opinion in which Mobil was underwriting culture was not a favorable one. Warner notes that executives were "being attacked by the press and public officials almost hourly. To be an oil company executive in a social setting during those periods was not a very happy experience . . . the regular attacks on the oil industry by those favoring divestiture, nationalizing oil companies, price control, windfall profits, simply had to be lived through to understand what we faced . . . it is simply impossible to recreate the environment in which we operated."[32] Pete Spina recalls, "We began to lose it as an industry, oil companies, in the '70s with the crisis and embargo period, then long lines in the latter part of the '70s."[33] Mobil saw itself as under siege from the opinion leaders of the establishment, and wanted to make friends and influence people to create sympathy for itself and the oil industry in the hostile corridors of power.

Yet other observers have not taken such a charitable view of Mobil's intentions and actions. Herbert Schiller argues that such public relations efforts were not defensive at all, rather "a direct outgrowth of the enormous expansion of corporate wealth and power in the postwar decades."[34]

By 1982, Mobil had in large measure succeeded in preserving its business interests. The corporation had withstood the assaults from its critics. A public opinion poll found it to be the most respected oil company, with the highest public reputation in the arts and culture area. Mobil also benefited among potential consumers, as noted in Warner's personal analysis of the poll data. Mobil was named by 31 percent of "upscale" customers as the gasoline they most often buy. This was 17 points, or 100 percent, greater than the expected market share. Warner concluded that Mobil was indeed established as "the upscale person's gasoline."[35] Mobil had created brand recognition among a prized target demographic. The corporation had not only done good—defending America by helping prevent nationalization and defending capitalism as an economic system—it had also done well for itself by promoting sale of its products to an important target demographic market.

In 1982, Warner judged Mobil's campaign a success, and promised that Mobil would maintain its efforts to reach opinion leaders. "We will continue to infuse our views, facts, and philosophy into the mix for their consideration . . . we expect to continue to attempt to influence events rather than react to them after the fact. If the pressures on us abate, this activity will not appear as intense, or strident to our opponents. But if conditions demand it, we have the know-how and willingness to meet them head on."[36]

Herbert Schiller critically comments on this "know-how" possessed by companies such as Mobil. He argues "the corporate 'voice' now constitutes the national symbolic environment. . . . It is not so much that one or another corporate giant utilizes the cultural industries to make its preferences known to the public. . . . Far more significant is the organic process by which the corporate voice is generalized across the entire range of cultural expression."[37]

When he concluded his analysis of the company's efforts, Mobil's chairman articulated the aims of Mobil's public affairs programs:

1) to build the reputation of an outspoken and responsible company, demonstrating an interest in major social issues and the energy future;
2) to stir debate on public issues of concern to Mobil;
3) to widen the sources of information available to the American public.[38]

From its perspective, Mobil had successfully faced, through its aggressive public relations campaign involving arts, culture, journalism, and the media, "major dislocations in supply, hostile federal administrations, and a climate in which politicians inflamed public doubts about our industry and company."

Mobil's chronology of its efforts breaks the events that affected the company—and that provided the context for its support of *Masterpiece Theatre*—into five time periods: 1) before the 1973–74 oil embargo, 2) during the embargo, 3) from the end of the embargo until the Iranian crisis, 4) during the Iranian crisis, and finally 5) events since the Iranian crisis.[39]

Mobil saw itself as simultaneously addressing several separate and overlapping audiences: 1) "opinion leaders," 2) "the general public," 3) "the investment community," 4) "our own employees," and 5) "foreign governments." Mobil sought to keep track of the impact of its public relations efforts—including *Masterpiece Theatre* —with these audiences by using polls, surveys, and assessments, as well as by commissioning specific studies. One such research project involved the effect of Mobil's op-ed advertising on the changing editorial policies of the *New York Times*. In addition to wanting to affect the general climate of opinion surrounding its activities, Mobil engaged in specific legislative battles over particular bills, such as the "fight against divestiture proposals in the mid-1970s," held by the official company history to be a "a signal success." Even anecdotal evidence as to the impact of its public relations work was carefully compiled by Mobil, down to recording in company records favorable comments about Mobil's *New York Times* op-ed campaigns and *New Yorker* cartoons made by seating companions on executive business flights, remarks that illustrated "the thesis that 'Mobil' has become synonymous with 'corporate good works.' "[40]

It was not only Mobil's official study that found the public relations campaign (of which *Masterpiece Theatre* was a significant part) to be successful. Advertisers and press agents were full of admiration for Mobil's achievement. In 1975, *Advertising Age* named Mobil's chairman, Rawleigh Warner, as "Adman of the Year." Its citation proclaimed Mobil "a company whose shoot-from-the-hip, gutsy 'idea' advertising has added a new dimension to corporate advertising during a period of unprecedented attacks by government, the media and consumer advocates, not only on the oil industry, but on American business in general." Warner told *Advertising Age* that although there was no way he could fully measure the effects of Mobil's effort, "I do know that if we hadn't done it, we would have left all the media to our critics. And I have to assume we'd be worse off today." In the article, Warner once again made clear the importance of sponsorship of *Masterpiece Theatre* on PBS to Mobil's corporate and political aims.

Warner said Schmertz "was able to sell me and others on it [*Masterpiece Theatre*] because he was producing quality TV at a cost that was so low and so attractive and which we'd have had trouble in not buying. . . . I think there was a very valid rationale for his suggestion that we do. Since we were going with our 'op-ed' ads to a very sophisticated and reasonably small audience, it was felt that if we could show the audience we were willing to produce for their benefit good entertainment and, at the same time reach them on the op-ed page, they would be a more receptive audience because these two things are fairly compatible and conceivably synergistic."[41] In other words, the people who would read the op-ed advertising would be more likely to believe what Mobil said once they knew Mobil was sponsoring *Masterpiece Theatre*. The television program would create good will which would make for a more understanding and receptive reading public.

The *Wall Street Journal* agreed with Warner's assessment of the impact of *Masterpiece Theatre*. Writer Michael J. Connor, in an article subtitled "Is It Brainwashing Public?" commented on the way the PBS series softened up public opinion for the advocacy advertising in the *New York Times*. "Presumably, the opinion leaders who should read Mobil's ads are among those who watch Mobil's commercial TV specials . . . and the Mobil-underwritten public-TV series—including *Masterpiece Theatre*."[42] There was other favorable publicity from underwriting PBS. ABC's often critical news magazine show, *20/20,* complimented Mobil's support of public television, singling out *Masterpiece Theatre* for bringing "the best in British drama" to American audiences. The broadcast said the corporation had "hitched its image to high-class television."[43]

Masterpiece Theatre was only one part of the consistent publicity profile, Schmertz's "mosaic," that Mobil was putting forward. The oil company's official report summed up the picture it wanted to project of its corporate personality as follows:

- Reasoning, intellectual, sensible, and attractive to many intelligent people.
- Demonstrating a well-defined economic philosophy, and a thoroughly expert awareness of our business and the world's energy realities.
- Showing social concern and sensitivity to environmental issues.
- Concerned with culture and other institutions of our broad society.
- Not just blindly trying to make a profit at any and all cost— damn the consequences—but certainly not operating to be loved.

- Willing and able to defend ourselves against misunderstandings or attacks, whether from malevolence or simple ignorance.
- And successful in presenting our belief in abundant energy and economic growth as the way to solve social problems.[44]

Frank Marshall was aware of the corporate image Mobil was seeking to portray when he recommended specific television programs for them to sponsor. He said he kept it in mind when he helped design the *Masterpiece Theatre* concept. Marshall said his view was that "any corporation is a direct reflection of its leadership. The people at Xerox felt that they wanted to be a socially conscious, socially responsible corporation, and it was only natural that they are not going to sponsor a golf tournament. Anybody can sponsor a golf tournament. . . . Now Mobil . . . was a totally different situation, where its management—and a very bright management—just wanted to separate themselves from the standard image of Big Oil, and to start dealing with its public policy issues and questions in a different manner, and wanted to build some credibility in the public mind, in the sense of not being this great gray corporation who never did anything for anybody—which was not a true image anyway. So *Masterpiece Theatre* helped give Mobil credibility in the realm of public opinion when they had something to say. I think it served its purpose very well."[45]

In its own internal study of the impact of its public relations campaign, Mobil agreed with Marshall that its effort was effective in matching the company's public image goals. As a result of sponsoring *Masterpiece Theatre,* and other efforts, Mobil was perceived as a good corporate citizen. The report concluded, "the nation may not always agree, but it definitely does respect our opinions." In summary:

- Mobil's image has greatly improved since the sixties among the general public and with key target groups, including journalists and government officials.
- Mobil is now recognized as an outspoken, highly responsible company with a high level of visibility and, very importantly, high credibility.
- Mobil has succeeded in reaching and influencing opinion leaders.
- Mobil has sparked public debate on many issues important to us.
- And Mobil has provided the public with an alternative source of information on major national issues.[46]

There was another dimension to Mobil's efforts. William L. Rivers and Wilbur Schramm point out that advertising support, because it creates a financial link, is a form of control over the media itself, despite claims of separation between editorial and advertising concerns. By purchasing ads in the *New York Times,* as well as sponsoring programs on PBS, Mobil was engaged in what Rivers and Schramm call "manipulation." They quote one television personality as saying "I know better than to make comments that offend advertisers." They conclude, "Only the most conscientious efforts imaginable and constant vigilance can ensure that the modern information system will not become hostage to the pressures, large and small, of money and profit."[47] If indeed Schmertz's public relations campaign was a form of manipulation, it was a successful one. Mobil's year-round presence on PBS was seen by contemporary observers as a major contribution towards a changed climate of opinion towards the oil company.

Mobil's place on public television was also significant in light of the corporation's running battle with the commercial networks, some of whom refused to run Mobil's advocacy advertising presenting the corporate point of view on energy policy. For example, while Mobil was placing fifty-two weeks of programming on *Masterpiece Theatre,* it was effectively banned from putting forth its corporate perspective regarding the causes of the energy crisis on CBS. This rejection was a sore point noted repeatedly in the Mobil study. In a speech to the 42nd annual convention of the Edison Electric Institute in New York, Mobil's chairman, Rawleigh Warner, complained that this problem was "the biggest roadblock we have encountered—the refusal of national television networks to sell us time in which to state our viewpoint on matters of great public import . . . as a result we have a very difficult communications problem, and we recognized that." In this same speech, Warner quoted from a rejection letter written by CBS stating, "it is the general policy of CBS to sell time only for the promotion of goods and services, not for the presentation of points of view on controversial issues of public importance."[48] By supporting *Masterpiece Theatre,* Mobil was very subtly finding an alternative way to promote a positive image of itself, in an alternate venue, free of network control.

PBS was only one of the public relations choices that Mobil was exploring as an alternative to the television networks. On PBS,

Masterpiece Theatre represented merely a single strand of Mobil's diverse media efforts. Simultaneously, Mobil was producing and distributing its own filmed news reports on the oil business. These clips, running about a minute and a half each, were syndicated to approximately one hundred commercial television stations around the country.[49] In addition, Mobil soon established the syndicated *Mobil Showcase Network,* presenting entertainment during prime-time to network affiliates. The affiliates would often preempt the network feed for Mobil's programming, depriving the networks of advertising revenues and giving Mobil the added satisfaction of "causing the networks pain."[50] The chain of stations making up the *Mobil Showcase Network* consisted of many of the same stations that eventually became the Fox network. Pete Spina of Mobil gives Schmertz credit for demonstrating that an alternative television network was possible.[51] As mentioned in the previous chapter, in October 1974 a full-page advertisement in the *New York Times* with the title *The Mobil Season* called attention to the range of Mobil's television programming on network, independent stations, and PBS.[52]

In 1978, Rawleigh Warner received the Columbia University Business School Alumni Association Award. He took the opportunity to once again talk about the development of Mobil's corporate personality. And he gave central importance to *Masterpiece Theatre* as the expression of Mobil's essence. In his speech, he outlined the reasons Mobil was "a good citizen, in every sense of the word, in the communities in which it operates."[53] Citing numerous good works, Warner concluded with the observation that "the cultural activity with which we seem to be most closely identified among the populace is our support of public broadcasting— most particularly *Masterpiece Theatre.* . . . In this connection I might mention that Mobil has from the outset of this effort been committed to building and strengthening public television. As I think the record will show, we have sought not only to underwrite programs of the first order of quality, such as *Upstairs, Downstairs,* but also to utilize our own corporate resources and skills to build a wider audience for public broadcasting. The promotion we put behind such series supports public television as an institution, and, we think, increases contributions to that medium from other sources, including individuals."[54] Here was a somewhat veiled reference to the work of Frank Marshall, Frank and Arlene Goodman, as well as to the history of how Mobil placed *Upstairs, Downstairs* on PBS despite the opposition of the station and system executives. By building up support and viewership for public television, Mobil was causing a simultaneous loss of support and viewership—small, but significant—for the competing commercial networks. Every television household tuned into PBS was a lower Nielsen rating for the competition on Sunday night. With PBS attracting one of the most desirable target demographics, that of affluent educated viewers, it was sure to hurt the public prestige of the networks as well. As Charles Paul Freund wrote in the *Washington Post,* "American intellectuals and cultural elite were once part of the audience the networks sought to serve. The networks once actually ran such highbrow programs as cinema verite documentaries and such series as *The Saga of Western Man* in prime time. With the establishment of PBS in the 1960s, the networks shrugged off that audience, thus marginalizing it in its own media ghetto. The access of intellectuals to the broader culture has since shrunk."[55]

As *Masterpiece Theatre* raised the reputation of PBS, it reduced the status of network television by contrast. With lowered reputations for quality, the commercial networks were not in as strong a position to resist the inroads of the independent stations, syndicators, and cable, for example. They may not have had as favorable a hearing from government bodies since losing their public service programming to PBS. There was, therefore, a synergy between the goal of creating a positive public image of "good works" for Mobil, and the corporate objectives Mobil had in breaking what Warner had described as a network "monopoly," one that refused to air Mobil's advocacy commercials. Warner referred to this goal in the conclusion of his Columbia University address when he noted, "We believe our outspoken support of the American system of democratic capitalism is all of a piece with our support of higher education and cultural programs. I am convinced that if our economic system is destroyed or fatally weakened by the relatively small but highly articulate elitists who seem bent on doing just that, whether from ignorance or for whatever reason, then our democratic society and our cultural institutions—including higher education—will be imperiled."[56] One might hypothesize that, in drawing a connection between the fate of business and the fate of cultural institutions, Warner was seeking to cement an alliance of commerce and civilization against leftist advocacy groups hostile to business and their publicists in the mass media. Mobil was seeking, in this view, to split cultural elites from policy elites and forge a new coalition on both the highest and broadest levels of American society. One key element in forming this alliance was *Masterpiece Theatre* and its appeal to the PBS audience.

Mobil's internal survey of the motivations for its public relations activities (including sponsorship of *Masterpiece Theatre*) gives some credence to this hypothesis. According to the corporation, in 1970 Mobil became convinced that corporate public relations would be a crucial factor in future development for the entire American oil industry. They characterized the negative publicity surrounding the Santa Barbara oil spill as creating "a bad year for the U.S. petroleum industry." The fallout from the "public and media reaction" included a slowdown in the granting of federal leases for offshore drilling, a tax reform that killed the percentage depletion tax allowance for oil, regulatory and court actions to block the construction of the Alaska pipeline, the imposition of environmental impact statements and proceedings required by them, licensing difficulties for nuclear power plants, and amendments to the Clean Air Act with the stage set for the switch to lead-free gasoline. In Mobil's opinion, the financial consequences of a negative public image were severe.[57] A bad press was directly costing the corporation money.

In 1971, things went from bad to worse, in Mobil's view. The Nixon administration imposed price controls on the economy, limiting oil company profits just as OPEC was being formed. That same year, the Teheran and Tripoli agreements raised prices by 25 percent. From 1972 to 1973, spot shortages developed in natural gas deliveries, caused, in Mobil's opinion, by the price differential between regulated interstate and decontrolled intrastate pricing. By 1973, Libya had nationalized its oil industry and OPEC had raised prices once again. The Nixon administration imposed new price controls on domestic oil while replacing previous import ceilings with a fee on imported oil. Mobil concluded that by 1973 "national energy policy was in total disarray and largely counterproductive . . . the public, government, and the media did not have the basic understanding to interpret what was happening and what would be happening."[58]

Mobil's lack of credibility because of the poor public image of oil companies was seen by the company as a major obstacle to the achievement of corporate goals. Mobil met these circumstances with a plan to promote its viewpoint through advertising on the op-ed page of the *New York Times,* because the corporation felt unable to get its views on the coming energy crunch across in conventional newspaper reporting, due to the hostile climate of opinion. The official account reads: "Lack of understanding of energy issues was made worse by the overall hostile attitude of the media to business in general and oil companies in particular."[59] The use of op-ed advertising was "a way that would assure control of the context of the message." At the same time as the op-ed program began, Mobil "also made the decision to provide large-scale funding for quality programs on public television, starting with a $1 million contribution [for both *Sesame Street* and *Masterpiece Theatre,* at that time the largest grant from any company] and providing a new dimension of quality on the airwaves. These two efforts worked together: op-ed ads were sometimes used to promote television programs . . . and the television programs created a climate of greater receptivity for the op-eds."[60]

The first Mobil ad appeared in the *New York Times* on October 19, 1970. It called for the expansion of mass transit and a program of energy conservation—issues designed to appeal to liberal readers.[61] Two days later, on October 21, 1970, Mobil announced its $1 million contribution to public television. In return, the company received public testimonials from Joan Ganz Cooney, president of Children's Television Workshop, and John W. Macy Jr., president of the Corporation for Public Broadcasting. Cooney stated, "Mobil Oil Corporation, in underwriting the costs of printing and distributing some 5,000,000 free copies of the four issues [of *Sesame Street Magazine*] . . . has demonstrated a sense of community concern and social awareness in the finest sense of those qualities . . . we are very pleased and we are very grateful to Mobil for their important contribution. We also share and admire their optimism for the youth of America."[62]

Macy, accepting on behalf of WGBH as well as CPB, expanded on Cooney's theme. He said, "The American viewing public is the beneficiary of this splendid contribution of the Mobil Oil Corporation. . . . The leadership of Mobil is to be commended for its decision which allows public broadcasting to dramatically increase its effectiveness. . . . Frankly, this grant will, in my opinion, give all of us in public broadcasting greater momentum. . . . I sincerely hope that this action by one of the world's largest industrial corporations . . . will spur continued involvement of the business community in support of public broadcasting's mission of providing programming for American audiences not available elsewhere."[63]

Mobil's Warner made clear the corporation's intention to link the programming to their corporate advertising. He noted, "We consider our participation in these two television projects more than simply a matter of providing funds. Both *Sesame Street* and *Masterpiece Theatre* hold considerable social value. . . . Of particular importance to Mobil, however, is the dimension we think we can add to these projects. What we plan to do is not merely to give money, but also to utilize some of our own corporate resources and skills in order to build a wider audience for public broadcasting. . . . For *Masterpiece Theatre,* we expect to do some national advertising, to work closely with the Public Broadcasting Service and Boston Station WGBH, and to engage in various promotional activities to support this program across the country. We hope we will be able to draw wide attention to what we believe are two superb television programs."[64]

Mobil's inaugural set of op-ed advertisements stressed the themes of mass transit, the need for an energy policy, the need for growth, the need for balancing environmental concerns against others, the need for conservation, and the value of capitalism as an economic system. "Our ads drew attention to the value of the free enterprise system in promoting economic growth. In a period of skepticism about business, we explained the role of profits in generating this growth."[65]

Janice Anderson has calculated that over the years Mobil ran some sixty-eight op-ed ads to publicize its television shows, forty-five of these for *Masterpiece Theatre* alone.[66] In the same space on the page, Mobil also dealt with foreign policy, advocating an "equitable" solution to the Arab-Israeli conflict. Although the ad drew a "huge volume of anti-Mobil mail," it also drew praise from Sheik Yamani, who conveyed the thanks of Saudi Arabia's King Faisal. Mobil was not alone in its suggestions for Middle East foreign policy. According to Daniel Yergin's history of the oil industry, Texaco, Chevron, and Exxon were also calling for a change in American foreign policy towards Israel and the Arabs.[67] Mobil characterized its mission as "reaching opinion leaders in government, the media, and elsewhere, as the key to changing public opinion as rapidly as possible."[68]

Erik Barnouw has described 1972 as a year of "collision" in public broadcasting, citing Nixon's veto of the CPB appropriation resulting in resignations and starvation budgets, and characterized the oil companies as the "rescuers" of the system, creating a permanent dependence on corporate underwriting. He points out how similar problems of "an image problem plus a glut of money" had given birth to DuPont's *Cavalcade of America* and Alcoa's *See It Now*. Barnouw notes that Mobil's *Masterpiece Theatre* and *Classic Theatre* were contemporaries of shows sponsored by Exxon, Gulf, and Arco, among others. He quotes a public television fundraiser who said, "We always tell ad agencies we are in the public relations business, not the advertising business, so we're not competing." But Barnouw's account differs from Mobil's in one important respect. He does not give Mobil the credit Mobil gives itself for planning and implementing its own public relations strategy. He writes, "Business corporations and their agencies were becoming a visible force in public television. They had not, in the first instance, sought this role. It had been virtually thrust upon them."[69] Barnouw paints Mobil as reactive, but it seems the evidence is to the contrary. Nothing was "thrusting" Mobil into public television except a corporate policy. Support for *Masterpiece Theatre* was a preemptive public relations strike. Herb Schmertz labeled the policy "affinity-of-purpose marketing."[70] Mobil chose to support public television because it wanted the "halo effect" such support would provide, and the corporation felt that *Masterpiece Theatre* would provide the biggest halo of all. Indeed, a rejected ad campaign for the series premiere announced "The Chairman of Mobil Oil is an Angel."[71]

It is apparent from the official history that Mobil actively sought out its role of benefactor to public television. Curiously, a Barnouw footnote quotes Schmertz as saying, "Our cultural broadcasting, like our institutional advertising in the *New York Times* and other newspapers, is designed to help us gain the understanding and support of important segments of the public." Barnouw's own reference contains the evidence that Mobil was a lot more considered, and a lot less passive, than the term "thrust" would imply.[72]

For example, at Carnegie-Mellon University in 1979, Warner discussed the amount of effort Mobil devoted to building up *Masterpiece Theatre*. He recalled, "We felt confident there were millions of Americans eager for the sort of fare proposed by public television—if only someone put enough muscle into advertising and promotion to reach them, to get them to test the water. We decided to do this even before we initiated *Masterpiece Theatre* at the beginning of 1971."[73] Warner pointed out in his speech that Mobil, in addition to advertising, used all the avenues of promotion the corporation had at its disposal, including 25,000 service stations, 200,000 shareholders, and several million credit card holders, employees, and retirees. He also noted in this same speech that Mobil arranged the cross-country publicity tours in the United States for the stars of *Upstairs, Downstairs*. He further pointed out that Mobil followed up on the success of the series with such educational shows as Jacob Bronowski's *The Ascent of Man* and Ben Wattenberg's *In Search of the Real America*. Warner also argued that Mobil's example had encouraged other companies to contribute to PBS. That is, Mobil had taken the initiative that created the phenomenon criticized as the "petroleum broadcasting system."[74]

At the time of its first PBS contribution, Mobil had felt the Nixon administration to be "sympathetic" to the oil industry, and described the atmosphere as one of "comparative calm" where even protests from church groups against operations in South Africa could be handled by "a special report to all stockholders on our operations in that country."[75] The relatively placid situation soon changed, due to the outbreak of the 1973 Arab-Israeli war and the ensuing oil embargo by OPEC.

With the start of hostilities on October 8, 1973, Arab oil producers closed off shipments to the United States, and OPEC increased prices by 70 percent and cut supplies by 10 percent. Mobil describes the oil shock as lasting until the lifting of the embargo in March 1974, and the effect of the embargo as doing "permanent damage to the credibility of the energy industries." The causes were to be found both in media and government, according to the corporation. Nixon's energy independence program, with the announced goal of eliminating imports by 1980, was seen as a major culprit. Mobil argued that price and allocation controls, lowered speed limits and canceling Sunday gasoline

sales, along with pressure on oil companies to husband invento-
ries, "exacerbated the hysteria and the shortage even though (in
retrospect) petroleum supplies would have been adequate for demand for that length of curtailment."[76]

Mobil's response, according to its report, was an advertising
campaign that explained some of the reasons for the gasoline
shortage, emphasized the need for profits, defended the industry
against the "obscene profits" charge (and the claim that Mobil was
cheating customers), and stressed additional conservation and increased production as a solution. It also ran a stream-of-con-
sciousness style ad entitled "Musings of an Oil Person" that expressed the dissatisfaction of the corporation with the commercial
networks. The ad gave Mobil's credo confronting its bad reputation through television (in a telegraphic style some might call
"Bush-speak"): "Much better to use TV to try to reach the millions
whose opinions about oil are swayed by what Cronkite, Chancellor, and Reasoner say every evening. Briefly! In thirty seconds
they can suggest enough wrongdoing that a year of full-page ex-
planations by us won't set straight. Hate to be on the defensive all
the time. . . . Speak out. Persuade them to listen. Never bore them.
If at first we don't succeed, bust a gut trying again. No other way.
Or we all end up working for the government."[77] One can hear Mobil's apprehension over the spectre of nationalization in the tone
of this ad. Perhaps the corporation had good reason to worry. Its
internal history notes some four thousand bills introduced in Congress between 1973 and 1974 "to break up, tax, and otherwise pe-
nalize the oil companies."[78]

Mobil found itself on the defensive against the Nixon administration, Congress, the media, and the public. Extremely galling to
the company was Senator Henry Jackson's public hearing in 1974,
where he called the heads of the seven largest oil companies in front
of his Permanent Subcommittee on Investigations "and insulted
them on national television, while labeling oil industry profits 'obscene.'" Daniel Yergin likened the event to Eugene O'Neill's play
A Moon for the Misbegotten, with Senator Jackson uttering the im-
mortal line "Down with All Tyrants! Goddamn Standard Oil!" and
proposing that oil companies be licensed and controlled by the federal government.[79]

Mobil's response was to reorganize its public affairs efforts and
coordinate media relations work with that of the American Petro-

leum Institute. Company executives were placed on television talk shows to "combat the negative image of the oil companies," and Mobil was openly proud of the part played by *Masterpiece Theatre* in this effort. The corporation's regard for the series is clear in Mobil's internal evaluation that, "On the cultural front, the highlight of this period was Mobil's introduction in January 1974 of the Bellamy family to the American public on *Upstairs, Downstairs,* perhaps the best remembered of all Mobil's television productions." The analysis notes that the series would add seven Emmys to Mobil's collection.[80] In 1975, Warner spelled out Mobil's strategy that, "it was not enough just to say the things we felt worthwhile, but to win a big enough audience that would read what we were saying."[81] That is, the credibility of the print advertising was enhanced by the prestige of the Mobil television presentations on *Masterpiece Theatre.* In a sense, the popularity of the Bellamy family helped keep Mobil out of the hands of the federal government.

Pete Spina recalls the sense of turmoil surrounding the Watergate period, noting, "Before Watergate you didn't need a massive lobbying effort with all kinds of grassroots help. The Ways and Means Committee of the House had no subcommittees." Spina said that old-fashioned lobbying had been personal. "You talked to the chairman of the House Ways and Means Committee, so what'd you do? Entirely different. You got close to [committee chairman] Wilbur Mills. Then came Watergate. Hundred new congressmen. One shot, a whole new breed came in. House Ways and Means Committee today is what, twenty-eight subcommittees? Or subsubcommittees? So the whole world has changed on you."[82] And in this changed world, Mobil's television efforts were more important than ever.

From Mobil's point of view, the four-year run of *Upstairs, Downstairs* coincided with the period "between crises" for the oil industry. Although supplies of oil were normal by March 1974, various administration programs resulted in additional fees and taxes on imported crude and refined products. Congress cut back special treatment for the industry. The foreign tax credit for oil companies was reduced, the depletion allowance eliminated for Mobil (but not for smaller producers). Mobil helped to defeat a bill to break up the oil companies introduced into the Senate in 1975. In 1976 and 1977 there was a natural gas shortage, and oil companies were accused of withholding supplies. Another unwelcome development, from Mobil's perspective, was the National Energy Plan introduced by the newly elected president, Jimmy Carter. This called for continued price controls on oil, increased taxes on oil, increased taxes on cars based on fuel efficiency, a tax on industrial oil users, and a standby gasoline tax. Then, in August 1977 the Department of Energy was created against the wishes of Mobil, which saw it as "a gigantic bureaucracy with many thousands of regulators." And Carter went further. "Adding insult to the NEP and DOE injuries, President Carter on October 13, 1977, accused oil companies of 'seeking to profiteer and grab money from the U.S. consumer.'" Mobil was especially unhappy that the Carter administration was emphasizing conservation at the expense of increased supply, and that it had failed to fill the Strategic Petroleum Reserve "despite two years of ample international supplies that would have permitted acquisition without disturbing the international market . . . the opportunity to take advantage of this breathing spell was lost."[83]

Mobil saw its biggest threat in the congressional moves to break up the big oil companies into separate exploration, producing, marketing, refining, and transportation companies. Corporation president William Tavoulareas had testified before the Church Committee on Multinational Corporations in 1974, and the Senate Judiciary Committee's Subcommittee on Antitrust and Monopoly in 1976. In 1974, "Tav" had opposed the efforts of Senators Church, Jackson, and others who were urging the formation of a national oil company, saying it "would be a hindrance rather than a help. . . . During the period prior to 1970 we had a surplus and we had a lack of political involvement. Today we have a lot of political involvement and we have a shortage. What we ought to be working toward is a better political atmosphere . . ."[84] Mobil, "Tav" said, recognized the importance of politics in determining the balance of supply and demand in the oil market.

Tavoulareas stated his position as, "We say that as a result of the political war and political events we had a boycott, therefore, we had a shortage."[85] Mobil was going into politics to get politics out of the oil business, in his view. Church Committee counsel Jerome Levinson disagreed, arguing rather that Mobil had "won nearly every objective they have sought in recent years. Either government or the marketplace has made possible one controversial development after another: approval of the Alaskan oil pipeline, rollback of environment timetables, etc. In what way has Mobil Oil Co. suffered as a consequence of this energy crisis?"[86] Levinson did not mention *Masterpiece Theatre*, but there can be little doubt that he was aware of the tremendous goodwill the series had generated for the corporation, goodwill that had paid off in protection from congressional attacks.

After attempts at nationalization had been defeated, Tavoulareas argued against those advocating the breakup of oil companies on grounds of antitrust legislation. In his 1976 testimony he said, "the ultimate question is whether divestiture would simply become the back door to nationalization of much of the oil industry. . . . Proponents of divestiture have produced no evidence that it would benefit the country."[87] Meanwhile, Mobil made "a strong public relations effort" to stop divestiture, mobilizing its ads, television appearances, news items, and to specifically rebut the Ford Foundation's energy study *A Time to Choose*, which attacked the oil industry. In addition to Mobil waging its most intensive public relations battle with the TV networks (who would not accept Mobil's advocacy commercials, as noted earlier), Mobil also began producing its own public service announcements, featuring "third-party commentators" speaking about oil issues. These were syndicated to 175 stations and supplied free by Mobil. Mobil continued to produce its own two-minute news clips for release to television journalists. Mobil produced spots that looked like news shows, "from the Mobil Information Center." Simultaneously, Mobil upgraded its "investor relations . . . taking the initiative to establish far greater personal contacts with key analysts and portfolio managers. . . . As a result Mobil is perceived as a company which keeps up its contacts with the investor community in both good times and bad."[88]

Mobil's official history argues the link between direct pressure on investors and Congress and the general climate of cultural opinion—in which *Masterpiece Theatre* figured prominently—when it states, "this heightened effort to get across Mobil's viewpoints on major issues was supported by a great expansion of the company's cultural programs. . . . Besides continuing to support *Masterpiece Theatre* and putting together an informal network to show quality drama on commercial television. . . . Mobil also increased sponsorship of art exhibits, catalogues, and community projects, in which Public Affairs wrote or produced backup art and culture ads and promotion. . . . These cultural activities were extended overseas with booklets and filmstrips designed to buttress Mobil's operations abroad. Thus in a period when Mobil was concerned with increasing its access to incremental supplies of Saudi Arabian crude oil, Mobil produced a major book, *The Genius of Arab Civilization,* which attracted much favorable attention in the Arab world."[89]

The Iranian crisis presented Mobil with its major Carter administration public relations challenge. By January of 1979, Iranian oil exports had fallen to nothing and gasoline lines soon began to form again at American filling stations. During the next year, prices of crude doubled. In 1980, Congress passed the Windfall Profits Tax, hurting Mobil's earnings. Mobil lobbied for, and received, a special tax incentive to increase its profitability. With this legislative favor, Mobil "parted company with the rest of the oil industry" and announced it would be willing "to forego decontrol of existing reserves beyond increases for inflation." One reason for the company's willingness to allow oil reserves to remain controlled might have been Mobil's reputation as a company long on brains and short on crude oil.[90]

Mobil had another problem. President Carter had singled out the company for a direct attack, a possible backfire of Schmertz's high profile for the company. The official history notes "while this might be considered a reverse tribute to our op-ed program, we had to correct the President's misstatements."[91] At the same time, Mobil went forward with its solution to the boycott of advocacy commercials by the networks. Schmertz expanded the Mobil Showcase Network, begun in 1974, with *The Magic Show.* Seven major series were syndicated from 1977 to 1980: *Ten Who Dared, When Havoc Struck, Between the Wars, The World of Magic, Minstrel Man, Edward the King,* and *Edward and Mrs. Simpson.*[92] Issue-oriented *Fable for Now* advertising accompanied the programs. They featured performances with growth and energy themes performed by, among others, the American Ballet Theater, the Pilobolus Dance Company, and mimes Shields & Yarnell. The dancers depicted squirrels, jungle animals, and mythical creatures faced with a shortage of nuts, grains, and other vital necessities. These were broadcast on fifty-four independent stations and network affiliates, reaching an estimated twenty-two million people. The official Mobil report comments, "these Mobil efforts to communicate our position in a new crisis were undergirded by cultural programs which continued to generate good will for the company."[93] That is to say, the corporate good will of the other efforts such as Mobil Showcase depended on the success, and credibility, of *Masterpiece Theatre*.

Despite the public attacks, Herb Schmertz enjoyed considerable personal access to the Carter White House, perhaps in part from Mobil's patronage of *Masterpiece Theatre* (and from Mobil having helped defray the expenses of President Carter's inauguration). Herb Schmertz would meet with Presidential Press Secretary Jody Powell as part of the Business Public Affairs Advisory Group, an informal association of fifteen corporate public relations executives put together by Frank Saunders, a Carter campaign worker who was director of corporate communications for Philip Morris, Inc. Members of this body paid for their own travel and lodging expenses, as well as a share of the cost of the White House dinner. After one such dinner, Powell wrote to Schmertz, "I think you and each member of the group should feel free to call me—as I hope I can feel free to call on you—for 'quickie' consultations on an ad hoc basis." Schmertz also had access to Carter aides Walter Wurfel, Greg Schneiders, and Anne Wexler.[94] Within the Carter administration, public confrontation with Mobil was matched by private consultation with Schmertz.

By 1981, Mobil reported that the world had moved into a period of a petroleum glut because of "price-induced conservation" and increased supplies from the North Sea and Mexico. President Reagan decontrolled the price of oil, and Mobil concentrated on foreign policy questions like the sale of AWACS to Saudi Arabia, relations with Mexico and Canada, and the struggle to maintain the foreign tax credit while staving off other proposed industry taxes. Mobil also fought losing takeover battles for Conoco and Marathon oil companies. On the television front, in the 1980s Mobil added *Mystery!* and *Life on Earth* to its offerings, to reach younger demographic groups.[95]

Mobil had carefully evaluated the effect of its efforts on the public sectors it targeted. The internal report claims success in reaching Mobil's prime target—the group they characterized as "opinion leaders," defined as "those people and institutions that influence the thoughts and actions of others." Mobil asserts that as a result of its media efforts, these elites "have changed their perceptions of national needs." Here Mobil sees the combination of print and television to be especially productive, perhaps because the audience for PBS also reads newspapers. "Our op-ed program and our support for *Masterpiece Theatre,* in particular, have enabled the company to become part of the 'collective unconscious' of the nation, as the changed views of opinion leaders have gradually molded general public opinion."[96] Again, Mobil's analysis explicitly ties *Masterpiece Theatre* to the op-ed campaign.

More specifically, Mobil's report subdivides the "opinion leaders" into different sectors. First, there are local, state, and federal government officials. The second group is the media, with print, radio, and television asserted to be "among the most influential opinion leaders." The third target are academics and members of think tanks, who "may eventually become part of a new national consensus." And the fourth sector are businessmen, church groups, consumer groups, and "others who have opposed business interests."[97]

Mobil claims success in affecting all of these, directly and indirectly, by tracing such factors as "credibility ratings." The oil company reports that "Mobil materials receive more direct attention from editorial writers, and that they are read, circulated, and used as reference sources." Further, in a Capitol Hill coup, the corporation succeeded in getting Senator Russell Long, chairman of the Senate Finance Committee, to distribute copies of a Mobil advertisement rebutting the Carter energy policy to every member of the Senate, *under his signature.* Finally, Mobil found it important to be noticed by the cartoonists, especially those of the *New Yorker,* "whose stock-in-trade is presenting humorously social and cultural developments of which the public is sometimes only dimly aware." These cartoons, Mobil argues, "attest to the extent of Mobil's impact by poking fun at our cultural programs and stances on the issues."[98]

Mobil found an indirect source of influence in the cultural arena when its public affairs executives, as a result of the success of *Masterpiece Theatre* and other projects, "have been called on to serve, in effect, as management consultants to other companies and organizations on how to run an effective advocacy or cultural campaign."[99] Mobil sees its influence in the academic community in the use of Mobil advertisements in textbooks, as well as "graduate students preparing theses and dissertations." The official history claims "an increased willingness to request and hear company speakers, indicates that Mobil is reaching this powerful set of opinion leaders—and future leaders—in a way unimaginable a decade ago."[100]

The oil company reprinted remarks from *Newsday*'s television columnist Marvin Kitman as evidence of its public relations success: "At the risk of being a sell-out, today I would like to thank the oil companies. As a special Thanksgiving 1977 tribute, I offer my thanks for past favors and future bounties. May the contributions multiply. I will be buying an extra cup of gas, driving the extra mile this holiday weekend in honor of the oil companies who gave. The Honor Roll (in order of contributions to American culture): 1. Mobil, 2. Exxon, 3. Arco, 4. Gulf, 5. Texaco."[101] Kitman's remarks, offered in jest, were received with great seriousness by Mobil, which appreciated the top ranking he gave the company.

Mobil's study also cites other favorable reviews of *Masterpiece Theatre* from the *Boston Globe,* the *Christian Science Monitor,* the *Washington Post,* and the *Dallas Times-Herald* to show how support of *Masterpiece Theatre* yields generally favorable press coverage of Mobil from newspapers normally critical of the oil industry in general.[102]

Such good will even affected news coverage of oil industry issues. Mobil's survey showed that the *New York Times,* over a ten-year span, "has altered or significantly softened its viewpoint to positions similar to Mobil's on at least seven key energy issues." The study noted Mobil's emergence as the leading spokesman for the oil industry.[103] Once more, op-ed advertising was working in coordination with *Masterpiece Theatre* to fulfill Mobil's corporate aims.

Mobil cites an independent 1977 survey as evidence for its improved public image. The results of the study examining the attitudes of the news media towards twenty-three companies by Opinion Research Corporation were based on interviews with 182 editors in all media. The poll ranked Mobil as the fifth most favorably viewed corporation in the United States, behind AT&T, Ford, Sears, and General Motors. It was the most favorably viewed oil company and received the highest credibility rating of any oil company. In order to quantify the corporate credibility, the poll

asked a specific question about Mobil's presentation of its side of
the divestiture issue. Thirty-five percent of the editors said Mobil
was the most credible in this case. The survey also did a demographic breakdown for Washington, DC, and New York editors.
Mobil was the most favorably rated with both groups. The ORC
study concluded that the oil industry had in fact improved its relations with the news media, and that Mobil's efforts had contributed
significantly to the entire sector's gain.[104]

In 1978, another survey was conducted by the American Petroleum Institute on behalf of Mobil. Fifty-two newspapers were contacted. Mobil was told that it was doing "the best job" in public relations. The editors read, circulated, and used Mobil materials.
Eleven of the editors reported that Mobil was their "main source
of information on the petroleum industry."[105]

In addition to print ads, Mobil had attempted to run the television equivalent of op-ed advertising on the commercial networks
(as mentioned earlier). These led to the 1974 formation of the Mobil Showcase Network. The creation of the network had been part
of the corporation's advocacy of a corporate "free speech" policy.
In 1974 Schmertz prepared a television spot with the following
text read over pictures of a seashore:

> Announcer's voice: According to the U.S. Geological Survey, there
> may be 60 billion barrels of oil or more beneath our continental
> shelves. Some people say we should be drilling for that oil and gas.
> Others say we shouldn't because of the possible environmental
> risks. We'd like to know what you think. Write Mobil Poll, Room
> 647, 150 East 42nd Street, NY 10017. We'd like to hear from you.

Although NBC accepted the ad, ABC and CBS refused to run it.
In response, Mobil ran a publicity campaign calling for the extension of First Amendment free-speech protection to corporations as
well as individuals, arguing for a right to media access. Mobil was
using the charge of censorship against the networks to encourage
a view of the corporation as victim. The landmark Supreme Court
decision in *Bellotti v. First National Bank of Boston* (1978) gave
some First Amendment protection to companies and was seen by
Mobil as a victory for its public relations efforts. Mobil's internal
report cites as evidence the American Management Association's

inviting a monograph from Herb Schmertz on the Bellotti case as public recognition of the corporation's role in creating the climate of opinion that made the Supreme Court decision possible. Mobil notes that the decision "opened entirely new vistas to the corporation engaged in such dialogue." Another example of Mobil's new found respect was the decision of CBS's *60 Minutes* to invite Schmertz as a panelist for a program on the role of the media. He was the only guest who was not a working journalist on the show, which aired in the 1981–82 season.

In 1980, Mobil commissioned the study, mentioned earlier, of the *New York Times* editorial positions over the last ten years. It found that the paper had come around to Mobil's point of view on issues of "conservation, monopoly and divestiture, decontrol, natural gas, coal, offshore drilling, and gasohol."[106]

In evaluating its impact on government officials, Mobil used the empirical test of legislation. The Mobil study points out that Senator Edward Kennedy's 1975 divestiture bill was defeated, as were 1976 and 1977 attempts. Mobil reports that in addition to promoting the corporation's viewpoint, Mobil's government relations staff also serves as a "meteorologist," tracking regulations and legislation. Mobil's Herb Schmertz worked as public relations man for the American Petroleum Institute, representing the entire industry. A study commissioned by Mobil found that between 1973 and 1977, two-thirds of government officials changed their view of oil companies from "unfavorable" to "favorable" and came to believe that the companies were the best source of information about energy issues. Among oil companies, Mobil was ranked highest.[107]

As Frank Marshall said, Mobil had sought to be differentiated from other oil companies in the public mind, while urging the country back on a course more friendly to business. Mobil's report confirms Marshall analysis. It says, "All of Mobil's communications activities—messages in the print media, our sponsorship of *Masterpiece Theatre*, special events of many kinds with which Mobil is associated, and other programs—have created a cumulative impact on the general public. We believe we have had some role in changing the nation's perception of the energy situation, and in steering popular sentiment toward a greater appreciation of the role of the free market in the nation's economy—changes reflected in the outcome of the 1980 presidential election."[108] In this statement, Mobil drew a connection between *Masterpiece Theatre* and the election of Ronald Reagan.

Mobil kept track of its impact on general public opinion through periodic surveys of *Parade* magazine readers. In regard to television, Mobil cites polling data that "have consistently shown that the company's advocacy advertising and sponsorship of *Masterpiece Theatre* have improved its image with the public, even during times when the oil industry has been viewed with general disfavor." In fact, the polls indicated that Mobil got credit for public television programs it did not sponsor, such as *Brideshead Revisited*. Mobil was also rated number one in polls for the "quality of the company's products and services."[109]

Mobil's analysis claims "While the public may not have been aware of it, Mobil's underwriting of *Masterpiece Theatre* on PBS has had a dual impact on television and its audience. First, the concept of the miniseries—a limited number of weeks devoted to a continuing drama—was pioneered by *Masterpiece Theatre* as illustrated by *Upstairs, Downstairs* or *I, Claudius*. There is good reason to believe that such commercial network miniseries successes as *Roots* and *Holocaust* were direct descendants of the Mobil-introduced technique [although *The Forsyte Saga* predates all of these shows]. Second, the substantial promotional effort behind Mobil's PBS presentations, especially *Masterpiece Theatre,* can safely be credited with educating the viewing public to the belief that public television is the natural habitat of quality dramatic and documentary programming. In summary, we have been able to demonstrate, on a continuing basis, that we have had a positive impact on public opinion in general."[110]

Mobil also studied its impact on investors. Mobil refers explicitly to the effect of *Masterpiece Theatre* in its *Annual Report* saying the series "is mentioned as a reason why some shareholders buy our stock."[111] The company commissioned a survey that found Mobil was ranked highly among stockbrokers and portfolio managers on issues of "believability," "social responsibility," and "trust." Eight percent of those surveyed specifically mentioned sponsorship of public television as a factor in making purchases of Mobil stock.[112]

Based on the success of the American public relations program, Mobil expanded its public relations efforts abroad, engaging in issue advertising in Britain, Norway, West Germany, New Zealand, and Canada, using cultural efforts such as the magazine *Pegasus* and sponsorship of art shows, films, and book series about Arab culture, Nigerian art, and other exploration-linked projects.[113] In fact, as a spin-off from the PBS series, the company started a *Mobil Masterpiece Theatre* television program on New Zealand's government-operated channel.[114]

In response to Mobil's prestige in the cultural arena, artists have attempted to influence Mobil through their creative work. Artist Hans Haacke's art comments ironically on the success of Mobil's public relations efforts. One of his works, entitled "Creating Consent" (1981), uses an oil drum with a television antenna, displaying the words "We spent $102 million last year in advertising. Mobil. We just want to be heard." Haacke also parodies the style of Mobil's op-ed advertising. A panel from "Upstairs at Mobil: Musings of a Shareholder" (1981) says, "One of Mobil's major assets is Herb Schmertz, our public relations genius and house philosopher. It was Herb who made Mobil a columnist of the *New York Times*. It was Herb who turned PBS into what our enemies call the Petroleum Broadcasting Service. And it was Herb who masterminded our entry into the art world. All this and more for little over $21 million annually. Herb's Democratic Party background and his connection with the Kennedy liberals we never saw before have been invaluable. He speaks their language and knows how to keep them off balance, even get their support."

Another panel says, "Mobil's public relations people make a killing through the support of the arts. Although our tax-deductible contributions are hardly equal to 0.1 percent of our profits, they have bought us extensive good will in the world of culture. More important, however, opinion leaders and politicians now listen to us when we speak out on taxes, government regulations, and crippling (sic) [in original] environmentalism. The secret for getting so much mileage out of a minimal investment is twofold: a developed sense for high visibility projects at low cost and well-funded campaigns to promote them. Mobil, in fact, ranks lowest among the 50 companies which give most in proportion to their pre-tax profits. Museums now hesitate to exhibit works which conflict with our views, and we need not cancel grants as we did at Columbia's Journalism School. The art world has earned our support. 'Art is energy in its most beautiful form!' Mobil makes my money grow!"[115]

Haacke's parody and Mobil's internal study agree with Schmertz on the effectiveness of the corporation's alliance with public television (and disagree with many scholarly accounts), though they differ in their attitude towards it. Both Haacke and Schmertz concur that in Mobil's public relations effort, "public broadcasting is the keystone." In another of his Mobil-inspired works, Haacke quotes from a Schmertz address claiming that *Masterpiece Theatre* "has helped us to achieve one of our major objectives—to make Mobil stand out as *different* [emphasis in original]. And in doing this, we have created an audience of opinion leaders who may be more disposed to listen to our viewpoint on energy issues."[116]

Haacke has injected Mobil's support of culture into the highbrow world of the international art discourse. For even by opposing Mobil, Haacke's work gives the oil company the very credibility and recognition it has sought through support of *Masterpiece Theatre*. As Herb Schmertz remarked, "Loving was not a consideration with us. Respect. Understanding. Being taken seriously. Participating in the dialogue. Those were the things that interested me."[117]

Notes

1. In a variation on this, Michael Mooney called it "the oil-can network." *The Ministry of Culture* (New York: Wyndham Books, 1980), 79.

2. Herb Schmertz, telephone interview, 11 September 1997.

3. Gregory Vitello, ed., *Twenty Seasons of Mobil Masterpiece Theatre, 1971–1991* (Fairfax: Mobil, 1991). In what is perhaps an effort to undo Herb Schmertz's highly public profile for the role of the company in the series, Rawleigh Warner's successor as chairman, Alan Murray, declared "much of the credit for *Masterpiece Theatre* must go to WGBH, Boston's public television station, which from the beginning has selected and packaged the programs for broadcasting. And certainly, special thanks go to Alistair Cooke, the series' urbane and inimitable host." (Vitello, 7).

4. Stanford Calderwood, memorandum to author, 27 January 1991.

5. Schmertz, personal interview.

6. Herb Schmertz, *Goodbye to the Low Profile* (Boston: Little, Brown, 1986), 210–12.

7. Peter Spina, personal interview, 17 April 1991.

8. William N. Greene, *Strategies of the Major Oil Companies* (Ann Arbor: UMI Research Press, 1982), 125.

9. Greene, *Strategies,* 140.
10. Greene, *Strategies,* 140–41.
11. *Current,* 24 June 1991.
12. Greene, *Strategies,* 154.
13. Greene, *Strategies,* 125.
14. Greene, *Strategies,* 143.
15. Janice Walker Anderson, *A Quantitative and Qualitative Analysis of Mobil's Advocacy Advertising in the New York Times,* Pennsylvania State University dissertation, 1984, 271.
16. Anderson, *A Quantitative and Qualitative Analysis,* 271.
17. Patricia Ann Davis, *A Description and Analysis of Mobil Oil Corporation Advertising on the Basis of Content and Context before, during, and after the Oil Crisis,* New York University dissertation, 1979, 348.
18. *Who's Who in America,* 1990.
19. Schmertz, *Goodbye to the Low Profile,* 22.
20. Schmertz, *Goodbye,* 22.
21. Rawleigh Warner Jr., "Excerpts from Remarks by Rawleigh Warner Jr., April 30, 1982," *Evolution of Mobil's Public Affairs Program: 1970–81* (New York: Mobil, 1981), 2.
22. ABC News, *20/20,* 12 February 1981.
23. Schmertz, *Goodbye,* 26–27.
24. Schmertz, *Goodbye,* 27.
25. Schmertz, *Goodbye,* 2–3.
26. Schmertz, *Goodbye,* 4.
27. Schmertz, *Goodbye,* 4.
28. Schmertz, *Goodbye,* 4.
29. Herb Schmertz, "Democracy, Tyranny, and Capitalism," in *Will Capitalism Survive?,* ed. Ernest W. Lefever (Washington, DC: Georgetown University Ethics and Public Policy Center, 1979), 17–21.
30. Mobil Corporation, *Evolution of Mobil's Public Affairs Programs* (New York: Mobil, 1982), 5.
31. Mobil Corporation, *Evolution,* 6.
32. Mobil Corporation, *Evolution,* 6–7.
33. Spina, personal interview.
34. Herbert Schiller, *Culture, Inc.* (New York: Oxford, 1989), 157.
35. Mobil Corporation, *Evolution,* 8.
36. Mobil Corporation, *Evolution,* 10.
37. Schiller, *Culture, Inc.,* 44.
38. Mobil Corporation, *Evolution,* i.
39. Mobil Corporation, *Evolution,* ii.
40. Mobil Corporation, *Evolution,* iii.
41. "Mobil's Rawleigh Warner is Adman of the Year," *Advertising Age,* 29 December 1975.
42. Michael J. Connor, "Arguing Back: Mobil's Advocacy Ads Lead

a Growing Trend, Draw Praise, Criticism: Firm, Like IBM and Others, Pushes Campaign to Tell Its Side of Controversies; Is It Brainwashing Public?" *Wall Street Journal,* 14 May 1975.

43. Tom Jarriel, *20/20,* 12 February 1981.

44. Mobil Corporation, *Evolution,* iv–v.

45. Frank Marshall, personal interview.

46. Mobil Corporation, *Evolution,* v.

47. William L. Rivers and William Schramm, *Responsibility in Mass Communication,* Third Edition (New York: Harper and Row, 1980), 105–41.

48. Mobil Corporation, *Evolution,* ix.

49. Mobil Corporation, *Evolution,* x.

50. Schmertz, telephone interview.

51. Spina, personal interview.

52. *New York Times,* 2 October 1974.

53. Mobil Corporation, *Evolution,* xi.

54. Mobil Corporation, *Evolution,* xi.

55. Charles Paul Freund, "Save the Networks! They May Be a Wasteland, but They're the Wasteland We Share," *Washington Post,* 28 July 1991.

56. Mobil Corporation, *Evolution,* xii.

57. Mobil Corporation, *Evolution,* I–A/2. Mobil had not faced any major public relations problems prior to the late 1960s. Indeed, until then the major issue had been that oil was becoming available too cheaply. New oil discoveries posed a threat to more expensive domestic crude, because of two-tier pricing policies. At the time, foreign oil accounted for only 20 percent of American supplies, and in the view of the corporation, the 1967 Arab-Israeli War was a successful demonstration that "America could protect itself and aid its allies when oil supplies were disrupted." ("Interpretative Chronology," I-A/1).

58. Mobil Corporation, *Evolution,* I-A/2-A/3.

59. Mobil Corporation, *Evolution,* I-A/3.

60. Mobil Corporation, *Evolution,* I-A/3-A/4.

61. Schmertz, personal interview. He notes, "People on the left went crazy over it, thought it was a terrible thing that we were espousing a liberal cause."

62. "Statement by Joan Ganz Cooney, president, Children's Television Workshop," press release, 20 October 1970.

63. "Remarks by John W. Macy Jr., president of Corporation for Public Broadcasting," press release, 21 October 1970.

64. "Remarks by Rawleigh Warner Jr., chairman of the board, Mobil Oil Corporation," press release, 21 October 1970.

65. Mobil Corporation, *Evolution,* I-A/6.

66. Anderson, *A Quantitative and Qualitative Analysis,* 73.

67. Daniel Yergin, *The Prize* (New York: Simon and Schuster, 1991), 596.

68. Yergin, *The Prize,* 596.

69. Erik Barnouw, *The Sponsor* (New York: Oxford University Press, 1978), 193.

70. Schmertz, *Goodbye,* 209.

71. Schmertz, *Goodbye,* 224.

72. Barnouw, *The Sponsor,* 193.

73. Rawleigh Warner and Leonard Silk, *Ideals in Collision: The Relationship between Business and the News Media* (New York: Carnegie-Mellon University Press, 1979), 34.

74. Warner and Silk, *Ideals in Collision,* 35.

75. Mobil Corporation, *Evolution,* I-A/7.

76. Mobil Corporation, *Evolution,* I-B/1-B/2.

77. *New York Times,* 28 February 1974.

78. *Evolution,* I-C/1.

79. Yergin, *The Prize,* 656.

80. Mobil Corporation, *Evolution,* I-B/2-B/3.

81. H. Lee Silberman, "Appeal to Reason," *Finance Magazine,* November, 1975.

82. Spina, personal interview.

83. Mobil Corporation, *Evolution,* I-C/2-C/6.

84. "Second Session on Multinational Petroleum Companies and Foreign Policy," Part 9, *Multinational Corporations and United States Foreign Policy,* 93rd Congress, 5 and 6 June, 25 July, and 12 August 1974 (Washington, DC: U.S. Government Printing Office, 1975), 87–88.

85. "Second Session on Multinational Petroleum," 91.

86. "Second Session on Multinational Petroleum," 109.

87. "Statement of William P. Tavoulareas," press release, 21 January 1976.

88. Mobil Corporation, *Evolution,* I-C/6-C/13.

89. Mobil Corporation, *Evolution,* I-C/13-C/14.

90. Mobil Corporation, *Evolution,* I-D/1-D/3.

91. Mobil Corporation, *Evolution,* I-D/5.

92. Marie Castillo, "Mobil Showcase Presentations," letter to author, 24 July 1991.

93. Mobil Corporation, *Evolution,* I-D/6.

94. Joseph L. Powell Jr., letter to Herb Schmertz, 22 November 1977, FG 1–3, Executive Files, Jimmy Carter Library, Atlanta, Georgia.

95. Mobil Corporation, *Evolution,* I-E/7.

96. Mobil Corporation, *Evolution,* II-A/1.

97. Mobil Corporation, *Evolution,* II-A/1.

98. Mobil Corporation, *Evolution,* II-A/2-A/3.

99. Mobil Corporation, *Evolution,* II-A/5.

100. Mobil Corporation, *Evolution,* II-A/5.

101. *Newsday,* 20 November 1977. Kitman later wrote amusingly about what the English watch on television in an article called "Mobilvision (The Sun Never Sets on *Dynasty*)." He remarked, "I had mixed feelings about the discovery that the upper classes of the U.K. and Europe were so into our soaps. Back home in New Jersey, I would have felt unpatriotic to admit this, a traitor to my class. Even worse, I was being disloyal to the company I keep, which is Mobil. . . . The sordid truth is that we probably watch more English television in New Jersey than they do in England. BBC-1 was broadcasting *The Towering Inferno* around Christmas time, and the announcer described it as "a masterpiece." Was this an attempt at sarcasm? Or were such shows *their* Masterpiece Theatre? Was it being introduced by Alistair Cooke? Could they understand Cooke's accent? Or did they get the stories un-Cooked? I liked to think—at first—that they watch *Dynasty* as comedy. No, they are very serious about it." Marvin Kitman, *I Am a VCR* (New York: Random House, 1988), 141–42.

102. Mobil Corporation, *Evolution,* II-A/Attachment 1d and 1e.

103. Mobil Corporation, *Evolution,* II-B/1.

104. Mobil Corporation, *Evolution,* II-B/5-B/6.

105. Mobil Corporation, *Evolution,* II-B/8-B/9.

106. Mobil Corporation, *Evolution,* II-B/11-B/14 and Attachments.

107. Mobil Corporation, *Evolution,* II-C/1-9.

108. Mobil Corporation, *Evolution,* II-D/1.

109. Mobil Corporation, *Evolution,* I-D/2-D/5.

110. Mobil Corporation, *Evolution,* II-D/7.

111. Mobil Corporation, *Mobil Annual Report: 1986* (New York: Mobil, 1986), 15.

112. Mobil Corporation, *Evolution,* II-E/1-E/10.

113. Mobil Corporation, *Evolution,* II-G/1-G/7.

114. Spina, personal interview.

115. Hans Haacke, *Upstairs at Mobil: Musings of a Shareholder, Creating Consent, Mobil: On The Right Track,* first exhibited at John Weber Gallery, New York, February 1981.

116. Haacke, *Upstairs at Mobil: Musings of a Shareholder, Creating Consent, Mobil: On The Right Track.*

117. Schmertz, personal interview.

7

Masterpiece Theatre and the Nixon Administration

He doesn't wear funny hats. The only time he was pictured dancing was at his daughter's wedding. You won't see a "beefcake" photo of him on a beach in a swarm of admirers, or a picture of him exhibiting a scar, or wearing a loud flowered shirt. He doesn't break out the bourbon at 5 o'clock and invite a bunch of the boys in for what is called in Washington "striking a blow for freedom."
— William Safire, memo to H. R. Haldeman

Although the United States has many able foreign service people, I have found in my travels to countries in which the British were influential that their diplomats have often been far more knowledgeable and better qualified than ours. I believe the American policymakers today can profit from actively seeking the advice of their European counterparts before making major decisions, rather than just "consulting" and informing them afterward. We must keep in mind that those who have the most power do not necessarily have the most experience, the best brains, the keenest insights, or the surest instincts.
— Richard Nixon, *Leaders*

When William Safire wrote the first set of these remarks for a 1971 White House memorandum called "The Nixon Style," it is doubtful he was considering its impact on public broadcasting policy. When Richard Nixon recorded his praise for British diplomacy, he probably was not thinking of English costume drama on public television. Yet it is clear from the history given in the preceding chapters that the PBS programming process was not insulated from either political or sponsor pressure, and that programming decisions were subject to influences other than solely the professional judgment of the PBS staff, including White House desires.

Therefore, it is my conclusion that *Masterpiece Theatre* is an enduring cultural artifact of the Nixon administration. In it are expressed, implicitly and explicitly, the values of the troubled commander-in-chief as he prepared America for a truly international presence in the world as the successor to the by-then bankrupt British Empire. If Jacqueline Kennedy's White House tour and Newton Minow's attack on the networks as a "vast wasteland" are to symbolize the relationship between the Kennedy administration and the television medium,[1] equally the Watergate hearings and *Masterpiece Theatre* will live on as Nixon's ambiguous and ambivalent televisual legacy. One need note only that both gavel-to-gavel coverage of Senator Sam Ervin's Watergate committee and *Masterpiece Theatre* were educational broadcasts presented on PBS.[2] Indeed, the Watergate coverage was funded by Nixon's old antagonist, the Ford Foundation.[3]

In Nixon's well-known hostility to public affairs programming on PBS, one can find a link not merely to self-interest, but also to his personal code of values. Nixon felt that education was an exposure to the classics, not to current events. He wrote, "When young people whose goal is political leadership ask me how they should prepare themselves, I never advise them to study political science. Rather, I advise them to immerse themselves in history, philosophy, literature—to seek to stretch their minds and expand their horizons. The nuts and bolts, whether of politics or of government, are best learned by experience. But the habits of reading, the disciplines of thinking, the techniques of rigorous analysis, the framework of values, the philosophical foundation—these are the things the would-be leader must absorb from the beginning of his educational process and must continue to absorb for the rest of his life."[4] Consistent with Nixon's educational philosophy, *Masterpiece Theatre* helped to educate the PBS audience for America's role of world leadership.

In addition to these circumstances there is direct evidence that *Masterpiece Theatre* was compatible with Nixon administration policy. It has been documented that the White House paid close attention to PBS and worked to eliminate from the system all programming of which it disapproved. By that measure, programming that survived on PBS must have been acceptable to the president. There were three interconnected Nixon administration goals for PBS:

1. End dependence on Ford Foundation money by seeking corporate support;
2. Replace National Educational Television (New York) with alternative production centers;
3. Make cultural and educational programming the franchise for the public broadcasting system, replacing public affairs shows.[5]

Masterpiece Theatre fit all three objectives perfectly.[6] As former White House aide Peter Flanigan, who was responsible for PBS policy, says, "Nixon believed that public funds should be used for things that were not being done in private television, but should not be used for things that were being done by private networks. Not news, which the networks did, but educational programs." Flanigan said this was a matter of principle to Nixon, who told him, "Peter, the government should not be competing against its own citizens."[7]

David M. Davis recalled, "The Nixon administration wanted to kill public television. When they installed Henry Loomis as the president of the Corporation for Public Broadcasting, I remember him coming into our Ford Foundation office and telling Fred Friendly and me that everything they did on public television should have shelf life. That is, you should be able to run it year after year. Which meant no public affairs. If you interpret that correctly. We later got access to all the White House memos . . . the fix was on. They were really going to do this thing. It should be educational television. Which means nobody watches."[8] As mentioned earlier, Nixon's opposition to public affairs programming was congruent with his belief in education based on classic literature and history. In his view, educational television should convey lessons from the past to the present generation.

Simultaneously, Nixon's telecommunications policy was promoting the establishment of cable television, independent stations as alternatives to the three networks (CBS, NBC, and ABC), and changes in the prime-time access rule (PTAR) to allow syndicated programming on network stations. The goal, as ABC founder Leonard Goldenson recalled, was "curbing network power."[9] Nixon was successful in all three areas.[10]

Masterpiece Theatre, therefore, fit into the Nixon administration's political "mosaic" as well as Mobil's. As David M. Davis points out, "That was the same time that Spiro Agnew was attacking the network news divisions . . . There was a meeting in the White House, one of our friends was there, where Nixon had brought in the heads of the groups, the television group ownerships . . . somebody brought up the question of, you know, these educational stations are beginning to get some audience, they're hurting us, locally. 'Cause you know, cost per thousand affects the rate card."[11] In other words, PBS was drawing viewers away from the networks.

It should be noted that Mobil was active as well, through its syndication efforts, in preempting network programming on affiliate stations. This was in conformity with Nixon administration goals. Time-Life, the BBC distributor through 1980, was a major investor in cable, and used English programming on its new services.[12] Such material benefited from the promotion and exposure provided by Mobil on PBS. And Mobil was certainly drawing viewers away from the networks to PBS when it promoted the original telecasts on *Masterpiece Theatre.*

PBS, with its use of *Masterpiece Theatre* during pledge week, was also promoting—in practice—the notion that television should be paid for by subscription rather than provided free through advertising. This type of subscription drive helped to create a climate of opinion favorable to the notion of cable television. As a result of its success with *Masterpiece Theatre,* WGBH Boston effectively replaced WNET as the largest single supplier of programs to the PBS network. A 1987–88 report noted that "WGBH supplied more prime-time hours to public television stations nationwide than any other program source—over 30 percent of the 8-to-11 P.M. PBS schedule."[13] And the fixed Sunday night slot meant that the highest sets-in-use period was reserved for Mobil and Alistair Cooke instead of, for example, the Ford Foundation and Fred Friendly.

This growth of WGBH can no doubt be traced to a November 4, 1969, White House memo from Peter Flanigan to the President, classified as "administratively confidential." It states, "I made it clear to [Frank] Pace [then chairman of the CPB] that the proposed $5 million increase in the funding for the Corporation was contingent upon the creation of new program production facilities to replace National Educational Television [NET] . . . I stated our position as being that government funding of CPB should not be used for the creation of anti-Administration programming or for the support of program-producing organizations which used other funds to create anti-Administration programs."[14]

The White House had a continuing interest in eliminating its antagonists from public television. An October 12, 1972, memo to the president in preparation for a meeting with then CPB chairman Thomas Curtis reads, "It is essential that they have a clear understanding of your goals for the public broadcasting system as soon as possible. In particular, they need to be informed of your strong desire to have the December meeting of the CPB take steps to eliminate public affairs programming from PBS activity."[15]

At a meeting early in his administration, Nixon had been told that the Ford Foundation was programming public television and he "was very anxious that this not be the case."[16] From 1974 to 1975 the Ford Foundation expenditures for support of public television dropped from $28,974,773 to $3,680,000.[17] By fiscal year 1989 only 4.8 percent of public television funds were provided by foundations.[18] Although the Ford Foundation says that it had always planned to reduce its funding independently of outside factors, it is a fair guess that the Foundation officers were aware of Nixon administration pressures. The support of alternative organizations by the Ford Foundation—the National Center for Public Affairs Television, to produce Watergate coverage, and the Station Program Cooperative, to distribute other programming to PBS stations—indicates that Ford found behind-the-scenes ways to produce programming, rather than the direct funding of PBS shows.[19]

Thus, the legacy of Nixon with regard to the role of *Masterpiece Theatre* is clear in all three respects:

1. Mobil and other corporations supplanted the Ford Foundation as major funders of public television programming;
2. WGBH replaced WNET as the largest production center in the PBS system;

3. Cultural and children's programming had become the priority of the PBS system. And cultural programming was historical and literary in emphasis.

It is not surprising that Larry Grossman, Hartford Gunn's successor as president of PBS from 1976–1984, says that broadcasting *Masterpiece Theatre* on the national schedule every year "was the easiest decision I had to make." Grossman, a former advertising man and NBC television executive who characterized the British dramas as "harmless fluff," explained the WGBH connection as natural, based on his perception that "the Boston Brahmins always had an affinity for British civilization." He further characterized *Masterpiece Theatre* as a "popular" series with "no controversy except for cleavage." This point was also made by the BBC's Mark Shivas, who said "there was a perception at a particular time, won't say anything about that now, but there was a perception that if it was going to offend anybody, then it wouldn't get onto *Masterpiece Theatre*."[20]

Grossman also pointed out that PBS benefited as a system from running *Masterpiece Theatre* because "Mobil took a lot of tune-in advertising." Grossman noted that, under the system that has evolved since *Masterpiece Theatre* joined the schedule, corporate funding could be used for cultural programming, freeing public funds to support documentaries and controversial programs.[21] However, what Grossman did not emphasize was that using public money for controversial programming gives the government leverage over the type and tone of the public affairs shows produced by public television.

What Nixon's actions had accomplished was the transformation of the public broadcasting system, in effect, into the structure of network television in the 1950s, where there were both "sponsored" and "sustaining" programs. Public affairs programs became the equivalent of sustaining shows, paid for by the Corporation for Public Broadcasting, PBS, or the local PBS stations, themselves recipients of CPB community service grants. Cultural shows have sponsors, called *underwriters* in the euphemistic language of public broadcasters (as they were called "subscribers" on the Ford Foundation program *Omnibus*). The history of *Masterpiece Theatre* is the story of how public television negotiated with the sponsors, local stations, and program suppliers to return a 1967 institution, PBS, to a 1950s-style television system. That is, *Masterpiece Theatre* is a restoration of a time when anthology drama, hosted by a celebrity, was routinely supplied by a sole sponsor for national broadcast as part of a corporate public relations campaign.

The British tend to think of the nostalgia element of the *Masterpiece Theatre* as part of their "heritage industry," the selling of bits of the British past to American consumers. That may be the case. But to an American audience there is a double nostalgia in *Masterpiece Theatre*. There is not only the nostalgia of the program content, with its detailing of life in the British Empire and the Edwardian Age, but also a more subtly propounded nostalgia for the America of the 1950s that is found in the very form of *Masterpiece Theatre*. The program is a traditional anthology drama hosted by a vintage 1950s celebrity, Alistair Cooke. And in this period, Nixon is inscribed both as a television personality and a politician. For the age of *Playhouse 90, GE Theatre, Armstrong Circle Theatre, Hallmark Hall of Fame, The U.S. Steel Hour,* and *Masterpiece Playhouse* was the age of Eisenhower's America, when Richard Nixon had a regular television role as vice president.

The connection between *Masterpiece Theatre* and the so-called golden age of television drama has been noted by *Boston Globe* critic Ed Siegel. In relation to the 1991 broadcast of *House of Cards,* he wrote: "In many ways, not all of them good, the profusion of banners such as these harks back to the '50s and early '60s, the so-called golden age of television, when single-advertiser programs were the rule rather than the exception. Sometimes they even went under banners such as *Kraft Mystery Theater* or *General Electric Theater* (with Ronald Reagan in the role of Alistair Cooke)."[22]

This link to the fifties was discussed by a roundtable of television producers put together by *Emmy* magazine in 1981. There, George Schaefer recounted producing *Macbeth,* which he called "the first television film ever made," for *Hallmark Hall of Fame* with British Lion Films in 1961. Pat Weaver recalled "a deal I made with Alexander Korda where, on *Producer's Showcase,* we got two movies made in England to show an American audience. One was with Rex Harrison and Kay Kendall, and the other was *Richard III* with [Sir Laurence] Olivier . . . the idea was that they would make certain kinds of movies over there, and, for really modest amounts of money that we would pay them because we couldn't really pay any big money then, they would gamble as an experiment. Now, Korda would do that."[23] This certainly sounds like Herb Schmertz talking about one of the reasons he sponsored English productions for *Masterpiece Theatre*.

Allen E. Murray, who followed Rawleigh Warner as chairman of Mobil, explicitly drew the connection between *Masterpiece Theatre, Studio One, Playhouse 90,* and the golden age of television in his foreword to a lavish coffee-table book the oil company published about the series.[24]

The return to the 1950s form of sponsored television anthology drama was perhaps the most significant aesthetic achievement of *Masterpiece Theatre*. For in so doing, no matter how feminist, working class, or even revolutionary the message of an individual show, the very format in which it would be presented defused any potentially explosive reaction from offended audiences or sponsors, for example, to the Marxist screenplays of Trevor Griffiths (*The Last Place on Earth*), whom British critic Edward Braun describes as a "socialist realist."[25]

In addition to the familiar format, the choice of Alistair Cooke as host played a similar role in reassuring the television audience. His personal presence served as an endorsement, and assured audiences that the dramas presented on *Masterpiece Theatre* were not offensive. In his distinctive way, Cooke filled the role of an intellectual bomb-disposal expert, much like the fictional characters on *Danger UXB*. Whether the subject was the revolt against imperialism in *The Jewel in the Crown,* Nazi S. S. atrocities in *Private Schulz,* or feminist revolution in *Shoulder to Shoulder,* Alistair Cooke was there to explain, patiently and calmly, that there was no cause for alarm.

The nostalgic and tranquilizing quality of *Masterpiece Theatre* fits in with the Nixon administration's agenda for confronting the radicalism it opposed. President Nixon's vision of his role in America was to "bring us together." As a White House memo notes, Nixon sought to portray "*A Dignified Man with a High Moral Purpose.* In an era of social permissiveness, the President is fighting to preserve the fundamental moral values and beliefs; he is successfully fighting the moral decay in our society. He will not tolerate permissiveness on crime and drugs; he is defending the country's old-fashioned virtues."[26]

In addition to fulfilling Nixon's domestic agenda, there was also, clearly, an international dimension to an Anglo-American series like *Masterpiece Theatre* that includes and also goes beyond the obvious connections to the Anglo-American heritage of the international oil industry, with its center at the London Policy Group described by Daniel Yergin. Oil and the British Empire were directly related. So too, oil was linked to America's new place in the world. As Yergin says: "The postwar petroleum order in the Middle East had been developed and sustained under American-British ascendancy . . . But Britain in the 1960s was a country preoccupied with its economic decline, which had combined with politics, both domestic and international, to make the liquidation of empire the central drama for Britain in the postwar world. Great Britain bowed out of the port city of Aden, at the southern tip of the Arabian peninsula . . . at the beginning of January 1968. . . . Prime Minister Harold Wilson announced the Britain would end its defense commitments east of Suez . . . The Amir of Bahrain was blunter. 'Britain could do with another Winston Churchill,' he said."[27] If one looks at the list of programs on *Masterpiece Theatre,* the theme of the British Empire and the role of Churchill loom very large indeed. There are clear parallels between the interest of the oil industry in these subjects, the interests of the Nixon administration, and the programs shown on *Masterpiece Theatre.*

As mentioned earlier, Nixon had for a long time expressed his feeling that America had much to learn from Great Britain. He had gone on record as early as 1958 as a defender of certain aspects of the British Raj. At that time, Nixon said, "The Free World is too often made to appear to be relying on our superior military power and economic strength. I know of no better example to illustrate the point I am trying to make than through an analysis of that much-maligned institution—British Colonialism . . . Colonialism has had its faults, but it has also had its virtues. I speak from some knowledge on this subject. I have visited twelve countries which at one time or another have passed through the status of British Colonialism. I have known personally and admired the dedicated and effective work of your superb colonial administrators. . . . Let us examine some of the benefits British colonial policy has produced. . . . It brought the military strength which provided the security from external attack. It brought in many areas the technical training which assured economic progress. But more

important than either of these, it brought the great ideas which provided the basis for progress in the future—ideas which will live on
for generations. . . . The common law, the English language, freedom of speech, assembly, press and religion—these are the institutions which are the proud legacy of the British people in lands
throughout the world. . . . May we, the English-speaking peoples,
proud in the heritage we share, join with the friends of freedom
everywhere and by our example save the cause of peace and freedom for the world."[28] By presenting the colonial period with nostalgia in its weekly dramas, *Masterpiece Theatre* helped to illustrate Nixon's point of view.

Herb Schmertz was also aware of the international ramifications
of changes in American commercial television since the 1950s.
With the decline of sponsor-supplied shows, there was a corre-
sponding decline in the image of corporate America. One point he
was particularly sensitive to was the portrayal of businessmen on
television. Many years after President Nixon had left office,
Schmertz arranged for Mobil to sponsor *Hollywood's Favorite
Heavy,* based on former Nixon speechwriter Ben Stein's book *The
View from Sunset Boulevard.* Schmertz says, "It was a piece that attacked the liberal persuasion of virtually all of Hollywood's producers. And if you go down the list of one show after another. . . .
when you start to look at it, every business person is a crook, is
fucking his neighbor, he'll steal anything that isn't nailed down. I
mean it's everything that's bad in society. You almost never see a
good business person doing anything socially redeeming in television during the period that I was watching. And I did a speech called
'The Balance of Trash,' which said, 'What do foreigners think
when they see all of these American shows on television? And what
kind of problems does that make for American foreign policy and
the American ambassadors in these countries, who are trying to
push themselves, the American philosophy, the American system
and all the rest, when everything they see about the American system in television says that it's rotten to the core and that the free
market system is simply a device for people to steal and commit
adultery and whatever?' And at the time I was on the President's
Advisory Commission on Public Diplomacy [Schmertz was appointed in 1983 by President Reagan], which is the oversight commission on the United States Information Agency, and here I'm
struggling on that commission with the problem, the USIA is talking

about the values of the American system with a minuscule budget, and here you see multimillion dollar television shows proliferating in every country around the world both in relatively free market places and also in nonfree market places, you say 'How does USIA stand a chance against *Dallas, Dynasty, Quincy* and all the rest of the shows that they're seeing?' I considered that a major foreign policy problem, and I simply tried to address it."[29]

In other words, PBS programming could compensate for the bias of the commercial networks against American business. It could be seen as a business equivalent of Nixon's declaration, "I am not a crook." And also, perhaps, direct relations between Mobil and foreign program suppliers, and the cash pipeline to produce British Empire nostalgia that was put in place, could help lubricate any friction these foreign broadcasters might feel towards the American corporations, and perhaps their own imperial pasts.

There was a larger international stake in *Masterpiece Theatre* than just the interests of Mobil or American corporations abroad. Until President Nixon assumed office, American relations with Britain were strained because of an English retreat from its role as an imperial power and British movement towards being part of a United Europe. That, and policy differences over Vietnam, created what Robert M. Hathaway calls "a more distant relationship" between the governments of the two nations during the Kennedy and Johnson years.[30] The newly elected president was determined to mend frayed transatlantic ties.

Nixon had met Sir Winston Churchill on several occasions. He writes about his encounters at length in his memoirs. He recalled vividly the tremendous personal impression Churchill made on him.[31] And on his initial trip to England (his first visit to any country after his election), President Nixon had tried to follow in Churchill's footsteps. At a dinner party given by Prime Minister Harold Wilson for the new British ambassador to the United States, John Freeman (later chairman of London Weekend Television, suppliers of *Upstairs, Downstairs* to *Masterpiece Theatre*), Nixon struck a conciliatory tone towards the former editor of the left-wing journal the *New Statesman*. Although Nixon still remembered that in 1962 the magazine had described his defeat by California Governor Pat Brown as "a victory of decency in public life," he took a dignified approach and proposed a toast to Freeman. President Nixon declared that the insult was a part of the past, and would be forgotten in the name of the Anglo-American special relationship. "After all," he concluded with a pun, "he's the new diplomat, and I'm the new statesman." Nixon cherished the note he received from Harold Wilson (later elevated to the House of Lords), and he quotes it in full in his memoirs. Prime Minister Wilson complimented Nixon on his sophistication and statesmanship, reading, "That was one of the kindest and most generous acts I have known in a quarter of a century in politics. Just proves my point. You can't guarantee being born a lord. It is possible—you've shown it—to be born a gentleman."[32] Apparently, Nixon appreciated not only the legacy of Churchill, the role of England in world affairs and diplomacy, but also valued the code of the English gentleman.

Nixon was inspired by British examples in his personal life as well as in politics. It is certain that Disraeli was one of his heroes. In his memoirs, Nixon notes reading Robert Blake's biography of the Victorian prime minister during his Watergate troubles.[33] He recorded, "I had been struck by Disraeli's description of Gladstone and his cabinet as 'exhausted volcanoes.' I announced that my second term would not suffer the same malady."[34]

When Nixon had arrived on English soil in February 1969, he delivered the following rather Churchillian address, revealing his sincere admiration for Britain's special relationship with the United States:

> In my travels abroad, going back over those 22 years when I first came here as a young congressman, I have had the opportunity not only to visit this country many times, but to visit every one of the countries of the Commonwealth, nations which—like the United States of America—share the language, the same great traditions that we in the United States share with the United Kingdom. I know the contribution, therefore, the contribution in ideals, the contribution in institutions, the contribution that has been made in so many respects by this nation around the world. . . . I know the wisdom that you and your colleagues can provide—wisdom which is essential for all of us as we attempt to find solutions. . . .
>
> Winston Churchill called ours a special relationship. He was not referring to legal obligations but to human intangibles. . . . And no two nations in the world more commonly and more closely share the means of communication than do the United States and the United Kingdom. We share a common language. We share the com-

mon law. We share the great institutions of the parliament. We share other institutions. Because we share those institutions we enjoy a means of communication which gives us a special relationship.

And so we shall strive on this visit and many others that we shall have over the years I will be in office; we shall strive for a mutual trust between our nation and other nations, the kind of trust that already exists between your nation and mine.[35]

The Churchillian language conveyed a Churchillian message. Nixon had called Winston Churchill "the largest human being of our time" and found his life an inspiration.[36] His book *Leaders* was modeled on Churchill's *Great Contemporaries*. During the ups and downs of his own career, Nixon often identified with Churchill as an example of the leader "in the political wilderness."[37] And Nixon clearly believed in Churchill's model for relations between Great Britain and the United States.

It is in this Churchillian regard—the sharing of a heritage, the sharing of institutions, and the sharing of a means of communication stressed by Nixon in the previous speech—that one can conclude: the politics of quality television as exemplified in Mobil's *Masterpiece Theatre* on PBS were the politics, foreign and domestic, of the administration of Richard Milhous Nixon.

Notes

1. For a history of Kennedy and television, see Mary Ann Watson, *The Expanding Vista: American Television in the Kennedy Years* (New York: Oxford University Press, 1990).

2. Erik Barnouw, *Tube of Plenty* (New York: Oxford University Press, 1982), 454–59.

3. Ford Foundation, *Ford Foundation Activities in Noncommercial Broadcasting: 1951–1976* (New York: Ford Foundation, 1976), 16.

4. Richard Nixon, *Leaders* (New York: Touchstone, 1990), 338.

5. John Witherspoon and Roselle Kovitz, *The History of Public Broadcasting,* eds. J. J. Yore and Richard Barbieri (Washington, DC: Current, 1987).

6. National Association of Educational Broadcasters, *The Nixon Administration Public Broadcasting Papers: A Summary, 1969–1974* (Washington, DC: NAEB, 1979).

7. Peter Flanigan, telephone interview, 11 March 1991.

8. David M. Davis, personal interview.

9. Leonard H. Goldenson, *Beating the Odds* (New York: Scribner's, 1991), 339.

10. H. R. Haldeman, "Memorandum for the File. Subject: Broadcasting Policy and Network Power," n.d., Nixon Presidential Papers, NARAS, Washington, DC.

11. Davis, personal interview.

12. George Mair, *Inside HBO: The Billion Dollar War between HBO, Hollywood, and the Home Video Revolution* (New York: Dodd, Mead, 1988), 33. Mair notes, "Also going on at the Time-Life Building in the spring of 1980 was the beginning of another cable network, which was to be known as 'BBC in America.'"

13. WGBH, *1987–88 Annual Report* (Boston: WGBH, 1988), 4.

14. Peter M. Flanigan, "Memorandum to the President," 4 November 1969, Nixon Presidential Papers, NARAS, Washington, DC.

15. Peter M. Flanigan, Schedule Proposal, "Meeting . . . to discuss the future direction and role for the Corporation for Public Broadcasting," 12 October 1972, Nixon Presidential Papers, NARAS, Washington, DC.

16. Peter M. Flanigan, "Memorandum for the President's File," 27 October 1969, Nixon Presidential Papers, NARAS, Washington, DC.

17. Ford Foundation, *Activities in Noncommercial Broadcasting: 1951–76* (New York: Ford Foundation, 1976), 23.

18. Public Broadcasting Service, *Facts about PBS* (Alexandria, VA: PBS, February 1991), 6.

19. Ford Foundation, *Activities in Noncommercial Broadcasting.*

20. Mark Shivas, personal interview.

21. Lawrence Grossman, telephone interview, 6 May 1991.

22. Ed Siegel, "'Quality' and the Single Sponsor," *Boston Globe,* 31 March 1991.

23. "Roundtable: Art to Business: TV Then, TV Now," *Emmy,* Summer 1981. For more on *Hallmark Hall of Fame,* see Ernest Roderick Deihl, "George Schaefer and the *Hallmark Hall of Fame:* A Study of the Producer-Director of a Live Television Drama Series," Ohio State University dissertation, 1964.

24. Greg Vitello, ed., *Twenty Seasons of Mobil Masterpiece Theatre: 1971–91* (Fairfax, VA: Mobil, 1991), 7.

25. Edward Braun, "Trevor Griffiths," *British Television Drama,* ed. George W. Brandt (Cambridge: Cambridge University Press, 1981), 79. The description reads, "socialist realist, that is, in the broad tradition of Gorky, O'Casey, Sholokhov, Steinbeck, and Brecht, aiming, as Lukacs says, 'to describe the forces working towards socialism *from the inside* [original emphasis] . . . to locate those human qualities which make for the creation of a new social order.'"

26. Charles Colson, "Presidential Image," memo to H. R. Haldeman, 6 July 1972, Nixon Presidential Papers, NARAS, Washington, DC.

27. Daniel Yergin, *The Prize* (New York: Simon and Schuster, 1991), 565.

28. Richard Nixon, "Text of Address of the Vice President of the United States of America Before the English-Speaking Union of the Commonwealth. 26 November 1958, Guildhall, London, England." *Six Crises* (New York: Touchstone, 1990), 429–33.

29. Schmertz, personal interview, 46.

30. Robert M. Hathaway, *Great Britain and the United States: Special Relations Since World War II* (Boston: Twayne, 1990), 74–117.

31. Richard Nixon, *RN: The Memoirs of Richard Nixon* (New York: Grosset and Dunlap, 1978), 153–59.

32. Nixon, *RN,* 371.

33. Nixon, *RN,* 681.

34. Nixon, *RN,* 768–89.

35. Richard Nixon, "Exchange of Remarks of the President and Prime Minister Wilson at the President's Arrival Heathrow Airport," Office of the White House Press Secretary, London, 24 February 1969, Nixon Presidential Papers, NARAS, Washington, DC.

36. Nixon, *Leaders,* 7.

37. Nixon, *Leaders,* xii.

Bibliography

ABC News. *20/20.* 12 February 1981.

Abramson, Albert. *The History of Television, 1880–1941.* Jefferson, NC: McFarland, 1987.

Ackerley, J. R. Letter to Alistair Cooke. 9 July 1931. BBC Written Archives Center, Caversham.

Adam, Christina. "Great Shows: *Omnibus.*" *Emmy,* October 1979.

Adam, Kenneth. "Kenneth Adam's View: British Is Best on U.S. Screens." *Evening News,* 13 December 1969.

Aleinikoff, Eugene. Letter to Richard Barovick, Esq., with attached agreement between WGBH Educational Foundation and Time-Life. 11 June 1971. Photocopy in author's collection.

"Alistair Cooke Sends BBC 1000th Letter on U.S." *New York Times,* 27 March 1968.

Allen, H. C. *Great Britain and the United States, 1783–1952.* London: Odhams, 1954.

Alvarado, Manuel and John Stewart. *Made for Television: Euston Films Limited.* London: BFI, 1985.

Amory, Cleveland. *The Proper Bostonians.* New York: Dutton, 1947.

Anderson, Janice Walker. *A Quantitative and Qualitative Analysis of Mobil's Advocacy Advertising in the New York Times.* Penn State University dissertation, 1984.

Anderson, Susan Heller. "Washington Sings 'Happy Birthday' to *Masterpiece Theatre.*" *New York Times,* 16 January 1991.

Angier, Jeanie. WGBH. Memo to author. 11 March 1991. Photocopy in author's collection.

Annan, Lord. *Evidence to the Committee on the Future of Broadcasting under the Chairmanship of Lord Annan.* London: IBA, 1974.

———. *The Politics of a Broadcasting Enquiry: The 1981 Ulster Television Lecture.* Belfast: Queen's University of Belfast, 1981.

Armes, Roy. *A Critical History of British Cinema.* New York: Oxford University Press, 1978.

Arnore, Robert F., ed. *Philanthropy and Cultural Imperialism: The Foundations at Home and Abroad.* Boston: G. K. Hall, 1980.

Aronson, Steven M. L. *Hype.* New York: Morrow, 1983.

Aufderheide, Patricia. "Public Television and the Public." Unpublished manuscript, 1991.

Bakewell, Joan and Nicholas Garnham. *The New Priesthood: British Television Today.* London: Allen Lane, 1970.

Baltzell, Digby. *Puritan Boston and Quaker Philadelphia.* New York: Free Press, 1979.

———. *The Protestant Establishment.* New Haven: Yale University Press, 1987.

Barnes, Harvey Elmer. *World Politics in Modern Civilization.* New York: Knopf, 1930.

Barnouw, Erik. *A Tower in Babel. A History of Broadcasting in the U.S.* (first of three vols.) New York: Oxford University Press, 1970.

———. *The Golden Web. A History of Broadcasting in the U.S.* (second of three vols.) New York: Oxford University Press, 1970.

———. *The Image Empire. A History of Broadcasting in the U.S.* (third of three vols.) New York: Oxford University Press, 1970.

———. *The Sponsor.* New York: Oxford University Press, 1978.

———. *Tube of Plenty.* New York: Oxford University Press, 1982.

BBC. *Annual Report and Handbook.* London: BBC, 1990.

———. D. S. W.'s office. Agenda: National Association of Educational Broadcasters, Visit to the United Kingdom, 8–18 September, 1952. E1/194 NAEB Visit May–August 1952. BBC Written Archives Center, Caversham.

———. Educational Television in the U.S. E1/1555 American Intelligence Bulletins. BBC Written Archives Center, Caversham.

———. *Guide to the BBC: 1990.* London: BBC, 1990.

———. North American Representative. Files, 1948–60. BBC Written Archives Center, Caversham.

———. TV: Foreign Countries. USA TV Development. Files, 1948–60. T8/88. BBC Written Archives Center, Caversham.

Bedell, Sally. *Up the Tube: Primetime TV and the Silverman Years.* New York: Viking, 1981.

Bell, Coral. "The Special Relationship." *Constraints and Adjustments in British Foreign Policy.* Ed. Michael Leifer. London: George Allen and Unwin, 1972.

Beloff, Max. "The Special Relationship: An Anglo-American Myth." *A Century of Conflict, 1850–1950.* Ed. Martin Gilbert. London: Hamish Hamilton, 1966.

Belson, William. *The Impact of Television.* London: Crosby, Lockwood, and Son, 1967.

Berlin, Isaiah. *Washington Despatches: 1941–45*. Chicago: University of Chicago Press, 1981.

Billington, Michael. "One of the Jewels in TV's 'Crown.' " *New York Times*, 23 December 1984.

Biryukov, N. S. *Television in the West and Its Doctrines*. Moscow: Progress, 1981.

Black, Peter. *The Mirror in the Corner: People's Television*. London: Hutchinson, 1972.

Blum, Daniel. *A Pictorial History of Television*. Philadelphia: Chilton, 1959.

Boman-Behram, B. K. *Educational Controversies in India: The Cultural Conquest of India under British Imperialism*. Bombay: DB Tavaporevala, 1943.

Bourdieu, Pierre. *Distinction: A Social Critique of the Judgement of Taste*. Trans. Richard Nice. Cambridge, MA: Harvard University Press, 1984.

————. *Homo Academicus*. Stanford: Stanford University Press, 1988.

————. *In Other Words: Essays Towards a Reflexive Sociology*. Trans. Matthew Adamson. Stanford: Stanford University Press, 1990.

Braun, Edward. "Trevor Griffiths." *British Television Drama*. George W. Brandt, ed. Cambridge: Cambridge University Press, 1981.

Brennan, Timothy. "*Masterpiece Theatre* and the Uses of Tradition." *Amerian Media and Mass Culture, Left Perspectives*. Ed. Donald Lazere. Berkeley: University of California Press, 1987.

Brett, Jeremy. Personal interview, Los Angeles, CA. 11 January 1991.

Briggs, Asa. *The Birth of Broadcasting. The History of Broadcasting in the United Kingdom*. 4 vols. Oxford: Oxford University Press, 1961.

————. *The Golden Age of Wireless. The History of Broadcasting in the United Kingom*. 4 vols. Oxford: Oxford University Press, 1965.

————. *Governing the BBC*. London: BBC Publications, 1979.

————. *A Social History of England*. New York: Viking Press, 1983.

————. *Sound and Vision. The History of Broadcasting in the United Kingdom*. Oxford: Oxford University Press, 1979.

Broadcasting Culture Research Institute. *Studies of Broadcasting*. Tokyo: NHK Broadcasting Culture Research Institute, 1991.

Broadcasting Research Unit. *Quality in Television—Programmes, Programme-makers, Systems*. London: John Libbey, 1989.

Brookhiser, Richard. *The Way of the WASP*. New York: Free Press, 1991.

Brooks, Tim. *The Complete Directory to Primetime TV Stars*. New York: Ballantine, 1987.

Brooks, Tim, and Earl Marsh. *Complete Guide to Prime-Time Network Shows: 1946–Present*. New York: Ballantine, 1988.

Brown, Les. *Encyclopedia of Television*. New York: Zoetrope, 1982.

————. *Television: The Business behind the Box*. New York: Harcourt Brace Jovanovich, 1971.

Brownmiller, Susan. "TV Series Exalts British Feminists."*New York Times,* 19 October 1975.

Buchan, Alistair. "Mothers and Daughters (or Greeks and Romans)." *Foreign Affairs* 54 (1976), 645–69.

Buckley, Tom. "TV: Duke Street Duchess." *New York Times,* 2 December 1978.

Bull, Hedley, and William Roger Louis, eds. *The Special Relationship: Anglo-American Relations since 1945*. New York: Oxford University Press, 1986.

Caine, Sir Sydney. *Statement on TV Policy: A Supplement to Hobart Paper 43*. London: Institute of Economic Affairs, 1969.

Calderwood, Stanford. Letter to Peter Robeck. 3 February 1971. Photocopy in author's collection.

————. Letter to Herb Schmertz. 3 February 1971. Photocopy in author's collection.

————. Response to your questions about *Masterpiece Theatre*. Memo to author (no. PVT 9935), 27 January 1991. Photocopy in author's collection.

Campaign, 14 April 1972.

Campbell, A. E. "The United States and Great Britain: Uneasy Allies." *Twentieth Century American Foreign Policy*. Ed. John Braeman. Columbus: Ohio State University Press, 1971.

Carnegie Commission on Public Broadcasting. *Public Television: A Program for Action*. New York: Carnegie Corporation, 1967.

Carnegie Commission on the Future of Public Broadcasting. *A Public Trust*. New York: Bantam, 1979.

Carnoy, Martin. *Education as Cultural Imperialism*. New York: Longman, 1974.

Carrington, C. E. *The British Overseas: Exploits of a Nation of Shopkeepers—Part One: Making of the Empire*. Cambridge: Cambridge University Press, 1968.

Castleman, Harry and Walter J. Podrazik. *Watching TV: Four Decades of American Television*. New York: McGraw Hill, 1982.

Chamberlin, Ward B., Jr. Letter to Samuel C. O. Holt. 11 January 1971. Photocopy in author's collection.

Chaplin, Charles. *My Autobiography*. New York: Simon and Schuster, 1964.

Clark, J. B., Memo to D. S. W. Re. NAEB. 26 September 1952. E1/194/2 NAEB Visit Aug-Nov. BBC Written Archives, Caversham.

Clark, Kenneth. *The Other Half*. London: Hamish Hamilton, 1989.

Cole, Barry G., ed. *Television: Selections from TV Guide Magazine*. New York: Free Press, 1970.

Colier, Basil. *The Lion and the Eagle: British and Anglo-American Strategy, 1900–1950*. London: MacDonald, 1972.

Collins, Richard, et al. *The Economics of Television: The UK Case*. Beverly Hills: SAGE, 1988.

Colson, Charles. Memo to H. R. Haldeman. Re: Presidential Image. 6 July 1972. Nixon Presidential Papers, NARAS, Washington, DC.

Comely, Basil. "Oiling the wheels of U.K. drama." *Broadcast,* 23 May 1986.

Cook, Philip S., ed. *American Media: The Wilson Quarterly Reader*. Washington, DC: Wilson Center, 1989.

Cooke, Alistair. *The Theatre, New York and London*. BBC 25 May 1938. BBC Written Archives Center, Caversham.

————. *Douglas Fairbanks, The Making of a Screen Character*. New York: Museum of Modern Art, 1940.

————. *A Generation on Trial*. New York: Knopf, 1950.

————. *A Commencement Address*. New York: Knopf, 1954.

————. "A Visitor Looks at Hollywood." USIS Feature. December, 1957.

————. "Letter to the Editor." *New York Times,* 18 September 1957.

————. *Talks about America*. London: Bodley Head, 1968.

————. *Garbo and the Night Watchmen*. London: Secker and Warburg, 1971.

————. *Alistair Cooke's America*. New York: Knopf, 1973.

————. *Edwardian Essays*. New York: Mobil, 1973.

————. *Six Men*. New York: Knopf, 1977.

————. "Did Rose Live Happily Ever After? Alistair Cooke Updates 'Upstairs, Downstairs.'" *New York Times Magazine,* 8 March 1977.

————. *The Americans*. New York: Knopf, 1979.

————. *Masterpieces: A Decade of Masterpiece Theatre*. New York: Knopf, 1981.

————. *The Patient Has the Floor*. New York: Knopf, 1986.

————. *America Observed*. Ed. Ronald A. Wells. London: Reinhardt-Viking, 1988.

————. *The Vintage Mencken*. New York: Vintage, 1990.

————. Personal interview, New York City. 19 June 1990.

————. "International Zone." *UN Dateline*. Executive producer George Movshon. UCLA Film and Television Archive.

————. "Introduction to *A Town Like Alice*." Episode one. Personal transcription. UCLA Film and Television Archive.

————. "Introduction to *Flickers*." Episode five. Personal transcription. UCLA Film and Television Archive.

————. "Introduction to *The Jewel in the Crown*." Episode one. Personal transcription. UCLA Film and Television Archive.

————. Talks File. BBC Written Archives Center, Caversham.

Cooke, John. "John Cooke Tells How It Was." *The Rolling Stone Rock and Roll Reader*. Ed. Ben Fong-Torres. New York: Bantam, 1974.

Cooney, Joan Ganz. Statement by Joan Ganz Cooney, president, Children's Television Workshop. Press release, 20 October 1970. Photocopy in author's collection.

Coppa, Frank J., ed. *Screen and Society: The Impact of Television upon Aspects of Contemporary Civilization*. Chicago: Nelson Hall, 1979.

Corporation for Public Broadcasting. *A Report to the People: 20 Years of Your National Commitment to Public Broadcasting: 1967–87*. Washington, DC: CPB, 1987.

—————. *Proceedings of the 1980 Technical Conference on Qualitative Television Ratings, Final Report*. Washington, DC: CPB Office of Communication Research, 1980.

—————. CPB/PBS/WGBH position on *Masterpiece Theatre*. Memo. 22 March 1971. Photocopy in author's collection.

Cosmopolitan, U.K. edition. February 1988.

Coveney, Michael. "D. H. Lawrence Comes to TV." *New York Times*, 15 May 1983.

Cowie, Peter. "The Man behind Many of Those British Gems." *New York Times*, 9 December 1984.

Cox, Michael. Personal interview, London. 20 August 1990.

Cross, Colin. *The Fall of the British Empire*. London: Hodder and Stoughton, 1968.

Cuddihy, John Murray. *The Ordeal of Civility*. New York: Basic Books, 1974.

Curran, Sir Charles. *The Fourth Network: A Question of Priorities*. London: BBC, 1974.

Current Biography. New York: Wilson, 1952.

Czitrom, Daniel J. *Media and the American Mind*. Chapel Hill: University of North Carolina Press, 1982.

Daily Telegraph (London), 22 October 1970.

Daily Variety, 10 January 1984.

Davis, David M. Letter to Samuel Holt. 14 June 1972. Photocopy in author's collection.

—————. Personal interview, Los Angeles, California. 12 January 1991.

Davis, Milt, Jr. DACS to all PTV Stations, Program Managers, PBS Programming. Re. Program Flags and Preview Dates, MPT: *I, Claudius*. DACS 09589. 1 May 1979. Photocopy in author's collection.

Davis, Patricia Ann. *A Description and Analysis of Mobil Oil Corporation Advertising on the Basis of Content and Context before, during, and after the Oil Crisis*. New York University dissertation, 1979.

Davy, Alexander. *Footnotes to the Film*. London: Lovett, Dickinson, 1938.

Dawtrey, Adam. "40 ITV license bids expected today." *Hollywood Reporter*, 15 May 1991: 4.

Deihl, Ernest Roderick. *George Schaefer and the Hallmark Hall of Fame: A Study of the Producer-Director of a Live Television Drama Series*. Ohio State University dissertation, 1964.

Deutsch, Karl. *Nationalism and Social Communication*. New York: Wiley, 1953.

Devine, Mary. "Sullivan's Job Is to Produce Masterpieces: Marblehead woman's won two Emmy awards." *North Shore Sunday,* 13 November 1977.

————. "The Mistress of *Masterpiece Theatre*." *Boston Magazine,* December 1982.

Dimbleby, David, and David Reynolds. *An Ocean Apart: The Relationship between Britain and America in the Twentieth Century*. New York: Vintage, 1988.

Docherty, David, ed. *Keeping Faith? Channel Four and Its Audience*. London: Broadcasting Research Unit, 1989.

"Drama Producer." London *Sunday Times,* 20 December 1987.

Eaton, Rebecca. Personal interview, Los Angeles, CA. 9 January 1991.

Eden, Anthony. *Full Circle*. London: Cassell, 1960.

"Epistles to the English." *Times Literary Supplement,* 24 October 1968.

Falk, Quentin. *Anthony Hopkins*. London: Columbus, 1989.

Fanning, David. Personal conversation, Los Angeles, California. 12 January 1991.

Fein, Esther B. "*Masterpiece Theatre* Is Honored." *New York Times,* 21 January 1986.

Fergenson, Susan, and Ron Devillier. Memo to Development Directors, Program Managers, PI Directors. Re. *Upstairs Downstairs Farewell . . . A Million Dollar Party.* 14 April 1977. Photocopy in author's collection.

Ferguson, Andrew. "The Power of Myth." *New Republic,* 19 and 26 August 1991.

Feuer, Jane, et al. *MTM: Quality Television*. London: BFI, 1984.

Fiddick, Peter. Column in the *Guardian,* 2 April 1974.

————. "A British Perspective," *The Museum of Broadcasting Celebrates Mobil and Masterpiece Theatre, 15 Years of Excellence*. New York: Museum of Broadcasting, 1986.

Fieldhouse, D. K. *The Colonial Empires,* 2nd ed. London: Macmillan, 1982.

Fisher, David Hackett. *Albion's Seed: Four British Folkways in America*. New York: Oxford, 1989.

Flanigan, Peter M. Memorandum to the President. 4 November 1969. Nixon Presidential Papers, NARAS, Washington, DC.

————. Memorandum for the President's File. 27 October 1969. Nixon Presidential Papers, NARAS, Washington, DC.

————. Schedule Proposal. Meeting . . . to discuss the future direction and role for the Corporation for Public Broadcasting. 12 October 1972. Nixon Presidential papers, NARAS, Washington, DC.

———. Telephone interview. 11 March 1991.

Floyd, Patty Lou. *Backstairs with Upstairs, Downstairs.* New York: St. Martin's Press, 1988.

Ford Foundation. *1955 Annual Report.* New York: Ford Foundation, 1955.

———. *Ford Foundation Activities in Noncommercial Broadcasting: 1951–76.* New York: Ford Foundation, 1976.

Freund, Charles Paul. "Save the Networks! They May Be a Wasteland, but They're the Wasteland We Share." *Washington Post,* 28 July 1991.

Frost, David, and Michael Shea. *The Rich Tide: Men, Women, Ideas and Their Transatlantic Impact.* London: Collins, 1986.

Frost, J. M., ed. *World Radio TV Handbook.* New York: Billboard Publications, 1990.

Fussell, Paul. *Class: A Guide through the American Status System.* New York: Summit, 1983.

Gander, L. Marsland. "BBC Finance: The Exports Factor." *Daily Telegraph,* 18 August 1969.

Gannett Center. "The Image Factory." *Gannett Center Journal,* 3.3 (1989 Summer).

———. "The New Media Barons." *Gannett Center Journal,* 3.1 (1989).

———. "The Opinion Makers." *Gannett Center Journal,* 3.2 (1989 Spring).

Gans, Herbert. *Popular Culture and High Culture, An Analysis of Evaluation and Taste.* New York: Basic Books, 1974.

Gardella, Kay. Personal interview, Los Angeles, CA. 12 January 1991.

———. "TV/Cable: A Class Act." *New York Daily News,* 19 January 1986.

Gascoigne, Bamber. *The Making of The Jewel in the Crown.* New York: St. Martin's, 1983.

Gerbner, George, and Marsha Siefert, eds. *World Communications: A Handbook.* New York: Longman, 1984.

Gilbert, Edward. Letter of agreement to Paul Gerken. Re. *Disraeli.* 16 April 1982. Photocopy in author's collection.

Gill, Brendan. *A New York Life.* New York: Poseidon, 1991.

Gill, Michael. Letter to Alistair Cooke, 18 May 1955. BBC Written Archives Center, Caversham.

Gitlin, Todd. *Inside Prime Time.* New York: Pantheon, 1983.

Glaser, Barney G., and Anselm L. Strauss. *The Discovery of Grounded Theory.* Chicago: Aldine Publishing Company, 1967.

Glick, Edwin Leonard. *WGBH-TV: The First Ten Years (1955–65).* University of Michigan dissertation, 1970.

"Global TV Series: 'International Zone' Shows UN Work." *New York Times,* 18 February 1962.

Goodman, Arlene. Personal interview, New York City. 14 March 1991.

―――. Unpublished interview with Joan Sullivan. Re. Music hall Epilogues, U/D. n.d. Photocopy in author's collection.

Goodman, Frank, and Associates. Draft letter to *Ms.*, n.d., no signature. Photocopy in author's collection.

Goodman, Frank. Memo Re. Audience Ratings for *Masterpiece Theatre* 1972–76. n.d. Photocopy in author's collection.

―――. *Masterpiece Theatre* Gets New Opening Look. Press release, n.d. Photocopy in author's collection.

―――. *Masterpiece Theatre* mixes comedy, drama for 1982–83. Press release, n.d. Photocopy in author's collection.

―――. Memo to the Staff. Re. Status Report on *Masterpiece Theatre* 15th Anniversary, 29 October 1985. Photocopy in author's collection.

―――. New *Masterpiece Theatre* Logo. Unpublished interview with Joan Wilson, n.d. Photocopy in author's collection.

―――. Personal interview, New York City. 14 March 1991.

―――. Press release draft, n.d. Photocopy in author's collection.

―――. Former TV Producer Confesses to Masterly Cover Up. Press release, 3 December 1990. Photocopy in author's collection.

Goodman, Frank, and Arlene Goodman. Memorandum to Peter A. Spina and Fran Michelman. 6 June 1988. Photocopy in author's collection.

Goodman, Walter. "TV: Churchill's Wilderness Years." *New York Times,* 15 January 1983.

Gould, Jack. "Omnibus Evaluated: Ford Foundation's TV-Radio Workshop's Contribution to Video Is Inestimable." *New York Times,* 16 November 1952.

Grade, Lew. *Still Dancing: My Story.* London: Fontana, 1988.

Gray, Arthur, and Frederick Brittain. *A History of Jesus College, Cambridge.* London: Heinemann, 1979.

Great Britain, Home Office. *Report of the Broadcasting Committee 1949.* London: Broadcasting Committee, 1949.

―――. *Report of the Committee on Broadcasting 1960.* London: Committee on Broadcasting, 1960.

―――. *Report of the Committee on the Future of Broadcasting.* London: HMSO, 1977.

―――. *Research on the Range and Quality of Broadcasting Services: A Report for the Committee on Financing the BBC.* West Yorkshire Media in Politics Group, Centre for Television Research, University of Leeds. London: HMSO, 1976.

Green, William N. *Strategies of the Major Oil Companies.* Ann Arbor: UMI Research Press, 1982.

Greenberg, Bradley, et al. *Production, Technological, Economic and Audience Factors in Assessing Quality in Public Service Television.* Michigan State University, Department of Telecommunications, February 1991.

Greene, Sir Hugh. Letter to George Probst. 26 September 1952. E1/193 NAEB, 1950–53. BBC Written Archives, Caversham.

———. *The Third Floor Front.* London: The Bodley Head, 1969.

Greenfield, Jeff. *Television: The First 50 Years.* New York: Crescent, 1981.

"Grinnell College News." 8 May 1980.

Grosser, Alfred. *The Western Alliance: European-American Relations since 1945.* London: Macmillan, 1980.

Grossman, Lawrence. Telephone interview, 6 May 1991.

Gunn, Hartford. Memo to Norm Sinel and Gerry Slater. Subject: TLF Quarterly and Holt's memo to Sinel of 8/17/73. 24 August 1973. Photocopy in author's collection.

Haacke, Hans. *Upstairs at Mobil: Musings of a Shareholder.* Art exhibit. First exhibited at John Weber Gallery, New York, February 1981.

———. *Creating Consent.* First exhibited at John Weber Gallery, New York, February 1981.

———. *Mobil: On The Right Track.* First exhibited at John Weber Gallery, New York, February 1981.

Halberstam, David. *The Powers That Be.* New York: Knopf, 1979.

Haldeman, H. R. Memorandum for the File. Subject: Broadcasting Policy and Network Power. n.d. Nixon Presidential Papers, NARAS, Washington, DC.

Hall, Stuart, ed. *Culture, Media, Language.* London: Hutchinson. 1980.

Halliwell, Leslie. *Halliwell's Television Companion.* London: Grafton, 1982.

Hardwick, Mollie. *The World of Upstairs, Downstairs.* New York: Holt, 1976.

Hare, Norman. "The World Buys from Britain." *Daily Telegraph,* 28 April 1969.

———. "British TV sales drive at Cannes festival." *Daily Telegraph* , 13 April 1970.

Harris, Patricia. Table 1: Highest Rated *Masterpiece Theatre* Programs. WGBH Research, n.d. Photocopy in author's collection.

Hasson, Nathan. Personal interview, Boston. 13 December 1990.

Hathaway, Robert M. *Great Britain and the United States: Special Relations since World War II.* Boston: Twayne, 1990.

Hawkesworth, John. Simon and Goodman interview. Transcript, tape 10. Frank Goodman Associates. Photocopy in author's collection.

————. Telephone interview, London. 24 August 1990.

Head, Sydney W. *World Broadcasting Systems*. Palo Alto: Wadsworth, 1985.

Head, Sydney W., and Christopher Sterling. *Broadcasting in America*. Boston: Houghton-Mifflin, 1986.

Henry, Brian, ed. *British Television Advertising: The First Thirty Years*. London: Century Benham, 1986.

Henry, Sarah. "Fighting Words: California's Official Language Law." *Los Angeles Times Magazine*, 10 June 1990.

Henry, William A., III. "*Masterpiece Theatre*'s Impresario." *Boston Globe*, 6 August 1978.

Hewison, Robert. *The Heritage Industry*. London: Methuen, 1987.

Hill, Doug, and Jeff Weingrad. *Saturday Night*. New York: Vintage, 1987.

Hill, Lord. *Behind the Screen*. London: Sidgwick and Jackson, 1974.

Hitchens, Christopher. *Blood, Class, and Nostalgia: Anglo-American Ironies*. New York: Farrar, 1990.

Holt, Samuel C. O. Letter to David M. Davis. 26 June 1972. Photocopy in author's collection.

————. Memo to the Files. Subject: Call from Michael Rice. 5 February 1973. Photocopy in author's collection.

————. Memo to Gerry Slater, 7 August 1973. Photocopy in author's collection.

————. Letter to Ward Chamberlin, 25 January 1971. Photocopy in author's collection.

————. Memo to Marlene, Re. Telegram to Shaun Sutton. 29 January 1971. Photocopy in author's collection.

————. Memo to Hartford Gunn, 1 March 1971. Photocopy in author's collection.

————. Memo to Hartford Gunn, 19 March 1971. Photocopy in author's collection.

Holt, Thaddeus. Memorandum to the record. Subject: Programs—*Masterpiece Theatre*. 24 March 1971. Photocopy in author's collection.

————. Memo to the record. Subject: Corporations—Mobil Oil. 9 April 1971. Photocopy in author's collection.

————. Letter to Frank Marshall, 23 June 1971. Photocopy in author's collection.

Independent Broadcasting Authority. *IBA Annual Report*. 1973–1990.

————. *IBA Comments on the Report of the Committee on the Future of Broadcasting*. London: IBA, 1977.

————. *IBA Guide to Independent Broadcasting*. London: IBA, 1977.

————. *Independent Broadcasting 4*. London: IBA, 1974.

————. *A User's Guide to Television Sponsorship for Programs on ITV, Channel 4, BSB*. London: IBA, 1988.

Innis, Harold. *The Bias of Communication.* Toronto: University of Toronto Press, 1951.

———. *Empire and Communications.* Oxford: Oxford University Press, 1950.

Isaacs, Jeremy. *Storm over Four: A Personal Account.* London: Weidenfeld, 1990.

ITCA. *Comments on the White Paper on Broadcasting.* London: ITCA, 1978.

ITV. *The Annan Report: An ITV View.* London: ITVA, 1977.

———. *ITV Evidence to the Annan Committee.* London: Independent Television Books, Ltd., 1975.

"Just the Job." *Daily Telegraph,* 14 November 1987.

Kay, John. "Battling BBC Bosses in a Telly Brawl." *Sun* (London), 11 December 1987.

Kaye, Evelyn. "More of Those Masterpieces from England on Ch. 2 List." *Boston Globe,* 7 July 1974.

Kendrick, Alexander. *Prime Time: The Life of Edward R. Murrow.* New York: Avon, 1969.

Kennedy, Ludovic. *On My Way to the Club.* London: Penguin, 1989.

Kitman, Marvin. *I Am a VCR.* New York: Random House, 1988.

———. *Newsday* , 20 November 1977.

Kurzbard, Gary. *Ethos and Industry: A Critical Study of Oil Industry Advertising from 1974–84.* Purdue University dissertation, 1984.

Labour Party. *The People and the Media.* London: British Labour Party, 1974.

Lambert, Stephen. *Channel Four: Television with a Difference?* London: BFI, 1982.

Lapham, Lewis. *Money and Class in America: Notes and Observations on Our Civil Religion.* London: Weidenfeld and Nicolson, 1988.

Lapping, Brian. *End of Empire.* New York: St. Martin's Press, 1985.

Larsen, Robert L. Letter to Hartford Gunn. 22 March 1972. Photocopy in author's collection.

———. Letter to Herb Schmertz, 23 April 1971. Photocopy in author's collection.

Larson, Joan. Memo to all PI directors, Re. Mobil *Masterpiece Theatre* Ad. 23 December 1970. Photocopy in author's collection.

Laughton, Roger. Personal interview, London. 15 August 1991.

Leapman, Michael. *The Last Days of the Beeb.* London: Allen & Unwin, 1986.

Leavis, F. R. *Mass Civilization and Minority Culture.* Cambridge: Cambridge University Press, 1930.

Ledbetter, James. *Made Possible By: The Death of Public Broadcasting in the United States.* New York: Verso, 1997.

Lee, Chin-Chuan. *Media Imperialism Reconsidered: The Homogenization of Television Culture.* Beverly Hills: SAGE, 1979.

LeMahieu, D. L. *A Culture for Democracy: Mass Communication and the Cultivated Mind in Britain between the Wars.* Oxford: Clarendon Press, 1988.

LeMahieu, D. L. "Imagined Contemporaries: cinematic and televised dramas about the Edwardians in Great Britain and the United States." *Historical Journal of Film, Radio, and Television,* 10.3 (1990).

Lerner, Max. *America as a Civilization.* New York: Henry Holt, 1987.

Levine, Lawrence W. *Highbrow/Lowbrow: The Emergence of Cultural Hierarchy in America.* Cambridge, MA: Harvard, 1988.

"Letters." *New York Times Magazine,* 29 May 1977.

Lewis, Anthony. "Reality in Romance." *New York Times,* 9 May 1977.

Liroff, David L. Letter to S. Anders Yocomb, 24 July 1975. Photocopy in author's collection.

Little, Frank. Memo to Karen Thomas, 26 September 1975. Photocopy in author's collection.

London Television Consortium. *An Application for the award of ITA Programme Contract B (London Weekend).* ITA, 1967.

Louis, William Roger. *The British Empire in the Middle East, 1945–51.* Oxford: Oxford University Press, 1984.

———. *Imperialism at Bay, 1941–45.* Oxford: Clarendon Press, 1977.

Lynes, Russell. *The Tastemakers.* New York: Grosset and Dunlap, 1954.

MacDonald, Dwight. *The Ford Foundation.* New York: Reynal and Company, 1956.

Macy, John W., Jr. Remarks by John W. Macy Jr., president of the Corporation for Public Broadcasting. Press release. 21 October 1970. Photocopy in author's collection.

Macy, Mrs. John W., Jr., Personal letter to author, 4 August 1990.

Mair, George. *Inside HBO: The Billion Dollar War between HBO, Hollywood, and the Home Video Revolution.* New York: Dodd, Mead, 1988.

Maltin, Leonard. *TV Movies and Video Guide.* New York: New American Library, 1988.

Mansell, Gerard. *Let Truth Be Told: 50 Years of BBC External Broadcasting.* London: Weidenfeld and Nicolson, 1982.

Marc, David. *Comic Visions: Television Comedy and American Culture.* Winchester, MA: Unwin, Hyman, 1989.

———. *Demographic Vistas: Television in American Culture.* Philadelphia: University of Pennsylvania Press, 1984.

Marshall and Bloom. Press release, 19 June 1973. Photocopy in author's collection.

Marshall, Frank. Personal interview, Key West, FL. 4 January 1991.

————. Personal resume, 1991. Photocopy in author's collection.

Marwick, Arthur. *Class: Image and Reality.* London: Collins, 1980.

Mattelart, Armand. *Multinational Corporations and the Control of Culture.* Brighton: Harvester, 1979.

McArthur, Colin. *Television and History.* Television Monograph No. 8. London: BFI, 1980.

McKay, Peter. "Cooke Stirs Up Row over Award." *Mail on Sunday,* 8 September 1985.

McKinley, John A. PBS Screening Report: *Masterpiece Theatre—Shoulder to Shoulder* no. 101. 1 November 1977. Photocopy in author's collection.

————. PBS Screening Report: *Masterpiece Theatre—Shoulder to Shoulder* no. 106. 15 November 1977. Photocopy in author's collection.

————. PBS Screening Report: *MT—Anna Karenina* no. 101. 5 January 1978. Photocopy in author's collection.

————. PBS Screening Report. 19 February 1978. Photocopy in author's collection.

————. PBS Screening Report. 27 February 1978. Photocopy in author's collection.

————. PBS Screening Report. 8 March 1978. Photocopy in author's collection.

————. PBS Screening Report. 12 March 1978. Photocopy in author's collection.

————. PBS Screening Report. 15 March 1978. Photocopy in author's collection.

————. PBS Screening Report. 22 March 1978. Photocopy in author's collection.

McMillan, Nancy Pomerene. "A Tenth Birthday for *Masterpiece Theatre.*" *New York Times,* 21 September 1981.

McPhail, Thomas L. *Electronic Colonialism: The Future of International Broadcasting and Communication.* Beverly Hills: SAGE, 1981.

Mills, C. Wright. *The Power Elite.* New York: Oxford University Press, 1956.

Milne, Alasdair. *DG: The Memoirs of a British Broadcaster.* London: Hodder, 1988.

The Mirror, 14 April 1969.

Mkherjee, Arun. *Towards an Aesthetic of Opposition: Essays on Literature, Criticism, & Cultural Imperialism.* Ontario: Williams-Wallace, 1988.

"Mobil Bankrolls Aussie-Produced 'A Town Like Alice' for PBS Air." *Variety* , 23 September 1981.

Mobil Corporation. *Evolution of Mobil's Public Affairs Programs: 1970—81.* New York: Mobil, 1982.

————. *1990 Annual Report*. Fairfax: Mobil, 1990.
Mobil Masterpiece Theatre, UCLA Film and Television Archives:
After the War
The Bretts, Series I–II
The Charmer
Danger UXB
Dickens of London
Disraeli
The Dressmaker
The Duchess of Duke Street
Edward and Mrs. Simpson
Elizabeth R
Flame Trees of Thika
Flickers
The Ginger Tree
House of Cards
I, Claudius
The Irish R.M.
Jeeves and Wooster
The Jewel in the Crown
Lillie
Lord Mountbatten: The Last Viceroy
Lost Empires
On Approval
Piece of Cake
Private Schulz
Scoop
Silas Marner
The Six Wives of Henry VIII
To Serve Them All My Days
The Shiralee
Sorrell and Son
Summer's Lease
A Tale of Two Cities
Testament of Youth
Tom Brown's Schooldays
A Town Like Alice
Traffik
The Unpleasantness at the Bellona Club
Upstairs, Downstairs, Series I–IV
A Very British Coup
"Mobil's Rawleigh Warner Is Adman of the Year." *Advertising Age*, 29
December 1975.

Montgomery, Kathryn. *Target: Prime Time. Advocacy Groups and the Struggle over Entertainment Television.* New York: Oxford University Press, 1989.

Mooney, Michael. *The Ministry of Culture.* New York: Wyndham Books, 1980.

Museum of Broadcasting. *The Museum of Broadcasting Celebrates Mobil and Masterpiece Theatre.* New York: Museum of Broadcasting, 1986.

Nathan, Wynn. Letter to Michael Rice. 9 February 1973. Photocopy in author's collection.

————. Letter to Herb Schmertz. 19 March 1973. Photocopy in author's collection.

National Association of Educational Broadcasters. *The Nixon Administration Public Broadcasting Papers: A Summary, 1969–1974.* Washington, DC: NAEB, 1979.

National Board for Prices and Incomes. *Costs and Revenues of Independent Television Companies.* London: HMSO, 1970.

Newcomb, Horace. *Television: The Critical View.* New York: Oxford University Press, 1987.

"Newcomers get BBC rights in U.S." *Broadcast* , 13 April 1981.

"News and Notes of TV and Radio: 'Omnibus,' " *New York Times,* 20 November 1960.

"News of TV and Radio: Alistair Cooke to Host Series Designed to 'Personalize' the UN." *New York Times,* 13 November 1960.

New York Times, 16 November 1957.

————. 25 February 1972.

————. 15 November 1972.

————. 12 April 1973.

————. 2 October 1974.

Nicholas, H. G. *The United States and Great Britain.* Chicago: University of Chicago Press, 1975.

Nixon, Richard M. *In the Arena: A Memoir of Victory, Defeat, and Renewal.* New York: Pocket Books, 1990.

————. *Leaders.* New York: Touchstone, 1990.

————. *RN: The Memoirs of Richard Nixon.* New York: Simon and Schuster, 1978.

————. *Six Crises.* New York: Touchstone, 1990.

————. Exchange of Remarks of the President and Prime Minister Wilson at the President's Arrival, Heathrow Airport. Office of the White House Press Secretary, London 24 February 1969. Nixon Presidential Papers, NARAS, Washington, DC.

Norback, Craig T., and Peter Norback, eds. *TV Guide Almanac.* New York: Ballantine, 1980.

Nunnerly, David. *President Kennedy and Britain*. London: Bodley Head, 1972.

O'Connor, John E., ed. *American History/American Television*. New York: Ungar, 1983.

O'Connor, John J. "Can Public Television Be Bought?" *New York Times,* 9 October 1974.

———. "TV: Notorious Woman, Public Network Presents BBC Series on Life and Loves of George Sand." *New York Times,* 20 November 1975.

———. "Imaginative Drama Captures Dickens Somber Comedy." *New York Times,* 14 May 1978.

———. "The Case of the Doting Dramatization." *New York Times,* 7 October 1979.

———. "TV Weekend: Marciano's Story Joins Live Sportsworld Bout." *New York Times,* 19 October 1979.

———. "When a Sequel Surpasses the Original." *New York Times,* 23 December 1979.

———. "TV Weekend." *New York Times,* 11 April 1980.

———. "Disraeli—More Evidence of the British Skill at Characterization." *New York Times,* 1 June 1980.

———. "TV Weekend." *New York Times,* 13 March 1981.

———. "TV Weekend." *New York Times,* 31 December 1982.

———. "A Searingly Honest 'Sons and Lovers.'" *New York Times,* 22 May 1983.

———. "Wicked Irish Wit Enlivens a New Mini-Series." *New York Times,* 29 January 1984.

———. "TV View." *New York Times,* 16 December 1984.

———. "'Bretts,' Britain Between Wars, on Channel 13." *New York Times,* 9 October 1987.

———. "The British Turn Out Duds, Too." *New York Times,* 19 May 1985.

———. "'The Last Place on Earth'—Not Just about the Antarctic." *New York Times,* 20 October 1985.

———. "'By the Sword Divided' on *Masterpiece Theatre*." *New York Times,* 21 March 1986.

———. "TV Weekend: 'Paradise Postponed,' a New Series on 'Masterpiece Theater [sic].'" *New York Times,* 17 October 1986.

———. "'Goodbye Mr. Chips' is Welcome Once More." *New York Times,* 4 January 1987.

———. "TV Weekend." *New York Times,* 23 January 1987.

Omnibus. UCLA Film and Television Archive:

　A Streetcar Named Desire. Number. 87. UCLA Film and Television Archive.

The Horn Blows at Midnight. 1953: 9. UCLA Film and Television Archive.

King Lear. Number 859. UCLA Film and Television Archive.

Oudes, Bruce, ed. *From: the President. Richard Nixon's Secret Files.* New York: Harper and Row, 1989.

Ovendale, Ritchie. *The English Speaking Alliance: Britain, the U.S. and the Cold War, 1945–51.* London: George Allen & Unwin, 1985.

Oxley, Bill. To All Stations. Re. Change in Preview Schedule. DACS 1182. 7 December 1970. Photocopy in author's collection.

Page, George H. Letter to Phil Bloom, Marshall and Bloom. 29 June 1973. Photocopy in author's collection.

Paignton Observer, 3 July 1931.

Paper, Lewis J. *Empire, William S. Paley and the Making of CBS.* New York: St. Martin's Press, 1987.

Patterson, Dean. Letter to Sam Holt, 26 March 1973. Photocopy in author's collection.

Paulu, Burton. *Television and Radio in the United Kingdom.* Minneapolis: University of Minnesota Press, 1981.

Pelletier, H. Rooney. Letter to FB Thornton, 31 July 1952. E1/194/NAEB Visit May–August 1952. BBC Written Archives, Caversham.

———. Report on the Visit of the National Association of Education Broadcasting to Britain. 14 November 1952. E1/194/2 NAEB Visit August–November 1952. BBC Written Archives, Caversham.

"People on Television." *New York Times,* 7 October, 1956.

Powell, Jonathan. Personal interview, London. 23 August 1991.

Powell, Joseph L., Jr. (Jody). Letter to Herb Schmertz, 22 November 1977. FG 1–3, Executive Files. Jimmy Carter Library.

"Power among Men." *New York Times,* 29 March 1959.

Prendergast, Curtis. *The World of Time, Inc.* New York: Athenaeum, 1986.

Price, Raymond. *With Nixon.* New York: Viking, 1977.

Price, Richard. Personal interview, London. 1 August 1990.

Public Broadcasting Service. Memo to All Member Stations, Subject: *Shoulder to Shoulder.* 3 February 1975. Photocopy in author's collection.

———. Memo. 2 February 1975. Photocopy in author's collection.

———. PBS Screening Report. *Masterpiece Theatre,* 101, *I, Claudius.* 6 November 1977. Photocopy in author's collection.

———. PBS Screening Report. *Masterpiece Theatre,* 108, *The Bretts 'Get Me To The Church On Time' (RAJ).'* 29 October 1987. Photocopy in author's collection.

———. Program Submission Form. *Private Schulz.* 24 January 1983. Photocopy in author's collection.

———. *Program Producers Handbook.* Alexandria: PBS, August 1990.

———. *Facts about PBS.* Alexandria: PBS, February 1991.

Pyenson, Lewis. *Cultural Imperialism in the Exact Sciences: German Expansion Overseas, 1900–1930. Studies in History and Culture, v.1.* New York: Lang, 1985.

"Radio Comment: Murrow, Morgan, Swing, Cooke Give Ideas Precedence over Pictures." *New York Times,* 9 October 1960.

Ranelagh, John. *The Agency: The Rise and Decline of the CIA.* New York: Simon and Schuster, 1987.

Ranney, Austin. *Channels of Power.* New York: Basic Books, 1983.

"RCTV Shakes Up Time-Life TV." *Adweek,* 15 December 1980.

Reith, J. C. W. *Into the Wind.* London: Hodder & Stoughton, 1949.

Reynolds, David. *The Creation of the Anglo-American Alliance, 1937–41.* Chapel Hill: University of North Carolina Press, 1982.

Rice, Michael. Memo to Sam Holt. 20 February 1973. Photocopy in author's collection.

—. Memo to PBS, CPB and Mobil. 2 August 1973. Photocopy in author's collection.

Rivers, William L., & Wilbur Schramm. *Responsibility in Communication,* Third Edition. New York: Harper and Row, 1980.

Robeck, Peter. Personal interview, New York City. 15 March 1991.

Robinson, David. *Chaplin: His Life and Art.* New York: McGraw-Hill, 1985.

Rogers, Dave. *The ITV Encyclopedia of Adventure.* London: ITV, 1988.

"Roundtable: Art to Business: TV Then, TV Now." *Emmy,* Summer 1981.

Ruch, Sandra. Personal interview, Los Angeles, CA. 22 February 1991.

Rusher, William A. *The Coming Battle for the Media.* New York: Morrow, 1988.

Russell, Derek. Report on 30th Anniversary Institute for Education by Radio-TV. 4–7 May 1960. E1/1565/1 NAEB 1955–66. BBC Written Archives, Caversham.

Russett, Bruce M. *Community and Contention: Britain and America in the Twentieth Century.* Cambridge, MA: MIT Press, 1963.

Saalbach, Louis Carl. *Jack Gould: Social Critic of the Television Medium, 1947–72.* University of Michigan dissertation, 1980.

Safire, William. *Before the Fall: An Inside View of the Pre-Watergate White House.* New York: Belmont Tower, 1975.

—. Memo to H. R. Haldeman: 'The Nixon Style.' 23 June 1971. Nixon Presidential Papers, NARAS. Washington, DC.

Sarson, Christopher. Memo to Michael Rice, 20 February 1973. Photocopy in author's collection.

—. Memo to Michael Rice, Re. Conversation with Schmertz, 10:45 A.M. 20 February 1973. Photocopy in author's collection.

—. DACS to Sam Holt, 4 January 1971. Photocopy in author's collection.

————. Memorandum to David Stewart (CPB) and Sam Holt (PBS), Re. *Masterpiece Theatre,* 1973–75. 1 May 1973. Photocopy in author's collection.

————. Letter to Richard Price and Arthur Marmor, 3 May 1973. Photocopy in author's collection.

————. Personal interview, New York City. 19 June 1990.

Schaefer, Richard J. "Public Television Constituencies." *Journal of Film and Video* 43 (1–2): 46–68.

Schiller, Herbert. *Mass Communications and American Empire.* New York: Augustus M. Kelley, 1969.

————. *Culture, Inc.: The Corporate Takeover of Public Expression.* New York: Oxford University Press, 1989.

Schmertz, Herb. *Corporations and the First Amendment.* New York: AMACOM, 1978.

————. "Democracy, Tyranny, and Capitalism." *Will Capitalism Survive?* Ernest W. Lefever, ed. Washington, DC: Georgetown University Ethics and Public Policy Center, 1979.

————. Official Biography. The Schmertz Company. New York. 1991.

————. Personal interview, New York City, 15 March 1991.

————. Telephone interview, 13 February 1991.

————. Telephone interview, 30 May 1991.

Schmertz, Herb, with William Novak. *Goodbye to the Low Profile: The Art of Creative Confrontation.* Boston: Little, Brown, 1986.

Schneider, Cynthia, et al. *Global Television.* Cambridge, MA: MIT Press, 1989.

Schuetz, Ralph. DACS to Gary Luddington, 8 April 1971.

Secrest, Meryle. *Kenneth Clark.* London: Weidenfeld, 1990.

Seldon, Anthony. *Churchill's Indian Summer.* London: Hodder and Stoughton, 1981.

Select Committee on Nationalized Industries. *Report of the Select Committee on Nationalized Industries.* London: HMSO, 1972.

Sendall, Bernard. *Independent Television in Britain, Volume 1: Origin and Foundation, 1946–62.* London: Macmillan, 1982.

Settel, Irving. *A Pictorial History of Television,* 2nd ed. New York: Ungar, 1983.

Shivas, Mark. Personal interview, London. 14 August 1990.

Shubik, Irene. *Play for Today: The Evolution of Television Drama.* London: Davis-Poynter, 1975.

Shulman, Milton. "Inside TV: These Churchills Won't Help Our Exports." *Liverpool Daily Post,* 25 October 1969.

Siegel, Ed. "An Adaptation Dulls Sons and Lovers: Something Weakened This Way Comes." *Boston Globe,* 14 May 1983.

————. "Ch. 2 to Repeat Citadel at 9." *Boston Globe,* 25 November 1983.

————. "*Masterpiece Theatre* Scores Again." *Boston Globe,* 27 October 1984.

————. "New British Series is No Jewel." *Boston Globe,* 30 March 1985.

————. "A Jewel in the Medium's Crown." *Boston Globe,* 11 July 1985.

————. "PBS Lineup: Too Many Valleys, Too Few Peaks." *Boston Globe* , 19 January 1986.

————. "Ch. 2 Plans Updated Masterpiece." *Boston Globe,* 1 May 1986.

————. "Silas Marner Has Many Virtues." *Boston Globe,* 14 March 1987.

————. "Noel Coward and the Gift of Dialogue." *Boston Globe,* 28 March 1987.

————. "PBS, Networks Reverse Roles." *Boston Globe,* 9 May 1987.

————. "Meet the Eccentric Bretts." *Boston Globe,* 10 October 1987.

————. Personal interview, Boston. 14 December 1990.

————. "Quality and the single sponsor." *Boston Globe,* 31 March 1991.

Silberman, H. Lee. "Appeal to Reason." *Finance Magazine,* November 1975.

Sinel, Norm. Memo to Hartford Gunn, Re. *Masterpiece Theatre*—Work Sheet. 23 March 1971. Photocopy in author's collection.

Singer, Aubrey. Letter to Barbara Halpern (Intelligence and Research), 29 July 1954. E1/27/6 America TV 4, 1952–54. BBC Written Archives Center, Caversham.

————. Memorandum to CP Tel., 6 November 1963. NETRC 1. BBC Written Archives Center, Caversham.

Slater, Gerry. Note to Sam Holt, 29 June 1972. Photocopy in author's collection.

Smith, Anthony. *British Broadcasting.* Newton Abbot: David and Charles, 1974.

————. *The Politics of Information: Problems of Policy in Modern Media.* Atlantic Highlands, NJ: Macmillan, 1978.

————. *The Shadow in the Cave: The Broadcaster, His Audience, and the State.* Urbana: University of Illinois Press, 1973.

————. *Television and Political Life.* New York: St. Martin's Press, 1979.

Smith, Hedrick. *The Power Game: How Washington Works.* New York: Ballantine, 1988.

Smith, Ned. "Interview: Alistair Cooke." *American Way Magazine,* Fall 1976.

Smith, Richard Norton. *The Harvard Century: The Making of a University to a Nation.* New Haven: Yale University Press, 1987.

Snowman, Daniel. *Britain and America: An Interpretation of Their Culture, 1945–75.* New York: Harper and Row, 1977.

Sperber, A. M. *Murrow: His Life and Times.* New York: Freundlich Books, 1986.

Spina, Pete. Personal interview, Alexandria, Virginia. 17 April 1991.

Stage and TV Today, 28 June 1973.

Standard Press. Burlington, Wisconsin. 6 October 1975.

Steiner, Gary A., ed. *The People Look at Television.* New York: Knopf, 1963.

Stevenson, William. *A Man Called Intrepid.* New York: Harcourt Brace Jovanovich, 1976.

Straight, Michael. *Nancy Hanks: An Intimate Portrait. The Creation of a National Commitment to the Arts.* Durham, NC: Duke University Press, 1988.

Streit, Clarence K. *Union NOW with Britain.* New York: Harper Brothers, 1941.

Style, Michael. "Programmes for Export." *Financial Times,* 21 August 1967.

Suber, Howard. *The Anti-Communist Blacklist in the Hollywood Motion Picture Industry.* University of California, Los Angeles, dissertation, 1968.

"Susan Cooke Will Be Married in December to Anthony Scoville." *New York Times,* 29 October 1968.

Sutton, Shaun. *The Largest Theatre in the World: Thirty Years of Television Drama.* London: BBC, 1982.

Syfret, Toby, ed. *Television Today and Tomorrow.* London: J. Walter Thompson—Europe, 1983.

Tabori, Paul. *Alexander Korda.* London: Oldbourne, 1959.

Tankel, Jonathan. *The ITV Thriller.* University of Wisconsin dissertation, 1984.

Tavoulareas, William P. Statement of William P. Tavoulareas. Press release, 21 January 1976. Photocopy in author's collection.

Tetreault, Mary Ann. *Revolution in the World Petroleum Market.* Westport, CT: Quorum Books, 1985.

Thomas, Barrie. NAEB Convention at Atlanta, 24 October 1956. E1/1565/1 NAEB 1955–66. BBC Written Archives, Caversham.

Thomas, James. "Boost for British Viewers as U.S. Foots the Bill." *Daily Express,* 30 June 1973.

Thomas, Karen. Memo to Jack Crutchfield and Frank Little, 23 September 1975.

Thornton, Basil. Three Wise Men of Gotham: A Progress Report on the NAEB Visit to London in September. 22 July 1952. 1/194 NAEB Visit May–August 1952. BBC Written Archives Center, Caversham.

———. NAEB Conference, Biloxi, Mississippi. 6 November 1951. BBC Written Archives Center, Caversham.

———. Report on NAEB Convention. 31 October 1955. E1/1565/1 NAEB 1955–66. BBC Written Archives Center, Caversham.

Times, London, 5 January 1967.
Times Literary Supplement 1 December 1950.
Trethowan, Sir Ian. *The Split Screen.* London: Hamish Hamilton, 1984.
Tunstall, Jeremy. *The Media are American.* New York: Columbia University Press, 1977.
TV Guide, 17 January 1981.
TV Today, London, 21 May 1970.
———. 28 May 1970.
UNESCO. *Many Voices, One World: Towards a New More Just and More Efficient World Information and Communication Order* (MacBride Report). UNESCO, 1980.
Unger, Craig. "House Proud." *New York,* 21 January 1991.
U.S. Patent and Trademark Office. Int. Cl: 4, US Cl:107. Service Mark, Principal Register: *Masterpiece Theatre.* Mobil Oil Corporation (New York corporation). Reg. No. 1,012,457. Registered 3 June 1975.
———. WBGH [sic] Educational Foundation (Massachusetts corporation). Reg. No. 1,132,403. Registered 1 April 1980.
U.S. Senate, *Multinational Corporations and United States Foreign Policy.* Part 9. 93rd Congress. 5 and 6 June, 25 July, and 12 August 1974. Washington, DC: U.S. Government Printing Office, 1975.
"U.S. Snaps up Edwardian drama." *Evening Standard,* 22 May 1978.
Variety , 1 November 1978.
———. 10 June 1981.
———. 29 January 1986.
———. 21 October 1987.
Varis, Tapio. "The International Flow of Television Programs." *Journal of Communication,* 34.1 (1984): 143–52.
Veeser, H. Aram. *The New Historicism.* New York: Routledge, 1989.
Vitello, Greg, ed. *Twenty Seasons of Mobil Masterpiece Theatre, 1971–91.* Fairfax: Mobil, 1991.
Wakeman, Frederic. *The Hucksters.* New York: Rinehart and Company, 1946.
Walker, Alexander. *Hollywood, U.K.* New York: Stein and Day, 1974.
Wallace, Vivien. Personal interview, London. 17 August 1990.
Warner, Rawleigh, and Leonard Silk. *Ideals in Collision: The Relationship between Business and the News Media.* New York: Carnegie-Mellon University Press, 1979.
Watson, Mary Ann. *The Expanding Vista: American Television in the Kennedy Years.* New York: Oxford University Press, 1990.
Watt, D. Cameron. *Succeeding John Bull: America in Britain's Place, 1900–75 — A Study of the Anglo American Relationship and World Politics in the Context of British and American Foreign Policy Making in the Twentieth Century.* New York: Cambridge University Press, 1984.

Webster, Lance. To All Station Program Directors, Re. *Masterpiece Theatre* Press Kits. DACS message no. 17144, 28 June 1973. Photocopy in author's collection.

Wedell, E. G. *Broadcasting and Public Policy*. London: Michael Joseph, 1968.

Wells, Ronald A. "Alistair Cooke: A Tocqueville for Our Time?" Unpublished paper presented to the European Society for American Studies. Seville, Spain, 1991.

WGBH. *Annual Report*. Boston: WGBH, 1989.

———. *1987–88 Annual Report*. Boston: WGBH, 1988.

———. Memorandum to Michael Rice, Re. An exuberant and somewhat illiterate draft of public information from the February–March 1972 Boston Neilsen Viewers-in-Profile Report. 29 March 1972. Photocopy in author's collection.

Who's Who (1990). London: A & C Black, 1990.

Who's Who in America (1990). Chicago: Marquis, 1990.

Will, George. Column in *Washington Post,* 11 September 1977.

Willey, Basil. *Cambridge and Other Memories*. London: Chatto, 1968.

———. *The "Q" Tradition*. Cambridge: Cambridge University Press, 1946.

Williams, Raymond. *Television: Technology and Cultural Form*. New York: Schocken, 1975.

———. *Raymond Williams on Television: Selected Writings*. Alan O'Connor, ed. London: Routledge, 1989.

Williamson, Larry Allen. *Transcendence, Ethics, and Mobil Oil: A Rhetorical Investigation*. Purdue University dissertation, 1982.

Wilson, James Q. *Bureaucracy: What Government Agencies Do and Why They Do It*. New York: Basic Books, 1989.

Wilson, Joan (Sullivan). Confidential Memo to Becton and Schmertz, Re. M.T., n.d. Photocopy in author's collection.

———. Memo to John Montgomery, 12 April 1974. Photocopy in author's collection.

———. Memo to Becton/Rice, Re. Piccadilly Circus, 27 November 1975. Photocopy in author's collection.

———. Memo to Henry Becton, 16 June 1977. Photocopy in author's collection.

———. Memo to Henry Becton, et al., Re. *Masterpiece Theatre*. 5 October 1979. Photocopy in author's collection.

———. Memo to Henry Becton, Re. *Masterpiece Theatre* 1977–78 Broadcast Schedule. 19 June 1977. Photocopy in author's collection.

———. Note to Frank Goodman, 24 August 1978. Photocopy in author's collection.

————. DACS To All Program Managers, PBS, Re. *I, Claudius.* 20 October 1977. Photocopy in author's collection.

————. Memo to Henry Becton, Re. Call from Bob Shay, 7 April 1983. Photocopy in author's collection.

————. Confidential Memo to Pauline Mercer, Re. *Wilderness Years.* Note on telephone conversation with Paul Gerken. 11 May 1982. Photocopy in author's collection.

————. Memo to Becton and Schmertz, Re. *Masterpiece Theatre* Potential Properties, 16 June 1980. Photocopy in author's collection.

————. Memo to Becton and Schmertz, Re. *Masterpiece Theatre*—1980–81 Season, n.d. Photocopy in author's collection.

————. Memo to Judy Becker, et al., Re. *Masterpiece Theatre* 10th Anniversary Season, 1980–81. 29 January 1981. Photocopy in author's collection.

Windlesham, Lord. *Broadcasting in a Free Society.* London: Basil Blackwell, 1980.

Winfrey, Carey. "Reunited Cast Bids Last Adieu to Eaton Place." *New York Times,* 2 May 1977.

Witherspoon, John, and Roselle Kovitz. *The History of Public Broadcasting.* Washington, DC: Current, 1989.

————. *A Tribal Memory of Public Broadcasting: Missions, Mandates, Assumptions, Structure.* Washington, DC: CPB, July 1986.

Woffinden, Bob. "A new genre of classics." *Independent,* 12 December 1987.

Wollen, Peter. *Signs and Meaning in the Cinema.* Bloomington: Indiana University Press, 1972.

Wright, Louis B. *The British Tradition in America.* Birmingham, AL: The Rushton Lectures, 1954.

Wyver, John. *The Moving Image: An International History of Film, Television, and Video.* London: Blackwell, 1989.

Yergin, Daniel. *The Prize.* New York: Simon and Schuster, 1991.

Yocomb, Andy. To All Stations. Re. *Masterpiece Theatre* 1978–79. DACS no. 17528, 10 August 1978. Photocopy in author's collection.

"Young bulls, down at the Bush." London *Times,* 16 December 1987.

Index

Abbott, George, 152
Ackerly, J. R., 61
Ackroyd, Dan, 47
Adam, Christina, 48
Adam, Kenneth, 127, 135
Adams Chronicles, The, x
Adventure Theatre, 8
Adventures of Sir Lancelot, The, 8
Advertising Age, 137, 175
advertising, 27, 40
"affinity of purpose marketing," 6, 166, 184
After the War, 21
Agee, James, 48
Ager, Ceclia, 70
Agnew, Spiro, 206
Alaska pipeline, 181
Alcoa, 35, 184
Alger, Horatio, 58
Aluminium of Canada, Ltd., 53
Alvarado, Manuel, 19
America. See Cooke, Alistair
American Ballet Theatre, 190
American Broadcasting Company (ABC), 8, 133, 176
American episodes of *Masterpiece Theatre,* ix
American foreign policy, 9, 183
American Language, The, 74
American Linguistic Atlas, The, 63

American Petroleum Institute (API), 37, 187, 194
American Playhouse, x, 33
American public, 165
American Telephone and Telegraph (AT&T), 36
American Trial by Jury, 51
American, The, x
An Age of Kings, 8, 34, 131
And Another Thing, 96
Anderson, Janice, 169, 183
Andy Pandy, 128
Anglo-American, 54, 57, 62, 71, 74, 125, 127, 129, 131, 211
Anglophilia, 47
Anna Karenina, 70
Arab-Israeli conflict, 183–84, 185
Aramco, 168
"Aristocracy of culture," 4
Armstrong Circle Theatre, 209
Art Institute of Chicago, 29
Ascent of Man, The, 185
Asner, Ed, 16
Associated Television (ATV), 7, 134
Astor, Brooke, 59
atomic bombs, 54
Auden, W. H., 63
Australian productions, x
Autobiography of Miss Jane Pittman, The, 37
Avengers, The, 8, 133

Baker, Russell, ix, xi–xii, 28, 47, 48
ballet, 51
Baltzell, Digby, 14
Barnes, George, 127
Barnouw, Eric, 4, 11, 19, 50, 51, 184
Baron, The, 8
Baroness Orczy, 135
Barr, Alfred, 76
Barrymore, John, 152
Baxter, Frank, 133
Beacon Wax, 31
Beatles, The, 8, 9
Becton, Henry, 28, 158–59
Beerbohm, Max, 72
Bellamy family, 187
Bellotti v. First National Bank of Boston, 194
Benchley, Robert, 71
Benny Hill Show, The, 9
Benny, Jack, 52, 53
Berlin Blockade, 29
Berlin, Isaiah, 127
Bernstein, Leonard, 29, 50, 51
Bernstein, Sidney, 70
Between the Wars, 190
Big Oil, 170
blacklist, 8
Blackpool Grammar School, 59
Blenheim Palace, 127
Blondell, Joan, 152
Blood, Class, and Nostalgia, 47
Bloom, Phil, 34, 96
Blumler, Jay, 11
Bond, James, 8, 55
Born to Dance, 70
Boston elites, 14, 208
Boston Gas Company, 30
Boston Globe, 20, 209
Boston Museum of Fine Arts, 29
Bourdieu, Pierre, 1, 2
bourgeoisie, 5

brainwashing, 176
Brennan, Timothy, 17, 58
Bretts, The, 21, 120
Brideshead Revisited: anti-Catholic impact of, x; homosexuality in, x; Mobil's credit for, 196; rejected by *Masterpiece Theatre,* x
Bridson, Gregory, 126
British Broadcasting Corporation (BBC), xii, 1, 8, 9, 15–21, 30, 31, 35, 37, 92, 96, 105; 1952 visit by American educational broadcasters, 126–29; BBC-2, 31, 34, 40; Board of Governors, 55; license fee, 134; Lime Grove, 127; North American representative of, 54; North American service, 54; PBS exposure as commercials for, 35; relationship with *Masterpiece Theatre,* 117–59; relationship with PBS, 99; sponsorship and, 117–25
British colonialism, 211
British cultural studies, 4
British drama, x, 32, 33, 37, 40, 47
British Embassy, 127
British Empire, 63, 204, 211
British Empire, The, 35
British Information Services (BIS), 131
British Lion Films, 209
British Overseas Airways Corporation (BOAC), 106
British Worthies, 128
Britishness, 9
Broadway, 15, 72, 135, 152
Bronowski, Jacob, 185
Brook, Peter, 52
Brown, Bryan, 154
Brown, John Mason, 72

Brown, Les, 152
Brown, Pat, 213
Bruce, David, 56
Brzezinski, Zbignew, 20
Buccaneers, The, x
Buckley, William F., x, 10
Business Public Affairs Advisory
  Group, 191
By the Sword Divided, 120
By the Sword Divided II, 120

cable television, 35, 206
Cafe Royal, 127
Calderwood, Stanford, 17, 29,
  48, 83, 99, 100; creation of
  Masterpiece Theatre, 31–44,
  166; resignation of, 95
"californication," 4
Cambridge University, 59
Camelot, 138
Campaign, 137
Campaign for Nuclear Disarma-
  ment, 9
Canada, 53, 54
Cannes television market, 134,
  135
Capitol Hill, 16
Capote, Truman, 59, 86n56
Carnegie commission, 18
Carnegie-Mellon University, 185
Carter, Jimmy, 188, 190, 191
casting, 119
Cather, Willa, x
Cavalcade of America, 184
censorship, 78, 110
Chamberlain, Richard, 38
Chamberlin, Ward, 97, 98
Chancellor, John, 186
Channel Four, 153
Chaplin, Charlie, 53, 63–67, 70.
  See also Cooke, Alistair
Charles II, 135
Charmer, The, 21

Chevron, 183
Child, Julia, 29, 30
Children's Television Workshop
  (CTW), 106, 182
Church Committee on Multina-
  tional Corporations, 188
Churchill, Winston, 9, 96, 104,
  127, 211, 214
Churchill: The Wilderness Years,
  120, 123, 159
cinéma vérité, 55
Civilization, 34, 37, 38, 57, 135,
  151
Claridges hotel, 31
Clark, J. C., 126
Clark, Kenneth, 34, 57
Clean Air Act, 181
Club Med, 93
Cold Comfort Farm, 42, 102,
  103, 113
color (in television), 40, 42, 133
Columbia Broadcasting System
  (CBS), 8, 29, 34, 133, 178
Columbia University Business
  School, 179
Commonwealth Conference, 126
communism, 80
Comora, Owen, 28
Conant, James, 15
confidential business records, 20
Congress, 187–89
Connor, Michael J., 176
Conoco, 191
Cooke, Alistair, ix–xii, 10, 27, 91,
  168, 206; abdication crisis and,
  68–69; *Alistair Cooke's Amer-
  ica,* 57; *America,* 56; *America:
  A Personal View,* 57; "The
  American Film," 54; acceptance
  of *Masterpiece Theatre* posi-
  tion, 91–94; authority of BBC
  and, 54, 71; biography of,
  47–90; Cambridge University

Cooke, Alistair (*continued*)
Mummers and, 59, 61; Chaplin, Charlie, and, 63–67; climb of, 59; clubs of, 58–59; Commonwealth Fund fellowship, 61–62, 67; complaints about, 78; condescension of, 52; credibility of, 48; cross-cultural comparison, 71; "The Critic in Film History," 70; as cultural headwaiter, 49, 50, 74; distinction of, 48; editor of the *Granta,* 61; emigration of, 71; as an Englishman, 48, 83; establishment credentials, 63; as establishment pillar, 55, 58; evangelical approach to English, 60; Fairbanks, Douglas, and, 76–77; fly-on-the-wall approach, 55; free expression as criterion, 71; *Garbo and the Night Watchmen,* 69; *A Generation on Trial,* 51, 79–82; "The Ghastly Sixties," 82–83; hard feelings at BBC towards, 77; Harvard University, 62; hired as BBC critic, 68; as host, 43, 48, 49, 95; ideas rejected by BBC, 75; indispensibility of, 48, 77, 83, 92; intelligence of, 48; *International Zone* and, 54–56; Knight Commander of the British Empire (KBE), honorary, 57; *Letter from America,* xi, 56, 57, 79; *London Letter,* 68; *Manchester Guardian* correspondent, 57, 79; Mencken, H. L., and, 74–76, 78–79, 81; modesty of, 72; moonlights with NBC, 68; as naturalized American citizen, xi, 57, 77, 78; as New Yorker, 59; *New York Times* editorial praise for,

56; Nixon and, 81–82, 209; *Omnibus* and, xii, 8, 21, 44, 48–54, 82, 83; as performer, 61; persona of, xi–xii, 47, 48, 49, 58, 59, 72, 92; philosophy of, 58, 70; presented to the Prince of Wales, 62; rejected by BBC talks department, 61; rejected by BBC television, 56; rejection of *Masterpiece Theatre* job, 72; relationship with Mobil, 44, 48; replacement of, ix, xi; selection of *Masterpiece Theatre* programs, 91, 113n1; self-made man, 59; as snob, 52, 53, 86n56; sophistication of, xi, 62, 92; as stand-in for Stanley Kowalski, 51; talent of, 48, 210; *Talks about America,* 56; "The Theatre: New York and London," 71–73; *Times* (London) correspondent, 71; *Times Literary Supplement* dubs him "British National Institution," 56; timing of, 94; visit with Wallis Simpson, 68; wedding, 67; Willey, Basil, and , 59–60, 69, 79; Yale University, 62
Cooke, Jane White Hawkes, 86n56
Cooke, John, 86n56
Cooke, Mary Elizabeth Byrne, 59
Cooke, Ruth Emerson, 86n56
Cooke, Samuel, 59
Cooke, Sarah, 92
Cooke, Susan, 86n56,
Cooney, Joan Ganz, 182
coproductions, x, 7–8, 9, 19, 129, 136
Cora Unashamed, x
corporate identity, 37
Corporation for Public Broadcasting (CPB): agreement with

Mobil, 111–13; grant for *Mobil Masterpiece Theatre's American Collection,* ix; Nixon veto of federal funding for, 10; official history, 18; relationship with *Masterpiece Theatre,* 2, 95–113; relationship with the Nixon administration, 207
Cosindas, Marie, 29
costume drama, 8, 18, 204
Court Martial, The, 8
Covent Garden, 127
credibility of journalists, 44
Crime and Punishment, 124, 159
Cronkite, Walter, 186
Cronyn, Hume, 51
Cukor, George, 63
cultural arena, 192
cultural capital, 1–4
cultural forum, 3
Culture, Inc., 6, 19
Current, 18
Curtin, David, 57
Curtis, Thomas, 207
Cymbeline, 63

Daily Herald, 71, 77
Daily Worker (London), 81
Dallas, 171
Daly, Joe, 36, 37
Dancing, 51
Danger Man, 8, 133
Danger UXB, 20, 210
Dateline London, 54
David Frost Revue, 8
David Niven Show, The, 8
Davis, David M., 33, 138, 205, 206
Davis, Patricia, 169
Day, James, 30, 43
de Mille, Agnes, 51
Dear Brutus, 51
Death of a Princess, 20

Death Valley Days, 34
Delibes, Leo, 127
demographics, 38, 93
Department of Energy, 3
Dick and the Duchess, 8
Dick Russell's Pontiac Village, 31
Dickens of London, 20
Disney, 47
Disraeli, 7, 20
Donat, Robert, 70
Dorchester hotel, 126
Douglas Fairbanks Jr. Presents, 8
downmarket, 17
Downs, Hugh, 57
Doyle, Dane, Bernbach, 36
Dressmaker, The, 21
Duchess of Argyle, 160n17
Duchess of Bedford, 121
Duchess of Duke Street, The, 20
Duke of Kent, 62
duopoly, 120
DuPont, 184
Dylan, Bob, 59

East Boston Tunnel, 31
Eastern Educational Network (EEN), 30, 98
Eaton, Rebecca, 93, 121
Ed Sullivan Show, 8
Edward and Mrs. Simpson, 20, 159, 190
Edward the King, 190
Edwardian, xi, 18
eggheads, 80
Eisenhower, Dwight, 209
Electric Company, The, 155
Eliot, T. S., 61
elite taste, 2, 4, 5, 8, 9, 170
elitism, 168
elitists, 180–181
Elizabeth R, 20, 99, 102, 103, 106, 110, 138

Index

Emmy award, 27, 58, 121
Empson, William, 80
*Englebert Humperdinck Show,
    The,* 8
English Speaking Union, 54
Englishness, 47
Ernte, 70
Ervin, Sam, 204
Esquire, 70
establishment, the, ix
etiquette, 74
Eurocentrism, 4
Euston Films, 19
Evans, Sir Maurice, ix
Evening Standard, 123, 134
Evolution of the Dance, 51
Exxon, x, 122, 131, 183

Fable for Now. See Mobil Cor-
    poration
Fairbanks, Douglas, 76–77
fascism, 83
Fashionable Frolic, 97
Federal Communications Com-
    mission (FCC), 95
Federal Theatre, 152
Ferguson, Otis, 70
Ferrer, Jose, 152
Feuer, Jane, 11
Fiddick, Peter, 125
Fifteen Maiden Lane, 70
filler, 28, 43, 44, 96, 103, 107
Financial Times, 133
First Churchills, The, 9, 42, 92,
    94, 95, 102, 135
First National Bank of Boston,
    31
Flames Trees of Thika, 7, 20
Flanigan, Peter, 205, 206
Flickers, 20
focus group, 28
Fonda, Henry, 152
football, 15

Footnotes to the Film, 70
Ford Foundation, 8, 10, 30, 33,
    48, 49, 91, 95, 126, 129, 130,
    138, 165, 189, 204–7. See also
    Cooke, Alistair, *Omnibus*
Forsyte Saga, The, 9, 29, 30, 31,
    33, 38, 42, 43, 96, 134
Forsythe, Robert, 70
Fortunes of War, 120
Fox network, 179
framing, 28, 103, 107
France-Musique, 2
Fraser, Antonia, 92
fraternity life, 15
free speech, 194
Freeman, John, 213
French Chef, The, 29
Freund, Charles Paul, 180
Friendly, Fred, 205, 206
Frontline, 131
Frost, David, 8
Funny Girl, 152
Fury, 70

Gambler, The, 42, 103
Gans, Herbert, 5
Gardella, Kay, 47
Garmes, Lee, 63
Garvin, J. L., 63
GE Theater, 152, 209
General Electric, 35
Genius of Arab Civilization, The,
    190
*George Sanders Mystery The-
    atre, The,* 8
George, Brian, 127
German productions, x
Germinal, 124
Gielgud, Val, 127
Gigi, 152
Gill, Brendan, 59
Gill, Michael, 54, 56
Ginger Tree, The, 21

Gitlin, Todd, 6, 91, 106
Gladstone, 214
Glick, Edwin, 31
"God Bless Harvard," 15, 28
Goddard, Paulette, 64, 67
"golden age" of television, ix, 209
Goldenson, Leonard, 206
Goodbye to the Low Profile, 16, 18, 27, 170
Goodman Associates, Frank and Arlene, 28, 98, 150–55
Gould, Jack, 51, 53, 54
Grade, Lew, 7, 134, 135
Grade, Michael, 153
Granada Television, 39, 70, 122, 137
Gray, Arthur, 59
Great American Dream Machine, The, 11, 151
Great Contemporaries, 215
Great Performances, x, 122
Greek pottery, 96
Greene, Graham, 70
Greene, Hugh Carleton, 126
Greene, William N., 169
Griffiths, Trevor, 3, 210
Grisewood, Harman, 126
Grossman, Larry, 208
Group W, 122
Guardian. See Manchester Guardian
Gunn, Hartford, 20, 30, 31, 36, 101, 103, 104, 105, 107, 110, 136, 137, 139
Gypsy, 152

Haacke, Hans, 197–98
Haiti, 54
Haldeman, H. R., 203
Hall, Stuart, 4
Hallmark Hall of Fame, ix, 8, 209

"halo effect," xi, 184
Hamlet, 52
Hampshire, Susan, 42, 96, 135
Hanley, Miles, 63
Harkness, Edward S., 61
Harlech Television, 137
Harley, William, 126
Harper's Bazaar, 5, 70
Harrison, Rex, 51, 209
Harvard Business School, 15, 28, 31
Harvard Poetry Library, 129
Harvard University, 14–15, 31. See also Cooke, Alistair, WGBH
Hasty Pudding Club, 63
Hawkesworth, John, 7
Hayes, Helen, 51
Heartbreak House, 61
Heath, Edward, 9
Henry VIII, 51
heritage industry, 7, 10, 106, 209
heritage, 9, 127, 212, 215
Herold, Don, 70
Herring, Robert, 70
Heston, Charlton, 50
Hicks, Seymour, 67
highbrow, 5, 50, 53, 82
Hirsch, Paul, 3
Hiss, Alger, 51, 79–82
History of Musical Comedy, 51
History of the English Speaking Peoples, 104
Hitchcock, Alfred, 70
Hitchens, Christopher, 47, 78
Hodsal, Sir John, 127
Hollywood's Favorite Heavy, 212
Hollywood Television Theatre, x
Hollywood, 2, 4, 8, 15, 54, 63, 135, 151
Holocaust, 196
Holt, Sam, 40, 97–113, 136, 138

Holt, Thaddeus, 100, 104–7, 110–13
homosexuality, x
Horn Blows at Midnight, The, 52
Hoskins, Bob, 154
House of Cards, 21
Houseman, John, 152
Hub of Two Worlds, 96
Hughes Television, 35
Hughes, Langston, x
Humble Oil, 34, 131
Hurt, John, 154
Hussey, Marmaduke, 15
Hutchins, Robert Maynard, 129

I've Been Reading, 31
I Remember Nelson, 120
I, Claudius, 7, 20, 74, 153, 196
Iliad, The, 50
image advertising, 38
In Search of the Real America, 185
Independent Broadcasting Authority (IBA), 118
Independent Television (ITV), 1, 8, 9, 15, 18, 19, 99, 100, 132, 135; relationship with *Masterpiece Theatre,* 117–59
Independent Television Commission (ITC), 15
Independent Television in Britain, 117
Inside Prime Time, 6, 91
interest groups, 1
international television trade, 53
International Zone, 21, 55, 82
Iranian crisis, 174, 179
Iraqi Army, 167
Irish R. M., The, 21
Isaacs, Jeremy, 130
Islamic art, 31
Italy, 54
Ives, David O., 33, 95, 168
Ivy, The, 127

Jackson, Henry, 186, 188
Jacobi, Derek, 154
James, Henry, x
Javits, Jacob, 59
jazz, 51, 71
Jeeves and Wooster, 21
Jesus College, 59
Jewel in the Crown, The, 18, 21, 70, 120
John Hancock Life Insurance Company, 31
Johns, Jasper, 59
Johnson, Samuel, 51
Jude the Obscure, 42, 102, 103
Judgement at Nuremberg, 152

Kellogg Fund, 130
Kelly, Gene, 51
Kendall, Kay, 209
Kennedy era, 55
Kennedy, Edward, 170, 195
Kennedy, Jackie, 59, 204
Kennedy, John F., 170
Kennedy, Robert, 170; assassination of, 82; and Ethel, 59
King and I, The, 152
King Faisal, 183
King Lear, 50, 52
kitchen-sink drama, 51, 104
Kitman, Marvin, 193
Korda, Alexander, 7, 209, 210
Korda, Vincent, 7
Kowalski, Stanley, 51
Ku Klux Klan, 80
Kuwait, 167

Labour Party (British), 77
Land camera, 36
Land, Edwin, 29
Larsen, Robert, 95, 97, 100, 107, 136, 137, 139
Last Days of the Beeb, The, 117
Last of the Mohicans, The, 102, 103, 113

Last Place on Earth, The, 120, 210
Last Tango in Paris, 152
Laughton, Charles, 129
Laughton, Roger, 123
Leaders, 203
Leapman, Michael, 117
Leavis, F. R., 60
left (political), 10, 70, 77
Leigh, Vivian, 152
LeMahieu, D. L., 18
Letter from America. See Cooke, Alistair
Levin, Meyer, 70
Levinson, Jerome, 188
liberal (political), 10, 11, 18, 30
life and literature, 60
Life magazine, 35, 70
Life Nature Library, 35
Life Science Library, 35
Lillie, 20, 123
Lincoln, Abraham, 48
Lisemore, Martin, 42
literary pedigree, 17
Little Hippo Goes a Long Way, A, 97
live television, 48
Liverpool Daily Post, 134
London Films, 7
London Weekend Television (LWT), 120, 121, 122, 213
London, England, xi, 8, 31, 33, 40, 47, 99, 100, 133
Long, Russell, 192
Loomis, Henry, 205
Lord Byron, 135
Lord Halifax, 62
Lord Mountbatten: The Last Viceroy, 21
Lord Reith, 15
Lord Simon, 127
Los Angeles Times, 34
Los Angeles, 52
Lost Empires, 21, 64, 71, 120

Love from a Stranger, 70
lowbrow, 52
Lowell Institute, 14, 130
Lubitsch, Ernst, 63
Luce, Henry R., 77
Lynes, Russell, 5

MacBeth, 209
MacCarthy, Desmond, 67
MacDonald, Dwight, 49–51
Mackenzie, Robert, 128
Macy, John W., 27, 100, 105, 110, 182
Magic Show, The, 190
Mail on Sunday, 117
Maisie, 102
Man from Interpol, The, 8
Man from Uncle, The, 8
Man in a Suitcase, 8
Manchester Guardian, xi, 55, 70, 71, 79
Manchester, England, 59, 127
Manhattan Madness, 70
Marathon Oil Company, 191
March, Frederick, 135
Mark Saber/Saber of London, 8
Marks, John, 70
Marsh, Jean, 154
Marshall and Bloom, 34, 57, 96, 98, 110
Marshall, Frank, 34, 37–43, 48, 57, 83, 119; control over program, 95–113, 139–40; controversy over *Upstairs, Downstairs,* 120–22, 156–59, 180; and Mobil's corporate image, 177, 195
Marxism, 3, 210
mass civilization, 60
Masterpiece Library, 106
Masterpiece Playhouse, 209
Masterpiece Theatre: advertising, 42; as an American institution, xii, 47; American productions

Masterpiece Theatre (*continued*) planned for, 43; as an anthology, xii, 9, 133, 209, 210; audience for, 2, 38; as the best television has to offer, 2, 4; budget of, 28; choice of Alistair Cooke, 44; deal memo, 141–42; franchise of, x, 38, 41; host, 42, 43; *Mobil Masterpiece Theatre's American Collection,* ix, 28; network, 42; origin of the name, 41; package, 41–44, 47, 95–6; payments, 43; premiere, 96; preview, 92–93; production and distribution of, 29–41; program agreement, 109–13; promotion, 42, 97, 98, 109, 183, 185; registered as a service mark, 41; as a symbol of PBS, 28; theme, 42, 43; time-slot, 103, 109; *Upstairs, Downstairs* controversy, 144–59, 180; and world leadership, 204

Matthews, Brander, 5

Maude, Cyril, 61

Max Liebman Spectaculars, 152

McAlpine, J. Warren, 126

McCarthy, Joseph, 51

McCarthyism, 67

McGhee, Peter, 28

McKay, Peter, 117

McKinsey and Company, 168

McLaren, Moray, 67

Mencken, H. L., 74–76. See also Cooke, Alistair

Mercer, Pauline, 159

Mercury Theatre, 152

Merman, Ethel, 68

Merrick, David, 152

Metro-Goldwyn-Mayer (MGM), 9, 35

Meyerhold, Vsevolod Emilievich, 62

Middle East, 9

middle-class, 51, 52

middlebrow, 48, 49, 51, 70

Mills, C. Wright, 5

minority culture, 60, 69

Minow, Newton, 204

Minstrel Man, 190

Mobil Corporation: advertising agencies, 37; advocacy campaigns, 19, 172; and energy policy, 181; as establishment pillar, 173; battle with commercial networks, 178; charges of gouging, 167; control over program, 98–113, 118–19; effectiveness of public relations, 169, 173–74, 191–97; extension of underwriting, 100; *Fable for Now,* 21, 170, 190; image, 29, 37, 176–77; "long on brains," 169, 190; Mobil Information Center, 170, 189; *Mobil Season, The,* 179; nationalization of, 172, 186; *New York Times* op-eds, 19, 182; "obscene profits" of, 186; personality of, 169; relationship with Alistair Cooke, 44; relationship with the British, 117–25; relationship with PBS, 95, 96–113; relationship with WGBH, 42; side agreements, 121, 159; as sponsor, x, 2, 3, 6, 7, 12, 16–19, 27, 165–98, 207

Mobil Masterpiece Theatre, 166

Mobil Showcase Network, 21, 37, 121, 159, 179, 190, 191, 194

Modern Times, 70

money-laundering, 160n29

Monroe, Marilyn, 152

Moon for the Misbegotten, A, 186

Moore, Henry, 128

Mountbatten: The Last Viceroy, 120

Mouret, Jean Jacques, 93
Mousterpiece Theatre, 47
Mr. Deeds Goes to Town, 70
MTM Television, 11
Muni, Paul, 152
Muppet Show, The, 8
Murray, Allen E., 210
Murrow, Edward R., 69, 78
Museum of Broadcasting, 18
Museum of Modern Art, 29
musicals, 62
"Music for the King's Supper,"
    93
Mystery!, 28; as a spinoff, 27,
    120, 141, 191; Diana Rigg as
    hostess of, 8; Mobil ceases
    funding of, ix

Nader, Ralph, 94, 107, 171
Nancy Astor, 120
Nathan, Robert, 71
National Academy of Television
    Arts and Sciences, 27, 57
National Association of Educa-
    tional Broadcasters (NAEB),
    125–30
National Broadcasting Company
    (NBC), 8, 29, 35, 37, 57, 92
National Educational Television
    and Radio Center (NETRC),
    125, 132, 134
National Educational Televsion
    (NET), 10, 30, 33, 34, 102,
    122, 125, 133, 205, 207
National Program Service. See
    Public Broadcasting Service
nature series, 32
NET Playhouse, 30
Neville, John, 135
New Masses, 70, 71
New Republic, 70
New Statesman, 70, 213
New York Daily News, 47
New York Life, A, 59

New York Television Playhouse,
    30
New York Times, xi, 2, 17, 19,
    20, 28, 47, 51, 53, 152, 171,
    176, 184, 193, 195
New York, 48, 133; cultural life
    of, 48
New Yorker, 5, 165, 192
Newcomb, Horace, 3
Newsday, 193
Nicholson, Harold, 61, 69
Nielsen ratings, 38, 138
Night and Day, 70
Nixon, Richard: administration,
    1, 9; Alger Hiss and, 80–82;
    BBC and, 131; Churchill and,
    213–15; Disraeli and, 214;
    code of the English gentleman
    and, 214; cultural legacy of,
    xii; educational philosophy of,
    204; energy crisis and, 185–87;
    foreign policy of, 211; "The
    Nixon Style," 203; policy to-
    wards PBS, 10, 11, 30, 205–15;
    values of, 210; Watergate im-
    peachment vote by House Judi-
    ciary Committee, 58
Noh drama, 63
Norway, 54
Nova, 28, 131

O'Connor, John J., 28, 47, 57
O'Neill, Eugene, 186
O. S. S., 8
Observer, 63
Official Films, 8
Oh, Boy, 8
oil crisis, 39
Olivier, Laurence, 152, 209
Omnibus. See Cooke, Alistair
On Approval, 20
On Opera, 51
OPEC embargo, 2, 174, 181, 185
Open End, 31

opinion leaders, 2, 175, 177, 184, 191
Orlando, Florida, 168
Oxbridge, 62
Oxford, 127

Pace, Frank, 10, 207
Page, George, 155
Pagett, Nicola, 154
Paignton Observer, 61
Pallisers, The, 125, 130
Palmer, Lilli, 51
Paradise Postponed, 120
Pearl Harbor, 77
Pelletier, Rooney, 126
Pere Goriot, 42, 92, 105
"perfidious Albion," 9
Perini Corporation, 31
"petroleum broadcasting system," 91, 165, 185
Philby, Kim, 9
Philip Morris, 191
Phillips, Mike, 19
Picadilly Palace, The, 8
Piece of Cake, 21, 120
Pilobolus Dance Company, 190
Pinth-Garnell, Leonard, 47
Piscator, Erwin, 62
Playhouse 90, 209, 210
pledge-night, 138
Point Counterpoint, 102
Polaroid Corporation, 29, 30, 36, 39
Poldark, 7
political advocacy, 17
Popular Culture and High Culture, 5
Portrait of a Lady, 38
Possessed, The, 42
Powell, Jody, 191
Powell, Jonathan, 1, 2, 123–25, 153
Power among Men, 54

pre-production deal, 160n9
Preminger, Otto, 152
President's Advisory Committee on Public Diplomacy, 6, 212
press agents, 150–54
pressures, 13
Price, Denis, 135
Price, Richard, 121, 122, 144–59
Priestly, J. B., 71, 72
Prisoner, The, 8
Private Schulz, 20, 210
Probst, George, 126
Producer's Showcase, 152, 209
product advertising, 38
Program Producer's Handbook, 12
propaganda, 54, 69, 131
Protestant Establishment, The, 14
public affairs, 4, 29, 204, 205
Public Broadcasting Service (PBS), 1, 2; as cultural oasis, 4; Dial Access Communications System (DACS), 92, 105, 109, 154; localism, 96; National Program Service standards, 12–14; network guarantees, 36; official history, 18; role in *Masterpiece Theatre,* 91–113; strains with Mobil and WGBH, 97–113; as target of the Nixon administration, 10
public relations, 6, 9, 37, 38, 165, 167, 178
public service, 15, 29, 38, 109
Pulitzer Prize, xi
Puritan Boston and Quaker Philadelphia, 14

"Q" (Arthur Quiller Crouch), 59–60, 69
quality: as an alternative, 4, 15; British, 7, 15–16; defined, 1, 2,

11–17; importance of, 39, 175; Mobil's identification with, 37, 168; television, xii, 27

Ralph Nader Report, The, 94, 107
Rank, J. Arthur, 135
Raven, Simon, 125
Read, John, 128
Reagan, Ronald, 152, 196, 209, 212
Reasoner, Harry, 186
Rebecca, 124
Reeves Communications, 37
Report to the People, 18
Resurrection, 42, 102, 103
revenue, 107, 118, 134, 137
Rice, Elmer, 71
Rice, Michael, 20, 33, 39, 138, 157–58
Richard III, 7, 209
Richardson, Ian, 154
Rigg, Diana, 8
Ritz Carlton Hotel, 93
Rivers, William L., 178
RKO General, 34
Road to War, The, 124
Robeck, Peter M., 34, 35, 37, 99, 100, 131,
Robin Hood, 8
Robinson, Lennox, 63
Rockefeller, John D., 61, 167, 168
Rodgers and Hammerstein, 152
Roman drama, 51
Roots, 121, 196
Rostow, Walt, 69
Roy Rogers Show, The, 34
Royal Opera, 127
Russian spies, 9

Safire, William, 9, 203
Saga of Western Man, The, 180

Saint Nicholas Magazine, 50
Saint, The, 8
Santa Barbara oil spill, 181
Sarson, Christopher, ix, 39, 40, 42, 43–44, 48, 72, 100; negotiations with Alistair Cooke, 91–94; negotiations with PBS, 95–113; reasons for choosing Alistair Cooke, 56–57, 83; resignation from *Masterpiece Theatre,* 120, 157–58; *Upstairs, Downstairs* controversy, 120–23, 144–50, 155–59
Sartre, Jean-Paul, 124
Saturday Night Live, 47
Saturday Review of Literature, 29
Saudek, Robert, 48–50
Saudi Arabia, 3, 190
Saunders, Frank, 191
Savile Club, 127
Say, Brother, 95
Scarlet Letter, The, x
Schaefer, George, 209
Schiller, Herbert, 6, 19, 173, 174
Schmertz, Herb, xi, 3, 6, 13, 16, 18, 27, 34, 37–44, 94, 210; access to the White House, 191; approval of key elements, 118–25; "balance of trash," 212; biography of, 169–70; control over *Masterpiece Theatre,* 95–113, 136–59, 165–98; reasons for choosing Alistair Cooke, 48, 83
Schram, Wilbur, 178
Scoop, 21
Scott, Robin, 31
Screen Actors Guild, 16
Scribner's, 70
scripts, 118, 119
Scupham, J., 127
Second World War, 9

Secret Agent, 8
See It Now, 184
Sendall, Bernard, 117
Sesame Street, 28, 47, 106, 182, 183
sets in use, 96
Seven Year Itch, 152
Seymour, Jane, 154
Shakespeare, William, 8, 123, 127
Shaw, George Bernard, 127
Shell Oil Company, 35
Shields and Yarnell, 190
Shiralee, The, 21
Shivas, Mark, 123
Shoulder to Shoulder, 210
Showtime, 8
Shulman, Milton, 134
Siegel, Ed, 209
Siegel, Seymour, 126, 127, 130
Siepmann, Charles, 15
Signs and Meaning in the Cinema, 1
Silas Marner, 21
Sinel, Norm, 103
Singer, Aubrey, 131, 133
Sir Francis Drake, 8
60 Minutes, 195
Six Wives of Henry VIII, 7, 20, 99, 101, 102, 103, 105, 106, 110
Slater, Gerald, 101, 102, 107, 108, 110, 136
slush fund, 29
Smith, C. Aubrey, 63, 66
snob appeal, 47
snobbery, 51, 168
Social Register, 167
socialist, 70
Socony-Vacuum, 167
Somerset Maugham TV Theatre, 8
Song of the Lark, x
Sonnenberg, Ben, 59
Sons and Lovers, 120

Sorrell and Son, 21
Sound of Music, The, 152
South Africa, 185
South Pacific, 152
Southern Pictures, 123
Soviet Union, 54
Speaking Personally, 127
"special relationship," 9, 104, 214
Spectator, The, 70
Spina, Peter, 28, 41, 121, 167, 168, 173, 187
spinoff (of *Masterpiece Theatre*), 27
Spoils of Poynton, The, 42, 92, 102
Sponsor, The, 6, 19
sponsorship, x, xii, 6–7, 13, 16–19, 29, 30, 31, 34, 37, 50, 117, 122, 125, 137, 190
Sports Illustrated, 35
spy stories, 8
Standard Oil Company, 167, 169, 186
station independence project, 138
Stein, Ben, 212
Stewart, John, 19
Strasberg, Susan, 51
Stratford, 127
Streetcar Named Desire, 51
Studio One, 210
Style, Michael, 133
Suez, 211
Summer's Lease, 21
Sunday, 48, 49, 55, 96
Sutton, Sean, 19, 99, 123
syndication, 137

Taffner, Don, 34
Tale of Two Cities, A, 21, 70
Tandy, Jessica, 51
Tankel, Jonathan, 19
"taste cultures," 5
Tastemakers, The, 5

Tavoulareas, William "Tav,"
 168, 169, 188
Telephone Time, 133
Television Today, 135
Tempest, The, 127
temporary hosts, xi
Ten Who Dared, 190
Testament of Youth, 20, 159
Texaco, 183
Thames Television, Ltd., 34
That Was The Week That Was, 8
The World We Live In, 35
Therese Raquin, 159
Things to Come, 70
Third Man, The, 8
This Is Tom Jones, 8
Thornton, Basil, 54, 126, 130,
 131
Time to Choose, A, 189
Time, Inc., 34–35; Time-Life
 books, 35; Time-Life Films,
 32, 34–35, 99, 100, 106, 137,
 206; *Time* magazine, 48, 77
Times (London), xi
To Serve Them All My Days, 20
Tokyo Television Festival, 133
Tom Brown's Schooldays, 20
Tom Jones, 152
Top Hat, 70
Total Quality Management
 (TQM), 16
tourism, 10
Town Like Alice, A, 20
Traffik, 21
Transatlantic Quiz, 79
Travelers Insurance Company, ix
Trevelyan, G. M., 135
Trials of Anne Boleyn, The, 51
20/20, 57, 176
Twin Peaks, 121

UN Dateline, 55
underwriter, 27, 31, 36
Union Jack, 93

Union Now with Britain, 77
United Nations, 54, 55, 79, 91
United States Information
 Agency, 212
United States Information Ser-
 vice, 54
University of California, Los An-
 geles (UCLA), 34; Film and
 Television Archive, 20
University of Chicago, 126
University of Wisconsin, 126
*Unpleasantness at the Bellona
 Club, The,* 20
upper middle-class, 48
Upstairs, Downstairs, 7, 14, 17,
 18, 57, 62, 66, 74, 113,
 120–22, 130, 144–59, 179,
 185, 187, 196, 213
U.S. Steel Hour, 209
Ustinov, Peter, 51, 152

Valenti, Jack, 133
value, 60
Vanity Fair, 92, 102
variety programs, 8
Variety, 16, 20
vaudeville, 49, 53
Very British Coup, A, 21
*View from Sunset Boulevard,
 The,* 212
Visions, x
Vogue, 70
Volksbuhne, 62
Von Sternberg, Josef, 7

Wall Street Journal, 33, 176
Wallace, Henry, 81
Wallace, Vivien, 122
Walt Disney World, 168
Walters, Barbara, 57
Warner, Rawleigh, 39, 121, 122,
 168–85
Washington Post, 165, 180
Washington, D.C., xi

Water, Wine, and Wisdom, 96
Watergate, 11, 86n52, 187, 204
Wattenberg, Ben, 185
Weaver, Pat, 209
Weekly Political Summaries, 127
Weinstein, Hannah, 8
Welch, Joseph N., 51
Welles, Orson, 50, 52, 152
Wells, H.G., 69
Wells, Ronald, 62, 67
West End, 72
Wexler, Anne, 191
WGBH, Boston, 1, 14, 18, 131, 206; hostility to large corporations at, 32; and origins of *Masterpiece Theatre,* 27–44; relationship with the British, 123–25; relationship with Mobil, 28, 42, 119; "sandbox," 32, 33, 39, 94
Wheatley, Parker, 126, 131
When Havoc Struck, 190
Whitehead, Clay T., 10, 11
Whyte, Sir Frederic, 69
Will, George, 165
Willey, Basil. See Cooke, Alistair
William Morris Agency, 129
Williams, Emlyn, 129

Williams, Raymond, 3
Wilson, Harold, 9, 211, 213, 214
Wilson, Joan (Sullivan), 64, 93, 119, 121, 124, 125, 158–59
Witherspoon, John, 18, 105
WNBC, New York, 55
WNET/ Channel 13, New York, 10, 30, 97, 98, 206
WNYC, New York, 126
Wolfe, Tom, 59
Wollen, Peter, 1
Woolcott, Alexander, 72
working-class life, 51
Works Progress Administration (WPA), 152
World In Action, 39
World of Jazz, The, 50
World of Magic, 190
World War II, 78, 127

Xerox Corporation, 34, 37, 57, 92, 151

Yamani, Sheik, 183
Yergin, Daniel, 183, 186, 211
Young People's Concerts, 29
Your Show of Shows, 152

Zoom, 39

About the Author

Laurence Jarvik has written *PBS: Behind the Screen* and edited both *Public Broadcasting and the Public Trust* and *The National Endowments: A Critical Symposium*. A graduate of the University of California, Berkeley, he received his Ph.D. and Master of Fine Arts from the School of Theatre, Film, and Television at the University of California, Los Angeles, and taught at UCLA and California State University, Los Angeles. Jarvik has published articles in scholarly journals as well as popular magazines and newspapers. He has appeared on *CNN Crossfire, ABC Nightline,* the *CBS Evening News,* and *C-SPAN,* and produced and directed the feature documentary *Who Shall Live and Who Shall Die?*, which was broadcast on PBS stations. Laurence Jarvik lives in Washington, DC.